Spectrum of Anthropological Perspectives of Northeast India

Spectrum of Anthropological Perspectives of Northeast India

Edited by
Sarthak Sengupta
Juri Borah

GYAN

Published, 2019

Published by

Gyan Publishing House
5, Ansari Road
Daryaganj, New Delhi-110002
Phone: 011-47034999, 9811692060
www.gyanbooks.com
E-mail: books@gyanbooks.com

Printed at: G. Print Process, Delhi.

Cataloging in Publication Data—DK
Courtesy: D.K. Agencies (P) Ltd. <docinfo@dkagencies.com>

Spectrum of anthropological perspectives of Northeast India /
edited by Sarthak Sengupta, Juri Borah.
pages cm
ISBN 9788121219433

1. Anthropology—India, Northeastern. 2. Ethnology—India, Northeastern. I. Sengupta, Sarthak, 1955- editor. II. Borah, Juri, editor.

LCC GN17.3.I4S64 2019 | DDC 301.09541 23

Dedicated
to the sacred memory of
Late Prof. Dr. Usha Deka,
a renowned anthropologist of our country
with respect, gratitude, and affection

Contents

Preface

The development of anthropological studies in India took place under the colonial patronage, and such interventions were more extensive in Northeast India which have been inhabited by numerous ethnic groups through ages with diverse biological and cultural attributes. The colonial government realized that for the effective administration of native Northeast Indians, understanding of their culture and custom was a must. During the colonial era, the British administrator initiated pioneering research in ethnography, archaeology as well as in biological anthropology among the population groups of the region.

India's Northeast is considered as a paradise for anthropological studies due to the diversities that exist in the realm of ethnic composition and landscape variation. There is a rich assembly of cultures and communities in this rugged expanse of the eastern Himalayas. This rainbow territory is a great meeting place of myriad racial and linguistic groups. Northeast India lays between 22° and 29°18' north latitude and 89°40' and 97°22' east longitude and are spread over an area of approximately 2,62,230 square kilometers and had a population of 45,772,188 persons and has over 220 varied ethnic groups. These represent some 7.9 percent of the country's total landmass and approximately 3.8 percent of its population. The average population density is 170 (approx.), the literacy rate is 68.5 percent and the urban population stands at 15.45 percent of the total population. More than 200 languages or mother tongues are spoken in the region, however, some of these languages have less than 10,000 speakers. The region has about 4,500 sq. km. international boundaries across Bangladesh, Myanmar, Bhutan, and Tibet. At present, in four of the eight states in Northeast India, the tribals constitute the majority. The mighty rivers, its tributaries, and its serried mountains have shaped its ecology and the lives of the people. Unfortunately, till date, information on this richly endowed and strategically important region and its population is scanty, sporadic, and sketchy, and this treatise is intended in part to fill that void.

The present anthology of research contribution accommodated in '*Spectrum of Anthropological Perspectives of Northeast India*' consist of eighteen research articles offered by distinguished and experienced anthropologists highlighting numerous issues covering biological, socio-cultural, prehistoric, ethnoarchaeological and several other aspects of varied ethnic groups living in diverse habitat of Northeast India. We have been fortunate to be able to convince the contributors to write about their allied field of researches. Both tribes and caste population reside in the Northeastern region of India is covered in this compilation and the areas of research includes the emergence and migration histories (*Khangembam Somibabu Meitei* and *Sanjenbam Yaiphaba Meitei*), understanding life in the inter-state borderlands (*Ratna Tayeng*), ethnographic text (*Charisma K Lepcha*), historical background and the population distribution (*P.K. Guha*), indigenous numeral system (*Somenath Bhattacharjee*), administration of village council (*Arifur Zaman*), corruption in the socio-cultural context (*Tame Ramya*), rice cake making practices (*Anamika Gogoi Duarah*), living megalithic practices (*Garima Thakuria* and *Manoj Kumar Singh*), sedimentary record of the pre-historic sites (*Sukanya Sharma*), demography (*Maitreyee Sharma*; *Tiluttoma Baruah*; *Dali Dutta; Juri Borah* and *Sarthak Sengupta*), women health related issues (*Suparna Shome*, *Susmita Bharati*, *Manoranjan Pal* and *Premananda Bharati*; *Zenia Thangjam* and *Sudipta Ghosh*; *Sumitabha Chakraborty*) and variation of angular photogrammetric analysis of the facial profile (*Debalina Roy*, *Priyanka Das, Kusum Ghosh*, *Diptendu Chatterjee* and *Arup Ratan Bandopadhyay*). Thus, a decent cross-section on emerging issues relating to man, society, and culture of the region is here reflected.

The effort expended in compiling this volume will be rewarded if this treatise proves to be informative, stimulus and of use to anthropologists besides other social scientists; administrators, planners, policy makers, academicians, scholars and indeed anyone with a concern about the land, environment, indigenous inhabitants of Northeast India.

The 31 December 2018

Sarthak Sengupta
Juri Borah

Acknowledgements

Several persons have contributed towards the undertaking and completion in the production and design of this comprehensive compilation and thanks are due to all of them in full measure.

First and foremost, we owe a special debt of thankfulness to all researchers who cheerfully volunteered to contribute their information for this edited volume in a timely manner. Without their help, this volume could not have been completed.

It has been possible for us to continue our academic pursuit for the infrastructural facilities provided by the authorities of Dibrugarh University. We avail of this opportunity to express our sincere thanks.

We would like especially to thank Dr. Samrat Sengupta who provided us with photographs to use in the jacket. Mrs. Neelanjana Barua cheerfully processed the manuscript through various modifications and got it ready for publication.

We also convey our special thanks to M/S Gyan Publishing House, New Delhi for providing excellent assistance during the final phases of preparation of the book in a printed form.

Finally, we must acknowledge the stimulus and encouragement given to us by our family members with their patience and unconditional support during the preparation of this compilation work.

The 31st December 2018

Sarthak Sengupta
Juri Borah

List of Contributors

Arup Ratan Bandopadhaya, Department of Anthropology, University of Calcutta, 35 Bullygunge Circular Road, Kolkata, West Bengal, 700019.

Tiluttoma Baruah, Department of Anthropology, Cotton University, Panbazar, Guwahati, Assam, 781001.

Premananda Bharati, Biological Anthropology Unit, Indian Statistical Institute, 203 Barrackpore Trunk Road, Kolkata, West Bengal, 700108.

Susmita Bharati, Sociological Research Unit, Indian Statistical Institute, 203 Barrackpore Trunk Road, Kolkata, West Bengal, 700108.

Somenath Bhattacharjee, Department of Anthropology, Assam (Central) University, Diphu Campus, Karbi Anglong, Assam, 782462.

Juri Borah, Department of Anthropology, Dibrugarh University, Dibrugarh, Assam, 786004.

Sumitabha Chakraborty, Anthropological Survey of India, Eastern Regional Centre, Salt Lake, Kolkata, West Bengal, 700064.

Diptendu Chatterjee, Department of Anthropology, University of Calcutta, 35 Bullygunge Circular Road, Kolkata, West Bengal, 700019.

Priyanka Das, Department of Anthropology, University of Calcutta, 35 Bullygunge Circular Road, Kolkata, West Bengal, 700019.

Kusum Ghosh, Department of Anthropology, University of Calcutta, 35 Bullygunge Circular Road, Kolkata, West Bengal, 700019.

Sudipta Ghosh, Department of Anthropology, Umshing – Mawkynroh, North Eastern Hill University, Shillong, Meghalaya, 793022.

Anamika Gogoi Duarah, Department of Anthropology, Arya Vidyapeeth College, Guwahati, Assam, 781016.

Dali Dutta, Department of Anthropology, Dibrugarh University, Dibrugarh, Assam, 786004.

P. K. Guha, Anthropological Survey of India, Government of India, 27 Jawaharlal Nehru Marg, Kolkata, West Bengal, 700016.

Charishma K. Lepcha, Department of Anthropology, Sikkim University, 6th Mile, Samdur, Tadong, Gangtok, Sikkim, 737102.

Khangembam Somibabu Meitei, Department of Anthropology, Guru Ghasidas Vishwavidhyalaya Bilaspur, Chattisgarh, India, 495009.

Sanjenbam Yaiphaba Meitei, Department of Anthropology, Manipur University, Canchipur, Imphal, Manipur, 795003.

Manoranjan Pal, Economic Research Unit, Indian Statistical Institute, 203 Barrackpore Trunk Road, Kolkata, West Bengal, 700108.

Tame Ramya, Department of Anthropology, Saint Claret College, Ziro, Lower Subansiri, Arunachal Pradesh, 791120.

Debalina Roy, Department of Anthropology, University of Calcutta, 35 Bullygunge Circular Road, Kolkata, West Bengal, 700019.

Maitreyee Sharma, Department of Anthropology, Dibrugarh University, Dibrugarh, Assam, 786004.

Sarthak Sengupta, Department of Anthropology, Dibrugarh University, Dibrugarh, Assam, 786004.

Sukanya Sharma, Department of Humanities and Social Sciences, Indian Institute of Technology, Guwahati, Assam, 781039.

Suparna Shome, Biological Anthropology Unit, Indian Statistical Institute, 203 Barrackpore Trunk Road, Kolkata, West Bengal, 700108.

Manoj Kumar Singh, Department of Anthropology, University of Delhi, Delhi, India, 110007.

Ratna Tayeng, Department of Anthropology, Rajiv Gandhi University, Rono Hills, Itanagar, Arunachal Pradesh, 791111.

Garima Thakuria, Department of Anthropology, Sikkim University, 6th Mile, Samdur, Tadong, Gangtok, Sikkim, 737102.

Zenia Thangjam, Department of Anthropology, North Eastern Hill University, Umshing-Mawkynroh, Shillong, Meghalaya, 793022.

Arifur Zaman, Department of Anthropology, Gauhati University, Gopinath Bordoloi Nagar, Jalukbari, Guwahati, Assam, 781014.

List of Tables

List of Figures

List of Plates

Chapter - 1

An Anthropological Outlook on the Emergence and Migration Histories of Northeastern Populations, India

Khangembam Somibabu Meitei and
Sanjenbam Yaiphaba Meitei

Introduction

The Northeastern part of India includes Arunachal Pradesh, Assam, Manipur, Meghalaya, Mizoram, Nagaland, Sikkim, and Tripura. The name 'Northeast India' is commonly used to refer to these regions. There are more than two hundreds of ethnic groups and sub-groups found in the Northeast region of India. It has also played an important role in the history of mankind, witnessing numerous waves of migration at different times and space, which is reflected in the presence of several ethnic groups with their specific identities. It has been hypothesized that all the Northeast tribes belonging to the Tibeto-Mongolian group might have come to present Northeast India from Southeast Asia through different waves of migration.

The strategic location of Northeast India region at the junction of South Asia, East Asia, and Southeast Asian countries and its natural and cultural interconnectivity may explain the cultural diversity among the population groups of this region. Besides this, it has played a crucial role in shaping the Indian nation especially the eastern part of the country (Chatterjee, 1970). Northeast India is known for its geographical and morphological diverse from mainland India.

In view of different ethnolinguistic histories, physical features and prehistoric elements of Northeast India from the mainland India, the present chapter tries to understand the peopling of Northeast India, their probable migratory histories and evolutionary relationship with neighbouring Southeast and East Asian countries from the archaeological and linguistic perspectives.

Archaeological Evidence

Till now very less archaeological exploration has been done because the entire Northeast region falls under the Tropical Rain Forest Zone (Sharma, 1972). The Archaeology of Northeast India is very important for the world archaeology, because of the fact that this region is known to have played a great role in the domestication of a number of food-producing plants essential for men, including rice (Sharma, 1991). The prehistoric tools have been studied by various scholars such as Goswami and Bhagabati (1959); Sharma (1972); Medhi (1987); and Sharma (2001). Sharma (1972) has divided the prehistoric cultures as a Palaeolithic, Mesolithic and Neolithic culture. The stone tools evidence from various regions of Northeast India shows similarity with various parts of East Asia and Southeast Asia (Dani, 1960). The three characteristic features of the Neolithic culture in Northeast India viz. celt making traditions, cord-impressed pottery, rice agriculture, are more or less similar to the Neolithic cultures of East Asia and Southeast Asia (Hazarika, 2006). Various excavated sites have yielded numerous potsherds like cord-impressed and other handmade wares from Daojali Hading (Sharma, 1967), Sarutaru (Rao, 1973), Parsi-Parlo (Ashraf, 1990), Garo hills (IAR, 1966-1967, 1967-1968), Manipur (Singh, 1983, 1993). The earliest evidence of pottery in China and Japan dates back to 21,000-18,000 yrs. BP (Yasuda, 2002:119,123). Nongpok Keithelmanbi of Manipur dated 4460 ± 120 yrs. BP (Singh, 1983), The pottery of the cultures of East Asia and Southeast Asia is remarkably alike and includes simple forms of cord-impressed, combed, fingertip-impressed or incised vessels, often on tripods and pedestals (Hazarika, 2006). The overall homogeneity of it makes it easy to visualize a common ancestral culture, located quite close in time, from which all the descendent cultures of the Yellow river basin originated (Bellwood, 2005). The occurrence of potsherds and stone tools related to the cultivation system in the same stratigraphic horizon at various sites like Daojali Hading, Sarutaru, Garo Hills, and Nongpok Keithelmanbi indicates similarity in the chronology for origin and evolution of pottery and agriculture during the Neolithic period. It is most likely that due to its proximity to China and Southeast Asian countries, Northeast India seemed to have the strong influence of these cultures during this period (Hazarika, 2006). The archaeological evidence based on the stone tools from the Garo hills of the Meghalaya region of Northeast India suggests that this region might have been inhabited as early as the Palaeolithic period (Sankalia, 1974; Ghosh, 1978). There is evidence for indigenous animal and plant domestication (Neolithic sites). Archaeological records show more connections between Northeast Indian Neolithic to Chinese Neolithic than the Southeast Asian Neolithic (vanDriem, 1998). Based on the archaeological findings, the ancestors who spoke Proto-Sino-Tibetan were estimated to live over 6000 years ago (Matisoff, 1991; Cavalli-Sforza et al., 1994). Su et al. (2000a, b) also suggested that the ancient people living in the upper-middle Yellow river basin *ca* 10000 years ago were the ancestors of modern Sino-Tibetan populations.

Linguistic Background

There are three linguistic families that appear to represent the primary dispersion of agricultural populations through the landscapes that were previously occupied mostly by hunting and gathering groups. These are the Sino-Tibetan, Austro-Asiatic and Austronesian families (Bellwood, 2005). Within the populations of Northeast India, two major linguistic groups are found i.e. Tibeto-Burman and Austro-Asiatic speaking populations with predominantly Mongoloid features. The linguistic similarity among Northeast India and East and Southeast Asia reveals an interesting possibility as to the migration of the Austro-Asiatic and Tibeto-Burman language families into Northeast India during the Neolithic time. This indicates strong connections between East Asian and Southeast Asian Neolithic cultures with their counterparts in Northeast India (Hazarika, 2006).

Enriquez (1932) claimed that Mongolian races, who now occupy Southeast Asia, and also Northeast India, originated from Western China and migrated in three waves which include Mon-Khmer, Tibeto-Burman and Tai Chinese. The route-chart of the Mon-Khmer group was that they followed the Mekong valley towards South into Cambodia and Thailand until they reached Myanmar where from some of them went further Westward up to the Bay of Bengal and then turned towards North. It is believed that Khasis are the remnants of the Mon-Khmer linguistic group while Tibeto-Burman speaking group initially moved towards the West and thereafter subdivided into several groups following different routes, one group reaching Tibet on the North where some of them stayed behind while others moved on the northward until they reached Myanmar (Gangte, 1993). The Tibeto-Burman tribes came through Myanmar and entered the hills and valleys of Assam in about 1000 B.C. They gradually encroached upon the Austric (Austro Asiatic) settlers who have been settling there since 2000 to 2500 B.C. and forced most of them to take refuge in mountainous homes.

That was how Khasis thrived in their mountainous homes high on the hills of Meghalaya (Moral, 1996). While migrating in various route they formed many isolated groups or tribes. Large-scale diffusion of linguistic innovations has been taking place among various linguistic families of Northeast India for a very long time resulting in many common linguistic features binding all these languages in a common thread even though they are not related genetically. This is a direct result of linguistic innovations originating in one language spreading to neighbouring varieties through the medium of bilingual speakers.

Distribution and History of Austro-Asiatic Linguistic Family

The vast majority of Austro-Asiatic speaking populations are distributed in Southeast and East Asia. But it is found scattering in pockets mainly in the Eastern and Northeastern part of Indian tribal population groups. There are about thirty tribal populations representing three broad subfamilies, the Munda (Munda, Santal, and Lodha), the Khasi-Khmuic (Khasis and Jaintia), and the Mon-Khmer (Andaman Island; Diffloth, 2005), representing the Austro-Asiatic linguistic family in India. While the Mundari populations are ethnically Australoid, the groups speaking Khasi-Khmuic and Mon-Khmer languages have Mongoloid features. The Austro-Asiatic speaking populations, however, are believed to be the earliest inhabitants of the region of Northeast India (Roy, 1991). A recent study by Kumar et al. (2007) suggests that the linguistic ancestor of Austro-Asiatic populations have originated in India and migrated to Southeast Asia. Other anthropologists, historians, and linguists (Risley, 1915; Rapson, 1955; Pattanayak, 1998) have supported the view that the Austro-Asiatic speaking tribal are the original inhabitants of India. Some also believed that the Austro-Asiatic speakers are exclusively tribal, which may be indicative of their being the oldest inhabitants of India (Pattanayak, 1998; Gadgil et al., 1998). But it is reported earlier that the Austro-Asiatic linguistic family is originated and evolved in southern China (Diamand, 1997). The Austro-Asiatic linguistic family can also trace back to rice cultivators of Southeast Asia (Higham, 2003; Bellwood, 2005). Some other scholars, however, argue that tribal groups speaking Dravidian and Austro-Asiatic language have evolved from an older original substrate of proto-Australoid (Keith, 1936). A recent study by Thom (2007) shows the relative closeness of the Munda languages to some of the other Asian families (Dravidian, Uralic, Altaic, etc.). Mundari language of the Austro-Asiatic language shows remarkable similarities with the Uralic languages of northern Europe and Asia, and it is still common to read that this is where the Munda languages originated (Muscat, 1989).

While the Mon-Khmer languages are grammatically close to Sino-Tibetan language. The key to this understanding has been the proposal that a 'pidginizing' event took place sometime around 6500-6000BC somewhere in the Bangladesh region (Thom, 2007).

Distribution and History of Tibeto-Burman Linguistic Family

Sino-Tibetan languages include Chinese and Tibeto-Burman and the linguistic connection between these two subfamilies is well established (Martisoff, 1991). The Tibeto-Burman-speaking populations of India are morphological, culturally, and ethnically distinct and are primarily restricted to the Northern and Northeastern parts of the subcontinent (Grierson, 1909; Ruhlen, 1991). According to the historical records, the Tibeto-Burman populations were derived from the ancient *Di-Qiang* tribes in Northwest China. About 2600 BP, the Tibeto-Burman populations embarked on a large-scale southward migration by the Tibetan-Burman Corridor (Wang, 1994). While the Northeast Indian Tibeto-Burman speaking groups are later immigrants from Tibet and Myanmar (Guha, 1935). Tibeto-Burman speakers are supposed to be recent migrants to the Indian subcontinent (Gadgil et al., 1998). They are assumed to have arrived at different periods from Eastern and Southeastern Asia (Rapson, 1955; Dani, 1960). These populations are important for understanding the genetic affinity of Indian populations with other Central and Southeast Asian Tibeto-Burman and Austro-Asiatic populations (Elwin, 1958; Roychoudhury and Nei, 1997; Blackburn, 2004).

The Indian population is extremely diverse due to the presence of different linguistic lineages (Grierson, 1927), ethnically distinct tribal and large caste groups (Singh, 1998), and varying extents of admixtures with different world populations (Habib, 2001; 2002). However, stringent mating patterns have led to the existence of thousands of endogamous populations within this diverse pool (Bahl et al., 2005). The mtDNA (Majumder, 2001) and Y haplogroups (Rosser et al., 2000) provides signatures of population movements into India from Central and West Asia. Irrespective of the geographical location, linguistic affinity or social proximity reveals a fundamental unity of mtDNA lineages in India in spite of the extensive cultural and linguistic diversity with relatively female founder lineage in India (Roychoudhury et al., 2000; Basu et al., 2003). However, based on a study of autosomal and mtDNA markers in eight Indian tribes speaking Austro-Asiatic, Dravidian and Tibeto-Burman languages, it was concluded that these different language groups represented distinct founding groups, with Austro-Asiatic speakers being the most ancient inhabitants of the region (Roychoudhury et al., 2001). Based on both mtDNA haplotype and HVSI sequence, Austro-Asiatic tribal show a higher diversity than Dravidian tribal (Roychoudhary et al., 2001).

Das and Das (1973) suggested that Khasis of Meghalaya have migrated from Southeast Asia. Based on the anthropometric measurement, Austro-Asiatic linguistic groups such as Khasi and Nicobarese are clustering along with Mongoloid population groups, reflecting geographical contiguity and ethnic similarity (Kumar and Reddy, 2003). The Khasi and Nicobarese though being ethnically Mongoloid and linguistically belong to the same linguistic Austro-Asiatic family cluster neither with the Mundari groups nor closely with each other (Kumar and Reddy, 2003). It seems probable that the Khasi and the Nicobarese genetically drifted apart, as geographically and social and cultural factors favoured prolonged isolation between the groups (Kumar and Mukherjee, 1975). The study was done by Dixon (1992) based on physical measurement of the Khasi and the surrounding Mongoloid populations concluding that the Khasi are racially related to the majority of the Tibeto-Burman linguistic tribes.

Conclusion

In spite of the fact that less archeological studies have been conducted among the Northeast Indian region, all the remained artifacts prove convincing evidence of human migration from East and Southeast Asian to Northeast India. It is evident from the present study that the two main linguistic groups of Northeast India i.e. Tibeto-Burman and Austro-Asiatic show archaeo-linguistic affiliations with East and Southeast Asian populations. The central theme that emerges from the present study is the complexity and diversity of the Indian population, as a whole.

References

Ashraf, AA 1990, *Prehistoric Arunachal: a study on prehistory and ethnoarchaeology of Kamla Valley*, Directorate of Research, Government of Arunachal Pradesh, Itanagar.

Bahl, S, Virdi, K, Mittal, U, Sachdeva, MP, Kalla, AK & Holmes, SE 2005, 'Evidence of a common founder for SCA12 in the Indian population', *Annals of Human Genetics*, vol. 69, pp. 528-534.

Basu, A, Mukherjee, N, Roy, S, Sengupta, S, Banerjee, S, Chakraborty, M, Dey, B, Roy, M, Roy, B, Bhattacharyya, NP, Roychoudhury, S & Majumder, PP 2003, 'Ethnic India: a genomic view, with special reference to peopling and structure', *Genome Research*, vol. 13, pp. 2277-2290.

Bellwood, P 2005, *First farmers: the origins of agricultural societies*, Blackwell Publishing, U.K.

Blackburn, S 2004, 'Memories of migration: notes on legends and beads in Arunachal Pradesh, India', *European Bulletin of Himalayan Research*, vol. 25, pp. 15–60.

Cavalli-Sforza, LLP & Piazza, MA 1994, *The history and geography of human genes*, Princeton University Press, Princeton.

Chatterjee, SK 1970, *The place of Assam in the history and civilization of India*, Gauhati University, Guwahati.

Dani, AH 1960, *Prehistory and protohistory of Eastern India*, Firma KL Mukhopadhyay, Calcutta.

Das, PB & Das, BM 1973, 'Incidence of child mortality in a Kachari village', *Society and Culture*, vol. 4, pp. 127-129.

Diamond, J 1997, *Guns, germs, and steel: the fates of human societies*, Jonathan Cape, London.

Diffloth, G 2005, 'The contribution of linguistic palaeontology to the homeland of Austro-Asiatic' in *The peopling of East Asia: putting together archaeology, linguistics, and genetics*, eds S Laurent, B Roger & SM Alicia, Routledge Curzon, London, pp. 77-80.

Dixon, RB 1992, 'The Khasi and the racial history of Assam', *Man in India,* vol. 2, pp. 2-13.

Elwin, V 1958, *Myths of the Northeast frontiers of India*, North-East Frontier Agency, Shillong.

Enriquez, CM 1932, *A Burmese arcady,* Service & Co., Ltd., Seeley, London.

Gadgil, M, Joshi, NV, Manoharan, S, Prasad, UVS & Patil, S 1998, 'Peopling of India' in *The human heritage*, eds D Balasubramanian & NA Rao, Hyderabad University Press, Hyderabad, pp. 100-129.

Gangte, TS 1993, *The Kukis of Manipur,* Manas Publications, Delhi.

Ghosh, AK 1978, 'What happens when cultural and biological adaptability of man fails? a case study with the Palaeolithic period in the Garo hills', *Bulletin of the Department of Anthropology, Dibrugarh University*, vol. VI (1977), pp. 6-15.

Goswami, MC & Bhagabati, AC 1959, 'A typological study of shouldered Celts from Rengchangre (Garo Hills)', *Journal of Gauhati University*, vol. 10, pp. 17-24.

Grierson, GA 1927 (1909), *Linguistic survey of India vol III Tibeto Burman family, part I,* Government Printing, Superintendent, Calcutta.

Guha, BS 1935, *The racial affinities of the people of India; in Census of India, 1931, part III – ethnographical*, Government of India Press, Simla.

Habib, I 2001, *People's history of India part 1: prehistory,* Aligarh Historians Society & Julika Books, Aligarh.

Habib, I 2002, *People's history of India part 2: the Indus civilization,* Aligarh Historians Society & Julika Books, Aligarh.

Hazarika, M 2006, 'Neolithic culture of Northeast India: a recent perspective on the origins of pottery and agriculture', *Ancient Asia*, vol. 1, pp. 25-43.

Higham, C 2003, 'Languages and farming dispersals: Austro-Asiatic languages and rice cultivation' in *Examining the farming/language dispersal hypothesis*, eds P Bellwood & C Renfrew, The McDonald Institute for Archaeological Research, Cambridge, pp. 223-233.

IAR 1967-68, *Indian archaeology: a review*, Annual Bulletin of Archaeological Survey of India, New Delhi.

IAR 1966-67, *Indian archaeology: a review*, Annual Bulletin of Archaeological Survey of India, New Delhi.

Jobling, MA 2000, 'Y chromosome diversity in Europe is clinal and influenced primarily by geography, rather than by language', *American Journal of Human Genetics*, vol. 67, pp. 1526-1543.

Keith, A 1936, 'Review of B S Guha's racial affinities of the peoples of India', *Man,* vol. 29, pp. 37.

Kumar, N & Mukherjee, DP 1975, 'Genetic distances among the Ho tribe and other groups of Central India', *American Journal of Physical Anthropology*, vol. 42, pp. 489-494.

Kumar, V & Reddy, BM 2003, 'Status of Austro-Asiatic groups in the peopling of India: an exploratory study based on the available prehistoric, linguistic and biological evidence, *Journal of Biosciences*, vol. 28, pp. 507-522.

Kumar, V, Reddy, AN, Babu, JP, Rao, TN, Langstieh, BT, Thangaraj, K, Reddy, AG, Singh, L & Reddy, BM 2007, 'Y chromosome evidence suggests a common paternal heritage of Austro-Asiatic populations', *BMC Evolutionary Biology*, vol. 7, pp. 47.

Majumder, PP 2001, 'Ethnic populations of India as seen from an evolutionary perspective', *Journal of Biosciences*, vol. 26, pp. 533-545.

Matisoff, JA 1991, 'Sino-Tibetan linguistics: present state and future prospects', *Annual Review of Anthropology*, vol. 20, pp. 469-504.

Medhi, DK 2003, 'Potters, and pottery of the Assam region' in *Earthenware of Southeast Asia*, ed J Miksic, University Press, Singapore.

Medhi, DK 1980, *Quaternary history of the Garo Hills, Meghalaya.* Ph.D. thesis, University of Pune, Pune.

Moral, D 1996, 'Northeast India as a linguistic area', *Mon Khmer Studies*, vol. 27, pp. 43-53.

Muscat, M 1989, *Santali: a new approach*, Vinay Press, Bihar.

Pattanayak, DP 1998, 'The language heritage of India' in *The Indian human heritage*, eds D Balasubramanian & NA Rao, Hyderabad Universities Press, Hyderabad, pp. 95-99.

Rao, SN 1973, 'The Neolithic culture of Sarutaru, Assam', *Bulletin of the Department of Anthropology, Dibrugarh University*, vol. 2, pp. 1-9.

Rapson, EJ 1955, 'People and languages' in *Cambridge history of India, vol. 1 ancient India*, ed EJ Rapson, S. Chand, Delhi, pp. 37-57.

Risley, HH 1915, *The people of India*, Thacker Spink, Calcutta.

Rosser, ZH, Zerjal, T, Hurles, ME, Adojaan, M, Alavantic, D, Amorim, A, Amos, W, Armenteros, M., Arroyo, E, Barbujani, G, Beckman, G, Beckman, L, Bertranpetit, J, Bosch, E, Bradley, DG, Brede, G, Cooper, G, Côrte-Real, HB, de Knijff, P, Decorte, R, Dubrova, YE, Evgrafov, O, Gilissen, A, Glisic, S, Gölge, M, Hill, EW, Jeziorowska, A, Kalaydjieva, L, Kayser, M, Kivisild, T, Kravchenko, SA, Krumina, A, Kucinskas, V, Lavinha, J, Livshits, LA, Malaspina, P, Maria, S, McElreavey, K, Meitinger, TA, Mikelsaar, AV, Mitchell, RJ, Nafa, K, Nicholson,

J, Nørby, S, Pandya, A, Parik, J, Patsalis, PC, Pereira, L, Peterlin, B, Pielberg, G, Prata, MJ, Previderé, C, Roewer, L, Rootsi, S, Rubinsztein, DC, Saillard, J, Santos, FR, Stefanescu, G, Sykes, BC, Tolun, A, Villems, R, Tyler-Smith, C, Jobling, MA 2000, 'Y chromosome diversity in Europe is clinal and influenced primarily by geography, rather than by language', *American Journal of Human Genetics*, vol. 67, pp. 1526-1543.

Roy, NN 1991, 'The tribes of Northeast India – a living museum of man', *Bulletin of Assam State Museum*, vol. 12, pp. 73-81.

Roychoudhury, AK & Nei, M 1997, 'The emergence and dispersal of Mongoloids', *Journal of Indian Anthropological Society*, vol. 32, pp. 1-49.

Roychoudhury, S, Roy, S, Basu, A, Banerjee, R, Vishwanathan, H, Usha Rani, MV, Sil, SK, Mitra, M & Majumder, PP 2001, 'Genomic structures and population histories of linguistically distinct tribal groups of India', *Human Genetics*, vol. 3, pp. 339-350.

Roychoudhury, S, Roy, S, Dey, B, Chakraborty, M, Roy, M, Roy, B, Ramesh, A, Prabhakaran, N, Usha Rani, MV, Vishwanathan, H, Mitra, M, Sil, SK & Majumder, PP 2000, 'Fundamental genomic unity of ethnic India is revealed by analysis of mitochondrial DNA', *Current Science*, vol. 79, pp. 1182-1192.

Ruhlen, M 1991, *A guide to the world's language*, Stanford University Press, Stanford.

Sankalia, HD 1974, *Prehistory, and protohistory of India and Pakistan*, Deccan College, Pune.

Sharma, HC 1972, *Prehistoric archaeology: stone age cultures of Garo Hills, Meghalaya*. Ph.D. thesis, Gauhati University, Guwahati.

Sharma, S 2001, *Cultural affinities between Southeast Asia and Northeast India during prehistoric times with special reference to Ganol and Rongram valleys in Meghalaya.* Ph.D. thesis, Deccan College, Pune.

Sharma, TC 1967, 'A note of the Neolithic pottery of Assam', *Man*, vol. 2, pp. 126-128.

Sharma, TC 1991, 'Prehistoric situation in Northeast India' in *Archaeology of North-eastern India*, eds JP Singh & G Sengupta, Vikas Publishing House, New Delhi, pp. 41-56.

Singh, KS 1998, *India's communities. people of India: national series, anthropological survey of India,* Oxford University Press, New Delhi.

Singh, OK 1983, *Archaeology in Manipur, Napachik: a stone age site in the Manipur valley*, State Archaeology, Government of Manipur, Imphal.

Singh, OK 1993, *Stone age culture of Manipur.* Ph.D. thesis, University of Manipur, Manipur.

Su, B, Jin, L, Underhill, P, Martinson, J, Saha, N, McGarvey, ST, Shriver, MD, Chu, J, Oefner, P, Chakraborty, R & Deka, R 2000a, 'Polynesian origins: new insights from the Y-Chromosome', *Proceedings of the National Academy of Sciences*, vol. 97, pp. 8225-8228.

Su, B, Xiao, C, Deka, R, Seielstad, MT, Kangwanpong, D, Xiao, J, Lu, D, Underhill, P, Cavalli-Sforza, L, Chakraborty, R & Jin, L 2000b, 'Y chromosome haplotypes reveal prehistorical migrations to the Himalayas', *Human Genetics*, vol. 107, pp. 582-590.

Thom, N 2007, *The origin of tongue*, Grosvenor House, Guildford.

Van Driem, GV 1998, 'Neolithic correlates of ancient Tibeto-Burman migrations' in *Archaeology and language II: archaeological data and linguistics hypotheses*, eds R Blench & M Spriggs, Routledge Taylor, and Francis Group, London, pp. 67-102.

Wang, ZH 1994, *History of nationalities in China*, China Social Science Press, Beijing.

Yasuda, Y 2002, 'The origins of pottery and agriculture in East Asia' in *The origins of pottery and agriculture*, ed Y Yasuda, International Research Centre for Japanese Studies, Japan, pp. 119-142.

Chapter - 2

Impact of Basic Amenities and Socio-economy on Women Health of Tribal Concentrated Zones in India

Suparna Shome, Susmita Bharati,
Manoranjan Pal, and Premananda Bharati

Introduction

Access to basic amenities like drinking water, sanitation, electricity, housing, and drainage is essential for human development. Housing conditions and access to basic amenities are closely linked to the health conditions of family members. Marsh et al. (2000), based on data from Great Britain, points out that poor housing conditions affect current as well as future health status. Therefore, access to reasonable housing conditions is essential for the family's overall welfare. Like other developing countries, India also experiences inequality in housing and basic amenities (Kundu et al., 1999; Srinivasan and Mohanty, 2004; Edelman and Mitra, 2006; Ahmad, 2012). There have been several initiatives, plans, and programmes like *Bharat Nirman, Indira Awaas Yojana, Rajiv Gandhi Gramin Vidyutikaran,* etc to improve basic amenities but that was not sufficient to reduce the gap among social groups.

India is a concentration of multi-ethnic group. And among these ethnic groups, the tribal community is numerically small but enormously diversified in respect of language, linguistic traits, ecological setting, population size, etc. A majority of the Scheduled Tribe population is concentrated in the eastern, central and western belt of India, covering the nine States of Orissa, Madhya Pradesh, Chhattisgarh, Jharkhand, Maharashtra, Gujarat, Rajasthan, Andhra Pradesh, and West Bengal. It is seen that Madhya Pradesh (14.69 %) has the largest percentage of concentration (Statistical profile of

Scheduled Tribe, 2013). Maharashtra, Orissa, Rajasthan, Gujarat, and Jharkhand having 8-10 percent concentration and in West Bengal, it is 5.0 percent. About 12.0 percent inhabit the Northeastern region, about 5.0 percent in the Southern region and about 3.0 percent in the Northern States (Ministry of the Tribal Affair, 2014).

Indian society is sufferers from different substantial inequalities in different aspects of life such as education, employment, health. And people are also very prone to get private health care but it is not only expensive but also it is urban-based. People in rural areas are more handicapped to get both public and private health facilities. These situations are more prevalent among the poor and uneducated population and also among the tribal population because tribes are considered as the weakest sections of the population in respect of socio-economic and socio-demographic aspects.

According to Deasi et al. (2010), that Indian people are suffering from fever, cough, diarrhea, etc., which vary frequently due to their impact on unhealthy basic amenities. Basic amenities like poor housing condition, unsafe drinking water, lack of sanitation, use of biomass fuel often increase the health problem which is also essential to assess the socio-economy and also fundamental to the assessment of health. The condition of health also differs due to substantial differences in the socio-economic condition of the household. Availability survey and census data proves that tribal people are mostly not used safe drinking water and sanitation. About 11.0 percent of tribal household uses tap water and also the availability of tap water in the tribal household ranges from 2.0 percent in Orissa to 49.0 percent in Sikkim and 54.0 percent in Goa. Only 17.0 percent of households have access to improved toilet facility whereas 44.0 percent among the non-tribal group (Census, 2011). Overall uses of non-smoky fuel are higher among the non-tribal people than tribal people. Uses of smoky or domestic fuel are maximum in Nagaland (80.0 %), followed by Kerala and Assam (79.0%), Meghalaya, Manipur, and Tripura, ranges from 70.0 – 77.0 percent.

On the other hand, undernutrition among the community is the major health problem in developing the world and mainly in Southern Asia and sub-Saharan Africa (WHO, 2002; 2004; FAO, 2004). Undernutrition is also responsible for the increase of infectious disease due to weak body immunity (Brasin and Counter, 2003; Pinstrup et al., 1993; Murrary and Lopez, 1997; Black, 2003). So, undernutrition is one of the most important risk factors for the burden of disease in developing countries (Murray and Lopez, 1997; Nemer et al., 2001). It is the direct cause of about 3, 00,000 of death per year (Nemer et al., 2001, Muller et al., 2003; Black, 2003; FAO, 2004).

And the majority of the tribes in India suffer from undernutrition and hunger since tribal communities are isolated from the general population and are socially and economically vulnerable (Laxmaiah et al., 2007). In this perspective, the study encompasses the impact of the differentials of basic amenities and socio-economy on women health in tribal concentrated zones of India like Northeast, Central, and East zones with the major objectives is to see the livelihood situation of the tribal which includes (1) basic amenities, (2) awareness, (3) the socio-economic factors (affecting the livelihood situation), and (4) inter-state comparison with high concentrated tribal people.

Methodology

For this study, we have used the National Family Health Survey (NFHS – III) data conducted by the International Institute for Population Sciences (IIPS), Mumbai, in 2005-2006. They collected data on reproductive-aged women of 15-49 years from 29 states in India and the population frame was based on the 2001 census. The data are cross-sectional and unit-level. Here our study is based on non-pregnant women. As our focused area of study are tribal concentrated three zones of India, such as Northeast, East, and Central zones of India along with the associated states, therefore, we have considered here only the data set of the same zones of India. The sample size consists of 8649 women from eight states in Northeast India, 1433 women of East India that includes the states of West Bengal, Orissa, and Jharkhand and for Central India, the sample size is 1746 and it includes two states such as Madhya Pradesh and Chhattisgarh. To measure the undernutrition, Body Mass Index (BMI) is considered as a basis for measuring undernutrition. It is classified into the following categories (WHO, 2003) as follows:

Categories	*Ranges of BMI (kg/m²)*
Chronic Energy Deficiency (CED)	<18.5
Normal	18.5 – 24.9
Overweight	25.0 – 29.9
Obese	≥ 30.0 only

For assessing anaemia, the levels of Hb in adult women were estimated using the HemoCue system. This system uses a single drop of blood from a finger prick, which is drawn into a cuvette and then inserted into a portable, battery-operated instrument. The Hb concentration appeared on a digital screen. Before the anemia testing was undertaken in a household, the respondent was asked to sign a consent form. Hemoglobin levels among women have been classified on the basis of International Standard as follows for non-pregnant women: normal, >12.0 g/dL; mild, 10.0 to 11.9 g/dL; moderate,7.0 to 9.9 g/dL; and severe, <7.0 g/dL. In this study, it is to be noted that in Nagaland no blood collection was done. Therefore, for anaemia, the sample size was lower due to exclusion of Nagaland.

The background explanatory variables are divided into two broad categories such as basic amenities and socio-economy. Under basic amenities, these are drinking water, having of toilet facility and electricity, the influence of mass-media, house type, and cooking fuel. And under socio-economy, these are (i) place of residence, (ii) respondent's occupation, (iii) respondent's education, (iv) wealth index of the family (following Rutstein, 1999), and (v) type of family.

Methods

To determine the association of undernutrition and anemia with the basic amenities and socio-economy, bi-variate table were done between tribe and non-tribe non-pregnant women to get clear ideas about non-tribe and tribe in the same locality. And also, to present the relative and effective intervention, binary logistic regressions were carried out. For this analysis, the binary values taken by the dependent variable are underweight and anemia when 1 for undernutrition or anaemic and 0 for others. We have used SPSS version 18.0, for analysis. An estimated odd ratio of 1 indicates that the nature of the dependent variable is no different from the reference category. If the estimated odd ratio is >1, the probability of becoming affected is more in this category compared to the reference category and if it is <1, then it is just opposite to that of >1 case.

Results

Indian women are generally vulnerable to poor nutrition, especially during pregnancy and lactation. The analysis is done to see the health vulnerability with that of some basic amenities along with some socioeconomic variables. It should be in mind that the emphasis is given on the tribal population and non-tribes are taken as a control group. Therefore, we have analyzed tribal first and then compare it with non-tribes.

Table 2.1 shows the percentage distribution of underweight and anaemic women among the tribes and non-tribes of Northeast, East and Central regions of the country. It is found from the table that overall percentage of underweight women is low (14.4%) in Northeast region compared to east

Table 2.1 Women health among tribal concentrated zones in India

Zones and states	*Tribe*			*Non-tribe*		
	No.	*Underweight*	*Anaemic*	*No.*	*Underweight*	*Anaemic*
Northeast India	8649	14.4	45.2	9952	24.9	55.5
Arunachal Pradesh	946	14.3	46.1	361	22.4	63.2
Assam	272	21.3	72.8	2866	36.2	68.6
Manipur	792	11.7	28.2	3157	15.0	38.5
Meghalaya	1340	12.0	46.3	293	23.5	41.0
Mizoram	1615	14.5	38.3	33	6.1	39.4
Nagaland	2835	15.8	---	625	21.9	---
Sikkim	605	8.9	57.7	1229	11.4	58.8
Tripura	244	25.0	74.6	1388	38.5	65.5
Eastern India	1433	50.6	78.5	10637	34.4	59.5
West Bengal	198	58.6	81.3	5731	31.6	59.6
Orissa	686	50.6	72.6	3022	36.8	57.3
Jharkhand	549	47.7	84.9	1844	39.3	62.9
Central India	1746	49.0	73.4	7328	36.0	47.9
Madhya Pradesh	845	49.0	73.1	4826	34.8	47.0
Chhattisgarh	907	49.2	73.6	2502	38.3	49.7

(50.6%) and central (49.0%) among the tribes whereas among non-tribe the proportion is 24.9 percent in Northeast and 34.4 percent in east and 36.0 percent in the central region of the country. The underweight percent among the tribes vary from 8.9 percent (Sikkim) to 25.0 percent (Tripura), whereas among non-tribe it shows 6.1 percent (Mizoram) to 38.5 percent (Tripura). For East and central region, the percentage is more or less the same among the tribe and non-tribe, though the percentage of underweight is lower among non-tribe compared to the tribe. Considering anaemia, the result shows that the overall percentage of anaemia among the tribe and non-tribe is 45.2 percent and 55.5 percent respectively in the Northeast region of the country. The percentage varies from 28.2 percent in Assam to 74.6 percent in Tripura among the tribal women whereas for non-tribe the percentage of anaemia varies from 38.5 percent in Manipur to 68.6 percent in Assam. Incidence of anaemia is quite high in the east (78.5%) and central zone (73.4%) compared to non-tribe of the same region. The percentage is higher in the eastern region (59.5%) compared to central zone (47.9%) among the non-tribes. The same scenario is observed in the case of the tribe also.

Table 2.2 describes the general condition of basic amenities along with their socio-economy among the tribal concentrated regions of India. The table shows that the use of safe drinking water sources is 70.0 percent or more among the tribes and non-tribes except tribes in the eastern region. It is also seen that the proportion of use of safe drinking water is almost the same among the tribes and non-tribes in the Northeast region, whereas the

Table 2.2 General condition of basic amenities and socio-economy among tribal and non-tribal

Basic amenities and socio-economy	*Northeast India (%)*				*Eastern India (%)*				*Central India (%)*			
	Tribe		*Non-tribe*		*Tribe*		*Non-tribe*		*Tribe*		*Non-tribe*	
	N	*Cond.*	*N*	*cond.*	*N*	*Cond.*	*N*	*Cond.*	*N*	*Cond.*	*N*	*Cond.*
Drinking water												
Unsafe	2585	29.9	2823	28.4	598	41.7	1374	12.9	517	29.6	1094	14.9
Safe	6064	70.1	7129	71.6	835	58.3	9263	87.1	1229	70.4	6234	85.1
Toilet facility												
Not-improved	2585	29.9	2669	26.8	1327	92.6	4784	45.0	1601	91.7	3810	52.0
Improved	6064	70.1	7283	73.2	106	7.4	5853	55.0	145	8.3	3518	48.0
Having electricity												
No	1398	16.2	2335	23.5	1097	76.6	3637	34.2	637	36.5	1053	14.4
Yes	7251	83.8	7617	76.5	336	23.4	7000	65.8	110	63.5	6275	85.6
Mass media												
TV watching	6733	77.8	8107	81.5	486	33.9	7658	72.0	710	40.7	5451	74.4
Newspaper reading	4579	52.9	5011	50.4	160	11.2	3856	36.3	243	13.9	3152	43.0
Listening Radio	4257	49.2	5852	58.8	408	28.5	4569	43.0	690	39.5	3370	46.0
House type												
Kancha	1692	19.6	1190	12.0	350	24.4	1296	12.2	254	14.5	635	8.7
Mixed	4533	52.4	6020	60.5	892	62.2	3646	34.3	1314	75.3	3039	41.5
Pucca	2424	28.0	2742	27.6	191	13.3	5695	53.5	178	10.2	3654	49.9
Cooking fuel												
Smoky	5417	62.6	5717	57.4	1387	96.8	7333	68.9	1638	93.8	4212	57.5
Non-smoky	3232	37.4	4235	42.6	46	3.2	3304	31.1	108	6.2	3116	42.5
Place of residence												
Rural	5486	63.4	5571	56.0	1231	85.9	5634	53.0	1557	89.2	3356	45.8
Urban	3163	36.6	4381	44.0	202	14.1	5003	47.0	189	10.5	3972	54.2
Respondent's occupation												
Not work/dom.	44.6	50.9	6053	60.8	390	27.2	7061	66.4	329	18.8	3786	51.7
Prof/serv	1483	17.1	1518	15.3	76	5.3	1234	11.6	77	4.4	761	10.4
Agro-related	2313	26.7	955	9.6	756	52.8	1373	12.9	1001	57.3	1832	25.0
Labour	447	5.2	1426	14.3	211	14.7	969	9.1	339	19.4	949	13.0
Education												
Illiterate	1867	21.6	2338	23.5	1018	71.0	3532	33.2	1195	68.4	2692	36.7
Primary	1594	18.4	1540	15.5	134	9.4	1970	18.5	232	13.3	1213	16.6
Sec. & Higher	5188	60.0	6073	61.0	281	19.6	5133	48.3	319	18.3	3423	46.7
Wealth index												
Poorer or poorest	1999	23.1	2163	21.7	1189	83.0	3981	37.4	1460	83.6	2680	36.6
Middle	2013	23.3	2709	27.2	138	9.6	1771	16.6	144	8.2	982	13.4
Richer or richest	4637	53.6	5080	51.0	106	7.4	4885	45.9	142	8.1	3666	50.0
Type of family												
Non-nuclear	4867	56.3	5921	59.5	760	53.0	5605	52.7	906	51.9	3791	51.7
Nuclear	3782	43.7	4031	40.5	673	47.0	5032	47.3	840	48.1	3537	48.3

difference is much higher in the east zone followed by the central zone. Use of improved toilet facility among the tribes is very poor in the east (7.4%) and central (8.3%) region compared to the Northeast region (70.1%). The proportion is quite higher among the non-tribes of those two zones, though the difference is negligible in the Northeast region. Having electricity among the tribes of the eastern zone is only 23.4 percent, whereas it is 63.5 percent in the central zone followed by Northeast zone (83.8%). The proportion of safe i.e. non-smoky cooking fuel is very low in the east (3.2%) and central (6.2%) zone and as usual large gap in use of safe cooking fuel found among the non-tribes of those two regions. Electricity is available only 23.4 percent among the tribal residence areas of east zone compared to other tribal and non- tribal areas of the central and Northeast region. Regarding mass media, the percentage of awareness through TV watching, newspaper reading and listening radio among the tribes are lower in east and central region compared to the Northeast region. Socio-economic factors also play an important role in differentiating the tribal and non-tribal situation in the said areas of the country. Percentage of tribes, residing in urban areas is only 14.0 percent and 10.5 percent in east and central region respectively. The situation is much better in the Northeast region where 36.6 percent of tribes reside in urban areas. The result clearly shows that the residence pattern makes a difference between tribe and non-tribe in their daily life. In the case of women's occupational status, the data indicates that the proportion of women in the tribal category, engaged in any occupational activities is more in east and central zone compared to the Northeast zone. In a similar pattern, illiterates are high in the east and central region. The result is reverse in case of Northeast where illiterate is only 21.6 percent among the tribes. Household economic status always plays a good role where we find the proportion of poor to the middle group is almost similar with that of the rich group in case of the Northeast zone for both tribe and non-tribe population. But in case of other two zones, i.e. east, and central zone, middle to the rich group is only 16.0 percent to 17.0 percent among the tribe and for non-tribe, it is more than 60.0 percent. No major difference in percentage is found in the family whether nuclear or non-nuclear.

Table 2.3 explains the condition of women's underweight and anaemia with respect to basic amenities and socio-economic factors. It is observed that the percentage of underweight and anaemia among the tribes of eastern and central India is quite similar in nature with some exception. But the condition is different in the Northeast states. Here, the percentage is much lower among the tribes compared to eastern and central region states. At

Table 2.3 Relationship between basic amenities and socio-economy with under-weight and anaemia

Basic amenities and socio-economy	*Northeast India (%)*				*Eastern India (%)*				*Central India (%)*			
	Tribe		*Non-tribe*		*Tribe*		*Non-tribe*		*Tribe*		*Non-tribe*	
	Under weight	*Anaemia*	*Under weight*	*Anaemia*	*Under weight*	*Anaemia*	*Under weight*	*Anaemia*	*Under weight*	*Anaemia*	*Under weight*	*Anaemia*
Drinking water												
Unsafe	15.8	52.7	26.2	51.8	50.7	82.4	42.8	64.5	48.4	74.7	44.3	52.3
Safe	13.8	42.6	24.3	56.9	50.5	75.7	33.2	58.8	49.4	72.8	34.5	47.1
Toilet facility												
Not-improved	14.9	46.6	33.1	56.2	52.1	78.9	47.5	64.4	50.4	74.1	45.5	52.9
Improved	14.2	44.5	21.8	55.2	32.1	73.6	23.7	55.6	34.5	65.5	25.7	42.6
Having electricity												
No	18.5	56.5	42.7	65.9	54.2	78.5	50.3	66.0	53.4	78.6	50.3	55.8
Yes	13.6	42.6	19.4	52.2	38.7	78.6	26.2	56.2	46.6	70.3	33.6	46.6
Mass media												
TV watching	14.1	43.3	21.8	53.6	45.3	74.9	29.1	57.0	45.8	70..7	32.2	45.8
Newspaper read	13.4	39.5	18.6	50.6	37.5	77.5	24.5	53.8	46.1	65.0	29.1	42.0
Listening Radio	14.3	42.0	22.6	50.5	49.8	73.8	32.7	58.7	51.0	73.8	33.9	45.8
House type												
Kancha	17.0	51.8	35.0	57.7	59.1	72.3	52.2	66.2	50.0	71.3	46.6	52.8
Mixed	15.3	44.1	26.9	54.3	48.3	80.6	45.6	64.3	51.1	74.3	44.6	52.0
Pucca	10.8	42.2	16.0	57.2	45.5	80.1	23.2	55.0	33.1	69.7	27.0	43.7
Cooking fuel												
Smoky	15.8	49.7	32.3	57.8	51.7	78.7	43.0	62.2	50.1	74.1	44.0	52.7
Non-smoky	12.0	38.7	14.9	52.1	17.4	71.7	15.4	53.7	34.3	63.0	25.2	41.5
Place of residence												
Rural	14.9	48.4	30.2	57.8	52.0	78.8	44.8	62.7	50.2	74.2	45.0	53.0
Urban	13.4	38.7	18.1	52.2	42.1	76.7	22.8	56.0	40.2	66.7	28.4	43.6
Respondent's occupation												
Notwork/dom.	15.9	48.1	26.4	58.6	44.6	77.4	31.7	58.3	45.0	71.7	31.6	45.1
Prof/serv	8.2	36.3	17.3	50.2	43.4	81.6	23.9	57.2	53.2	64.9	27.7	46.9
Agro-related	15.1	44.7	24.3	49.1	53.3	80.2	52.1	67.2	50.6	75.4	45.3	52.0
Labour	16.3	47.8	26.6	52.7	54.5	73.5	43.0	60.7	47.5	70.8	42.1	51.9
Education												
Illiterate	16.3	52.0	32.7	60.8	53.3	78.3	44.8	65.6	51.0	75.6	40.5	53.0
Primary	14.9	14.9	30.1	59.7	50.7	82.8	37.0	60.6	47.4	69.4	39.2	52.3
Sec. & Higher	13.5	40.7	20.5	52.4	40.6	77.2	26.3	55.0	42.9	67.7	31.3	42.3
Wealth index												
Poorer or poorest	17.0	54.0	42.1	64.5	52.9	78.6	51.3	66.2	50.5	75.1	48.2	53.8
Middle	16.9	46.4	28.5	54.6	47.8	76.1	36.4	60.3	47.2	67.4	40.7	52.6
Richer or richest	12.1	40.5	15.6	52.0	28.3	80.2	19.9	53.8	35.9	61.3	25.8	42.3
Type of family												
Non-nuclear	14.3	43.3	24.4	54.8	47.8	80.5	32.9	60.0	47.3	74.3	34.7	47.9
Nuclear	14.5	46.8	25.1	56.0	53.0	76.7	35.8	59.1	50.8	72.5	37.2	47.9

this point, it is better to say that the percentage of underweight is lower compared to anaemia for all the said regions both for tribe and non-tribe. In the Northeast region, the proportion of underweight is lowest (8.2%) among the women engaged in professional or service category and highest (17.0%) among poorest wealth index categories. Considering basic amenities, it varies from 10.8 percent (*Pucca* house type, an indicator may be of a household economic factor) to 18.5 percent (having no electricity). The result of the east region shows that underweight for basic needs ranges from 17.4 percent (for that tribe use non-smoky cooking fuel) to 59.1 percent (for *kachcha* house type). The trend is similar for the tribes of central region where it varies from 34.3 percent (non-smoky fuel) to 53.4 percent (having no electricity). Underweight is low among the women of higher education and rich wealth index categories, though intensity is different for the regions. It is surprising that the proportion of underweight among the non-tribe of the Northeast region is high irrespective of basic amenities and socio-economic factors. The result shows a similar trend with respect to anaemia also in the Northeast region. But for the other two regions like east and central, the result is reversed. The percentage of underweight and anaemia is lower among the non-tribe compared to the tribe for all the factors.

Table 2.4 and 2.5 describes the association of basic amenities and socioeconomic variable on underweight and anaemia through logistic regression analysis. Table 2.4 explains the association with basic amenities. The table shows that cooking fuel is an important parameter for both the condition of underweight and anaemia in the Northeast region. The odds of non-smoky fuel user are significantly lower than the smoky fuel category for both tribes and non-tribes for both underweight and anaemia among the tribes and non-tribes of Northeast region. For the eastern region, the odds of underweight are significantly lower among tribes of non-smoky (odds: 0.314), having electricity (odds: 0.643) and mixed type of house (odds: 0.694) and for anaemia, odds are significantly lower (odds: 0.703) among the user of safe drinking sources compared to unsafe and the risk is significantly higher among the tribes who are staying in mixed or *pucca* household compared to *kancha* house. The result is reverse for non-tribe when compared with house type both for underweight and anaemia. It is also observed from the analysis that for non-tribes, underweight is significantly lower among the user of improved toilet facility compared to non-improved (odds: 0.708), having electricity (odds: 0.718), and who are watching TV (odds: 0.888) and for non-smoky cooking fuel (odds: 0.441). Central region shows association both for underweight and anaemia only among the user of non-smoky fuel for non- tribe. Role of mass media through newspaper reading is found to be significant both for tribe and non-tribe among the anaemic women.

Table 2.5 shows an association of underweight and anaemia among the tribe and non-tribe of tribal concentrated regions of the country with respect to socio-economic variables. The analysis shows that women's occupational status is significantly associated both for tribe and non-tribe in the Northeast region of the country. It is found that for underweight, odds are significantly lower among the women of having occupation compared to not working category. The odds of labour does not show any significance compared to the reference category. The picture is clear for anaemia. The odds are significantly lower both among tribe and non-tribe in Northeast region. Role of education and wealth index also play an important role in the determination of underweight and anaemia for the Northeast region. It is also found that underweight is significantly low among the women of urban resident pattern compared to rural. In this study, regional variation is prominent where we observe that the Northeast region shows something different than that of east and central to the Northeast. For east zone, underweight is significantly lower (odds: 0.447) among the rich wealth index group compared to poor category among the tribe, whereas underweight are significantly higher (odds 1.223) among nuclear family type and anaemia is significantly lower (odds: 0.803) compared to non-nuclear family. The table describes that among non-tribe, the odds of underweight of professional or service category is significantly lower (odds: 0.784) and significantly higher among agro-related and labour compared to the non-working category. The education and wealth index has a positive role in the reduction of underweight and anaemia. The odds are significantly low compared to illiterate and poor wealth index category in the eastern region. Tribe in the central region shows a mixed and scattered result. It is found that odds of wealth index are significantly lower when considering for underweight and anaemia among the tribe and for non-tribe underweight shows significance in urban residence pattern. The odd ratio is significantly higher in labour (odds: 1.232) compared to the domestic working group, significantly in higher education compared to illiterate (odds: 1.151, 1.241) category and underweight significantly lower among the higher wealth index group (odds: 0.762, 0.401) compared to poor wealth index group. It is also seen that anaemia in the central region is significantly low (odds: 0.830) in an urban area compared to rural, higher education (odds 0.771) compared to illiterate, rich wealth index (odds the 0.795) compared to poor wealth index categories.

Table 2.4 Categorical logistic regression between basic amenities with underweight and anaemia.

Basic amenities	*Northeast India*				*Eastern India*				*Central India*			
	Tribe		*Non-tribe*		*Tribe*		*Non-tribe*		*Tribe*		*Non-tribe*	
	Under weight	*Anae-mia*	*Under weight*	*Anae-mia*	*Under weight*	*Anae-mia*	*Under weight*	*Anae-mia*	*Under weight*	*Anae-mia*	*Under weight*	*Anae-mia*
Drinking water												
Unsafe (R)	1.00	1.00	1.00	1.00	1.00	1.00	1.00	1.00	1.00	1.00	1.00	1.00
Safe	0.962	0.832**	1.047	1.148*	1.067	0.703*	1.056	0.932	1.167	1.043	1.053	1.032
Toilet facility												
Not-Improved (R)	1.00	1.00	1.00	1.00	1.00	1.00	1.00	1.00	1.00	1.00	1.00	1.00
Improved	1.197*	1.363**	0.994	1.153*	0.770	0.781	0.708**	0.90	0.659	0.870	0.642**	0.868
Having electricity												
No (R)	1.00	1.00	1.00	1.00	1.00	1.00	1.00	1.00	1.00	1.00	1.00	1.00
Yes	0.753**	0.681**	0.494**	0.585**	0.643**	1.074	.718**	0.867*	0.835	0.687**	0.837*	0.883
Mass media												
TV watching												
No(R)	1.00	1.00	1.00	1.00	1.00	1.00	1.00	1.00	1.00	1.00	1.00	1.00
Yes	1.148	1.067	0.938	0.965	0.779	0.758	.888*	0.892*	0.896	0.936	0.890	0.960
Newspaper reading												
No (R)	1.00	1.00	1.00	1.00	1.00	1.00	1.00	1.00	1.00	1.00	1.00	1.00
Yes	0.979	0.730**	0.836**	0.836**	1.031	1.155	1.007	0.835**	1.129	0.695*	1.019	0.812**
Listening Radio												
No (R)	1.00	1.00	1.00	1.00	1.00	1.00	1.00	1.00	1.00	1.00	1.00	1.00
Yes	0.943	0.804**	0.754**	0.679**	0.900	0.764	0.987	1.019	1.199	1.076	0.961	0.958
House type												
Kancha (R)	1.00	1.00	1.00	1.00	1.00	1.00	1.00	1.00	1.00	1.00	1.00	1.00
Mixed	0.943	0.945	1.024	1.085	0.694*	1.567**	0.863*	0.953	1.035	1.159	1.051	1.071
Pucca	0.660**	1.017	0.864	1.339**	1.119	2.032**	0.651**	0.821*	0.576*	1.603	0.843	1.129
Cooking fuel												
Smoky (R)	1.00	1.00	1.00	1.00	1.00	1.00	1.00	1.00	1.00	1.00	1.00	1.00
Non-smoky	0.843*	0.739**	0.554**	0.842**	.314*	0.690	0.441**	1.009	1.194	0.703	0.741**	0.789**

Table 2.5 Categorical logistic regression between socio-economy with underweight and anaemia

Basic amenities and socio-economy	*Northeast India*				*Eastern India*				*Central India*			
	Tribe		*Non-tribe*		*Tribe*		*Non-tribe*		*Tribe*		*Non-tribe*	
	Under weight	*Anaemia*	*Under weight*	*Anaemia*	*Under weight*	*Anaemia*	*Under weight*	*Anaemia*	*Under weight*	*Anaemia*	*Under weight*	*Anaemia*
Place of residence												
Rural(R)	1.00	1.00	1.00	1.00	1.00	1.00	1.00	1.00	1.00	1.00	1.00	1.00
Urban	1.125	0.808**	0.779**	0.900*	0.950	0.952	0.789**	1.071	0.849	1.176	0.856*	0.830**
Respondent's occupation												
Not work/dom.(R)	1.00	1.00	1.00	1.00	1.00	1.00	1.00	1.00	1.00	1.00	1.00	1.00
Prof/serv	0.505**	0.696**	0.735**	0.776**	1.002	1.311	0.784**	0.976	4.415	0.727	0.879	1.120
Agro-related	0.839**	0.649**	0.612**	0.585**	1.160	1.154	1.195**	1.089	1.020	0.971	1.072	0.902
Labour	0.962	0.820*	0.843**	0.739**	1.226	0.814	1.193*	0.949	0.898	0.768	1.232**	1.094
Education												
Illiterate(R)	1.00	1.00	1.00	1.00	1.00	1.00	1.00	1.00	1.00	1.00	1.00	1.00
Primary	0.954	1.005	0.968	0.949	0.961	1.281	0.893*	0.869*	0.899	0.752*	1.151*	1.023
Sec. & Higher	0.989	0.754**	0.873*	0.790**	0.787	0.896	0.892*	0.792**	0.831	0.794	1.241**	0.771**
Wealth index												
Poorer/ poorest(R)	1.00	1.00	1.00	1.00	1.00	1.00	1.00	1.00	1.00	1.00	1.00	1.00
Middle	0.985	0.756**	0.583***	0.711**	0.953	0.891	0.623**	0.814**	0.941	0.696*	0.762**	1.039
Richer / richest	0.664**	0.691**	0.293**	0.668**	0.447**	1.254	0.319**	0.641**	0.636*	0.511*	0.401**	0.795**
Type of family												
Non-nuclear(R)	1.00	1.00	1.00	1.00	1.00	1.00	1.00	1.00	1.00	1.00	1.00	1.00
Nuclear	0.974	1.070	0.919*	1.005	1.223*	0.803*	1.038	0.920*	1.155	0.901	1.096*	0.971

Discussion

It is evident from the above results that poor tribal people have worse health indicators than the general population. Household risk factors affecting health, particularly underweight and anaemia are mainly due to lack of proper basic amenities like drinking water, toilet facility, fuel used for cooking, etc. The study makes an attempt to see the effect of factors under basic amenity and socioeconomic condition on risk factors of women health among the tribes of the Northeast, Central, and Eastern region of the country. Nontribes are taken as a control group to compare and understand the actual situation of the tribes with respect to non-tribe. The result shows that women health risk in Northeast is much lower than that of the eastern and central region among the tribes of India. Not only have that, in the Northeast region, tribe non-tribe difference also lowered than other two aforesaid regions. It is found that overall percentage of underweight women is low (14.4%) in Northeast region compared to East (50.6%) and Central (49.0%) among the tribes whereas among non-tribe the proportion is 24.9 in Northeast and 34.4 in East and 36.0 in the Central region of the country. Considering anaemia, the result shows that the overall percentage of anaemia among the tribe and non-tribe are 45.2 and 55.5 respectively in the Northeast region of the country. The result shows that the use of safe drinking water sources is 70.0 percent or more among the tribes and non-tribes except tribes in the eastern region. Use of improved toilet facility among the tribes is very poor in the East (7.4%) and Central (8.3%) region compared to the Northeast region (70.1%). The proportion is quite higher among the non-tribes of those two zones, though the difference is negligible in the Northeast region. Regarding mass media also, awareness through TV watching, newspaper reading and listening radio among the tribes are lower in the east and central region compared to the Northeast region. Use of cooking fuel is very important for women health. It is found that use of safe i.e. non-smoky cooking fuel is very poor in the east (3.2%) and central (6.2%) zone among the tribes compared to Northeast region (37.4%). It is said that India's poor tribal people have far worse health indicators than the general population because most tribal people live in remote rural areas where illiteracy, adverse physical environment, lack of personal health and hygiene make them more vulnerable to health risk. Our result shows that tribes residing in urban areas are only 14.0 percent and 10.5 percent in east and central region respectively compared to 36.6 percent in the Northeast region. Regarding education, illiterates are high in the east and central region. The result is reverse in case of Northeast where illiterate is only 21.6 percent among the tribes. Educational facilities are to be improved in the tribal areas to eradicate illiteracy so that they can aware themselves in the risk of health vulnerability. It is also found that women's underweight is lower in all the regions compared to anaemia, may be variation in food pattern. Underweight is quite low in the Northeast region compared to the other two regions. The result clearly shows that the factors of basic amenities have a significant relationship in the condition of underweight and anaemia among the population. Socioeconomic factors including household economic condition and women's occupational status also make a difference in the health risk of the women. The study also reveals that tribes in the Northeast region are in a better position compared to an east and central region in all aspects. This may perhaps possible due to a special drive from the Governmental side and personal level local people involvement.

Indian tribe constitutes 104.3 million people out of a total of 1.21 billion populations (Census, 2011) and it constitutes 8.6 percent of the total population of the country. Tribal people in India are living in different transitional phases of development in respect of socio-culture and socio-economy in different parts of India and majority of them are lives in remote areas and generally detached from the mainstream population in respect of poverty, illiteracy, lack of developmental healthcare facilities (Thakur et al., 1991; Basu, 1994) excepting Northeast region. So, it is the main reason for differences in basic amenities and socio-economy between tribe and non-tribe of the same region as well as between tribe and non-tribe of different regions.

In conclusion, it can be said that to reduce the gap, there must be taken some acceptable strategies to improve the access of basic amenities so that the health status of the tribal women could be better. And also, along with the Govt. policies and programmes, emphasis should be given more to the targeted group who are lagging behind. Moreover, the tribal development agencies should also take care of the development of tribes to uplift basic amenities and socioeconomic status to improve tribal health in other parts of the country.

References

Ahmad, S 2012, 'Housing inequality in socially disadvantaged communities: evidence from urban India, 2009', *Environment and Urbanization Asia*, vol. 3, no. 1, pp. 237-249.

Basu, S 1994, 'A health profile of tribal India', *Health Millions*, vol. 2, no. 2, pp. 12–14.

Black, R 2003, 'Micronutrient deficiency-an underlying cause for morbidity and mortality', *Bulletin of the World Health Organization*, vol. 81, no. 2, pp. 79.

Brabin, BJ & Coulter, JBS 2003, 'Nutrition-associated disease' in *Manson's tropical diseases*, eds GC Cook & AI Zumla, Saunders, London, pp. 561–580.

Desai, SB, Dubey, A, Joshi, BL, Sen, M, Shariff, A & Vanneman, R 2010, *Human development in India: challenges for a society in transition*, Oxford University Press, New Delhi.

Edelman, B & Mitra, M 2006, 'Slum dwellers' access to basic amenities: the role of political contact, its determinants, and adverse effects', *Review of Urban and Regional Development Studies*, vol. 18, no. 1, pp. 25-40.

FAO/WHO/UNU 2004, *Report of a Joint Expert Consultation Human Energy Requirements*, FAO, Food and Nutrition Technical Report Series 1, Rome. Available from http://www.fao.org/docrep/007/y5686e/ y5686e00.HTM. [20 October 2014].

Food and Agriculture Organization of the United Nations 2004, 'Undernourishment around the world', *The State of Food Insecurity in the World* 2004, The Organization, Rome.

International Institute for Population Sciences (IIPS) and ORC Macro 2007, *National Family Health Survey (NFHS-3), 2005-06*, vol.1, IIPS, Mumbai, India.

Kundu, A, Bagchi, S & Kundu, D 1999, 'Regional distribution of infrastructure and basic amenities in urban India: issues concerning empowerment of local bodies', *Economic and Political Weekly*, vol. 34, no. 28, pp. 1893-1906.

Laxmaiah, AK, Rao, M, Harikumar, RN, Arlappa, VK & Brahmam, GNV 2007, 'Diet and nutritional status of the tribal population in ITDA project areas of Khammam district, Andhra Pradesh', *Journal of Human Ecology*, vol. 21, no. 2, pp. 79–87.

Marsh, A, Gordon, D, Heslop, P & Pantazis, C 2000, 'Housing deprivation and health: a longitudinal analysis', *Housing Studies*, vol. 15, no. 3, pp. 411-428.

Ministry of Tribal Affairs 2014, *Report of the High-Level Committee on socio-economic, health and educational status of tribal communities of India*, Govt. of India. [May 2014].

Müller, O, Garenne, M, Kouyaté, B & Becher, H 2003, 'The association between protein-energy malnutrition, malaria morbidity and all-cause mortality in West African children', *Tropical Medicine and International Health*, vol. 8, pp. 507–511.

Murray, CJL & Lopez, AD 1997, 'Global mortality, disability, and the contribution of risk factors: global burden of disease study', *Lancet*, vol. 349, pp. 1436–1442.

Nemer, L, Gelband, H & Jha, P 2001, 'The evidence base for interventions to reduce malnutrition in children under five and school-age children in low- and middle-income countries', *CMH Working Papers Series*, Paper No WG5:11, Commission on Macroeconomics and Health, WHO, Geneva.

Pinstrup–Andersen, P, Burger, S, Habicht, J & Peterson, K 1993, 'Protein-energy malnutrition' in *Disease control priorities in developing countries*, 2nd edn, eds DT Jamison, WH Mosley, AR Measham & JL Bobadilla, Oxford University Press, Oxford (UK), pp. 391–420.

Rutstein, S 1999, *Wealth versus expenditure: comparison between the DHS wealth index and household expenditures in your departments of Guatemala*, ORC Macro, Calverton, Maryland, USA.

Srinivasan, K & Mohanty, SK 2004, 'Deprivation of basic amenities by caste and religion: an empirical study using NFHS data', *Economic and Political Weekly*, vol. 39, no. 7, pp. 728-735.

Statistical Profile of Scheduled Tribes in India 2013, Ministry of Tribal Affairs, Statistics Division, Govt. of India.

Thakur, DS, Thakur, DC & Saini, AS 1991, 'Socio-economic impact of tribal development programmes in Himachal Pradesh', *Journal of Rural Development*, vol. 10, pp. 823–830.

World Health Organization 2002, *World Health Report*, the World Health Organization, Geneva.

Chapter - 3

Corruption in the Socio-cultural Context of Arunachal Pradesh: An Anthropological Understanding

Tame Ramya

Introduction

In recent years, anthropology has provided innovative and insightful accounts of corruption, at the levels of practices and ideas, in different countries of the world (Shore, 2005; Sewanta, 2009; Torsello, 2014). It has not been easy for anthropologists to study corruption through direct observation. This has called for a problem requiring the solution of the phenomenon in terms of both its salience as a universal vs. relativistic phenomenon and of the mainstream definitions of corruption itself. This chapter has attempted to solve the theoretical impasses brought about by these two issues in the discipline of anthropology.

Anthropological and ethnographic accounts of corruption in different socio-cultural settings suggest that, although a relativistic standpoint is the most likely to be encountered when studying this phenomenon, its manifestation, perceived impact into local societies and degree of moral refusal, there exist a number of reasons why relativism is insufficient an explanation.

The study analyses the phenomenon of corruption in the socio-cultural context of Arunachal Pradesh, one of the less-developed states in India's Northeastern region. After twenty-eight years of statehood, most of the districts in Arunachal Pradesh have made little progress regarding economic development, eliminating poverty, and creating more jobs for their populations. In addition to these historical handicaps, corruption, in many of these districts has become an integral part of the social fabric and how business is conducted. Among the Northeastern states, Arunachal Pradesh had been leveled at 'Alarming Situation' together with Assam and Nagaland (RGICS, 2012: 12).

Despite Arunachal Pradesh being one of the highest recipients of per capita central government assistance, it impoverishes in poverty and backwardness. The socio-economic indicators are terribly poor, and thus the question arises how and at what level the money is being utilized in the state. Due to the misappropriation of development fund and rising unauthorized expenditure (CAG reports), the state's fiscal structure is at peril. Various illegal and unauthorized activities have led to large-scale corruption across the state. Thus, illegal border trade, timber trade, illegal poppy seed cultivation, extortion of underground extremists, a strong nexus between politicians, business groups, and underground extremists, and unaccountable governance are the major causes of corruption in the state. This has halted economic development despite having high resource potentials. Corruption is a major problem with respect to economic growth, political democracy, efficient public administration, education, health, and sustainable environmental economic development. However, corruption is not only a matter of Arunachal Pradesh only. It is everywhere in each society, but it affects societies differently.

A high degree and extent of corruption is a symptom (or rather a cluster of symptoms indicating) of, in words of Sztompka (1993), 'civilizational incompetence' (Murdoch, 2009: 49). Corruption may be defined as the misuse of power for private gain (Transparency International, 2006). In this perspective, corruption is the abuse of public office for private or personal benefit. It has many forms that include bribery, extortion, fraud, and embezzlement. In Arunachal Pradesh, it also covers relations between individuals in their daily life. For instance; street vendors and other small business owners are also involved in the corruption of police officers, and other bureaucrats who deal with them. In this practice, these small business owners circumvent the red tape of bureaucracy to get their paperwork done quickly. Corruption has many forms. They include economic, political and social. It is vertical, between top leaders and subordinates in the context of public administration, but it is also horizontal, involving many public agencies in the government and between private individuals and citizens (Shehu, 1999). Corruption is, therefore, a serious issue with respect to Arunachal Pradesh. Its effects have already impacted or impeded the economic development of the state. It is difficult to know the monetary impact of corruption on Arunachal Pradesh, because of its nature, corruption is a secret transaction and it is difficult to measure. The elimination of corruption must be a priority for Arunachal Pradesh to foster a solid economic development policy that precludes any political and social sustainability across the state. Corruption is rampant in Arunachal Pradesh but it is also an inherent part in the modern society of Arunachal Pradesh which faces a high increase of poverty, joblessness and low educational skills. High conditions of poverty and misery across Arunachal Pradesh are motivating factors for corruption. To understand corruption in the context of Arunachal Pradesh, this chapter focuses on some theoretical aspects that highlight the analysis. Most theoretical literature treats corruption as a principal-agent problem. This chapter focuses on two theoretical frameworks. First, the Sociological theory that contrasts traditional and modern society highlights the social structure in which corruption has evolved and was analyzed since Durkheim (1893). In that perspective, clients who influence the behaviour of the bureaucrats by complaining to political leaders may lower the level of corruption. Second, Social Capital theory, which emphasizes social structure and the quality of government by creating a 'civic society' (Putnam, 1993), can also decrease corruption through democratic values. Finally, this chapter concludes by exploring some strategies to combat or to curb the epidemic like phenomenon call 'corruption' in Arunachal Pradesh.

Corruption in Socio-cultural Context

Before reviewing the concept of corruption and its development across Arunachal Pradesh, we must first look at the cultural behaviour of the people of Arunachal Pradesh and what is acceptable and unacceptable behaviour in society. In many instances, Arunachal Pradesh and its peoples had developed highly sophisticated cultural norms and behaviours before the arrival of outsiders. For many observers, corruption, particularly, in Arunachal Pradesh, is understood as a cultural phenomenon, which would be inherent to contemporary societies of the people of Arunachal Pradesh. However, if one would look at the cultural heritage, history shows that this is not the case, but rather corruption is a new phenomenon that stems from the collision between the colonial heritage and the indigenous culture of the people of Arunachal Pradesh during the colonial era. To further this analysis, we refer to the cultural behaviour of the people of Arunachal Pradesh before the cultural confrontation between Arunachal Pradesh and outsiders particularly the colonial administrators. Through the lenses of a historical review of the cultural heritage of Arunachal Pradesh, this chapter analyzes the development and expansion of corruption that stems from cultural integration or confusion between the indigenous cultural norms and the cultural norms that the alien society imposed on societies of Arunachal Pradesh.

Historical Background

Arunachal Pradesh is the largest state in Northeast states. It is located between latitudes 26° 28' N and 29° 30' N and longitudes 91° 30' E and 97° 30'E. It spreads over an area of 83,743 sq. km touching the international boundary with Bhutan in the West, China in the North and Myanmar in the South-East. On the south, it is linked with Assam and Nagaland. The state is presently divided into 22 districts namely, Tawang, West Kameng, East Kameng, Kurung Kumey, Kra Daadi, Papum Pare, Lower Subansiri, Kamle, Upper Subansiri, West Siang, East Siang, Upper Siang, Lower Siang, Siang, Dibang Valley, Lower Dibang Valley, Anjaw, Lohit, Namsai, Changlang, Tirap, and Longding.

The territorial and administrative evolution of Arunachal Pradesh dates back to 1875 when the Inner Line Regulation of 1873 was drawn up. But the territory assumed administrative significance in 1914; a year the frontier line (the Mac Mahon line) between the then Tibet and Northeast India was defined. Further, a territorial entity emerged in the name of North East Frontier Tract (NEFT). The areas either inhabited or frequented by the tribes mentioned in 1880 Acts were included in this track. The Act mentions of such tribes as Abors, Miris, Mishmis, Singphos, Nagas, Khamptis, Bhutias, Akas, and Daflas. Following the Act and subsequent knowledge on the region, the Notification of Presidential Order, 1950 listed 12 tribes namely, Abor (now Adi), Aka, Dafla (now Nyishi), Apatani, Galong (Galo), Monpa, Khampti, Singpho, Khowa, Sherdukpen, Mishmi and any Naga tribes. In another Notification in 1989, based on the proposal of the State Government, 25 tribes were enlisted.

In 1954 NEFT was brought under a single administrative unit and re-designated as North East Frontier Agency (NEFA). Frontier Tracts were renamed as frontier divisions. In this year Balipara Frontier Tract was divided into Kameng and Subansiri Divisions; Abor Hills and Mishmi Hills Districts were changed to Siang and Lohit Frontier Divisions; Sela sub-Agency to Kameng Frontier Division and Subansiri Area into Subansiri Frontier Division. In 1957 the Tuensang Frontier Division was excluded from NEFA and included in Naga Hills. In 1965 the divisions of the NEFA were designated as districts and Political Officers as Deputy Commissioners.

Another development took place in 1965. As has been said the NEFT assumed an administrative and territorial recognition in 1914 by a notification by the Foreign and Political Departments of the Government of British India. In other words, the affairs of the territory remained with foreign department thereafter. Though the present Arunachal Pradesh was linked with Assam administration, it was placed under the Ministry of External Affairs even after the Independence of the country. On August 1, 1965, the Ministry of Home Affairs, Government of India took the charge of the administration of NEFA from the Ministry of External Affairs.

On January 20, 1972, NEFA was renamed as Arunachal Pradesh and became a Union Territory. In 1974 the capital of Arunachal Pradesh was shifted from Shillong to present Itanagar. On February 20, 1987, Arunachal Pradesh became the 24th state of Indian Union.

The territorial and administrative evolution of the present state dates back to the pre-independence period. But the political development began at two phases before the territory became a Union Territory. The first one is the nomination of Shri Choukhamoon Gohain (Namchoom) as M.P. to Lok Sabha in 1952 and the second the introduction of Panchayati Raj in 1967. In 1971 the representation to Lok Sabha was increased by one and one seat was provided in Rajya Sabha. In 1977 people of the present state exercised their franchise for the first time to elect their representative to Lok Sabha. At present, there are two representatives to Lok Sabha and one to Rajya Sabha.

On August 15, 1975, an elected provincial Legislative Assembly with 30 members was constituted and the first council of Ministers assumed office. The first general election to the Assembly was held in February 1978. When Arunachal Pradesh attained full-fledged status in 1987 the seats in State Assembly increased from 30 to 60.

It was during the long period of colonial domination that Arunachal Pradesh and its people faced colonial rules through administration, police and other religious domination, that has forever changed the history of this state. During the colonial period, there was cultural conflict and confusion across Arunachal Pradesh. Resistance and defeat were both parts of the struggle coming from indigenous people of Arunachal. This struggle was fought through the prism of a cultural dominant/subordinate. Arunachal Pradesh developed as it was forced to cooperate with foreign forces. Therefore, in some instances, this struggle led to cultural confusion and in others, a cultural integration that resulted in adopting all the behaviours from the dominant cultural force, in this case, the Colonial one. In order to understand this struggle, one must first, define culture and what is acceptable behaviour or unacceptable behaviour from the indigenous perspective of Arunachal Pradesh.

Cultural Heritage of Arunachal Pradesh

Culture is defined as a system of values, norms, and techniques that society has developed and that link it to future generations. The transmission of these elements is carried out through languages and other means of communications that the society has developed throughout its history. This definition, although universal, must be analyzed through lenses of the people of Arunachal Pradesh. Even though this definition is academically accepted, it does not take into account the way in which many cultural heritages of Arunachal Pradesh have developed while maintaining a certain tolerance pertaining to behaviour in economics, politics, and social affairs. The confrontation of two different societies (Arunachal Pradesh and Europe) resulted in the confrontation of two opposing values, norms and behaviours. This conflict has generated confusion concerning what is correct behaviour, in other instances, it allows integration. In this context, politics or policy becomes a very divisive field in Arunachal Pradesh because people are still confusing the new behaviours with kinship and ethnic solidarity. Furthermore, social solidarity is a necessary element of the cultural basis of Arunachal Pradesh. Giving a gift to someone else is the most honourable gesture in a relationship. It is commonly accepted due to the fact that indigenous people believe in prior anticipation of new relationship even before things have taken place. Therefore, gift- giving is a part of social solidarity in order to maintain harmony and peace across all the spheres of society. This symbolic interaction plays a vital role in many societal settings including the workplace, government, and politics. It is also a part of social relationships, including finding a mate or making friends. For many indigenous people, gift -giving is not corruption and it never leads to bribery or embezzlement. It is simply a way to maintain peace and harmony in society. This social norm that characterized Pre-colonial Arunachal Pradesh has swept away when Europeans colonized the State. Local cultures are simply diluted or transformed into a new cultural norm that becomes totally confusing for many intellectuals and everyday people of Arunachal Pradesh as well. In many instances, refusing a gift from another becomes an anathema in relationships. Further, it is seen as an insult. This situation is well described in African socio-cultural context by the Nigerian novelist Chinua Achebe (1960) in his book 'No Longer at Ease', where his main character Obi Okonkwo said the following: 'They said a man expects you to accept 'kola' from him for services rendered, and until you do, his mind is never at rest.... A man to whom you do favour will not understand if you say nothing, make no noise, and just walk away. You may cause more trouble by refusing a bribe than by accepting it'.

Even though this statement stems from an Igbo society from Nigeria, it equates most Arunachalee people's understanding of gift-giving in society. In addition, it also describes what is acceptable in Africa and societies of Arunachal Pradesh, even though for many Westerners, it constitutes corruption or a bribe. Finally, the dilemma from that Igbo man stems from a confusion of an entire society which was losing its basic cultural foundations, while it has not fully embraced the new culture. The new foundations of the colonial norms are based on the concept of individualism and elitism that are now the core foundations of the new public services or administration. These elements constituted the new paradigm for many public servants of Arunachal Pradesh. Another transformation of the society of Arunachal Pradesh, which led to confusion and the development of corruption, stems from the colonial political system imposed upon Arunachal Pradesh. First, European colonists carved societies of Arunachal Pradesh without considering the different ethnic groups or ethnic alliances. They then created artificially new administrative zones that did not take into consideration cultural and ethnic differences between these diverse groups of people. This situation leads to a lack of respect for public services, or institutions, due to their illegal characteristics. Consequently, no one in public service would respect public office as an essential factor for the common good of the nation. Even today, more than twenty-eight years after statehood, this situation is common in Arunachal Pradesh and it creates conditions for corruption or bribery.

Today, corruption is rampant in Arunachal Pradesh and it is mainly analyzed from the Westerners' viewpoint. The majority of the literature focuses on the principal-agent client model. This chapter insists on examining the contrast between traditional and modern societies of Arunachal Pradesh, which is necessary to understand corruption patterns in Arunachal Pradesh. The second aspect includes the social capital theory that creates conditions for a 'civic society' where people are engaged or included in solving everyday problems.

Theoretical Framework

Most of the literature on corruption has focused on the principal-agent-client model. Without elaborating extensively on this model, this chapter will briefly review a few articles concerning this model. This model is also known as agency theory. The principal-agent client model stems from two notions developed around the study of the economics or organizational and institutional behaviour. It comes first, from the public choice theory that claims that self-interest motivates the activities of individuals and organizations (Gauld, 2007). It is also believed to be exclusively used in public administration, implementation analysis, and political science to examine the problems associated with management and administration in a decentralized environment (Alvarez and Hall, 2006). This principal-agent client model may be used to understand and combat corruption across Arunachal Pradesh. In this model, corruption occurs when an agent betrays the principal's interest in pursuit of his own by accepting or seeking a benefit from the service seeker, the client (Carr, 2009). Further, this analysis argues that the conditions of corruption are prevalent when the principal is in a powerful position to entrust the agent to carry out the services with discretion and with less accountability. This situation is prevalent in all corruption settings across Arunachal Pradesh. Principal-agent client model presents a powerful argument concerning corruption in modern public administration and services, but also it concerns modern institutions which are centered on Western conceptions, based on individualism, market economy and liberal democracy's tenants based on elections, the participation of the civic society, etc. This model may not explain the underlying factors that have motivated corruption in Arunachal Pradesh since it encountered west through colonialism. In Pre-colonial Arunachal Pradesh, there was the existence of many realities that created conditions for a democratic society, where ethics of justice and good governance prevailed. These conditions are based on cultural values, norms, and behaviours developed by indigenous people across the state.

It may be posited that the state had created good governance in the pre-colonial era, although in today's norms of liberal democracy, the state never prevailed much in this field. In addition, a pre-colonial tribal society in which there is a dual existence of reality represents the worldview of the tribals of Arunachal Pradesh. In that perspective, there are two worlds, the visible and the invisible; material and immaterial; male and female; good and bad; etc., and in both of these worlds, there are objects, people, events and situations. This division of the world leads to knowledge that does not privilege one aspect of the duality over the other. Further, this duality in the traditional society of Arunachal Pradesh provides the relationship between the individual and the community. In this perspective, both the individual and the community have an inter-relation of dependency and freedom concerning individual and community decisions regarding public services. Further, it may be asserted that this complementary and non-hierarchical system allows justice and good governance to prevail due to this interdependency inactions regarding the conduct of public officials and their community roles (public service) or in their individual daily life in the community (personal responsibility in one's own life). In such indigenous political system, justice is not whether social rules are obeyed, but whether the rules themselves are fair in the way they contribute benefits and burdens between a set of claimants. In addition, this political model in traditional societies of Arunachal Pradesh pinpointed the role of an individual and the responsibility he/she must follow in each position that person may hold in the society. Therefore, this political system or model emphasizes and increases one's standing and responsibility pertaining to the public services or institutions that one intends to serve. Furthermore, the role of the community (whole society) is to ensure that the community works to help the individual to carry out his/her duties without much interference, but also to enable that individual not to overstep his/her role or responsibility while in public service. This means, that the traditional society of Arunachal Pradesh creates conditions to control but at the same time, lets each individual exercise their own judgment by following the society's guidelines regarding ethics, morality and good governance. This political model in traditional indigenous societies of Arunachal Pradesh created conditions for harmony and respect due to sacred and shared values that each community across the state had created long before the coming of Western values. These shared values conditioned a stable society with various codes that enabled traditional indigenous societies to thrive and combat corruption and other unacceptable behaviours in the community. During these periods, when someone broke the law or moral codes, this offender of the sacred was punished by the moral codes established by the community and accepted by both the community and the individuals. This kind of moral, ethical, and good governance formula allowed the traditional societies of Arunachal Pradesh to establish social control and mechanisms for punishment when a rule or social code was broken. Under this prism of knowledge and consensual society, everyone in the indigenous traditional society of Arunachal Pradesh knew about the rules and codes. In this perspective, corruption, across Arunachal Pradesh was not as rampant as today.

Mazman (2008) analyzed the impact of knowledge and religion in society. His observation reveals many contrasts between traditional and modern societies. Further, he presents many different sociological analyses, from Karl Marx, Karl Mannheim, and Berger-Luckmann to Emile Durkheim and Max Weber. These theoretical frameworks insist on knowledge and religion. In addition, these observations show that knowledge and religion play an important role in society. He indicates that all these sociological theories have contrasted the traditional society and modern society regarding the phenomenon of knowledge, culture, ethics, and religion. Furthermore, he asserts that each of these elements defines a specific role and therefore, determines the political, economic and social configurations that are characteristic of different social settings in which they exist. Applying these sociological analyses of knowledge to Arunachal Pradesh, this chapter concludes that corruption in modern Arunachal Pradesh results from this contrasting scheme that the state went through when it encountered west. During this cultural confrontation between Arunachal Pradesh and West, traditional values, ethics, morals and the religions of Arunachal Pradesh, faced enormous pressure and ultimately, deteriorated. Further, under Karl Marx's analysis, knowledge is material, because what is real is material (Mazman, 2008). Extrapolating this view to Arunachal Pradesh, this study shows that the Westerners' cultural invasion was detrimental to the indigenous local cultures, which were strong and thriving before. Once they settled in, the reality changed in favour of the invaders, and they began destroying local norms, beliefs, and religion in favour of their own. Concretely, the traditional society gave away to a new society, that became real and as such, it meant the new reality. Therefore, Europeans or Westerners imposed new norms, beliefs, religion, institutions, and bureaucracies. These new institutions and social norms constituted the materials or ideas that would determine the future of this state with all the consequences that follow. Knowledge now stems from the colonial perspective and determines the behaviour, moral and ethical codes imposed by the new masters of the state. The indigenous society of Arunachal Pradesh was a highly sophisticated one, due to a social control norm based on the shared and sacred values that governed all aspects of the indigenous society. Knowledge was transmitted through the traditional system based on initiation, elderly conventions, etc. With colonialism, indigenous people of Arunachal Pradesh lost their ability to maintain their social values and norms due to the brutality and repression. One can assume that knowledge, in that context, was learned from the colonial viewpoint. It determined all the aspects of the indigenous people's life during that period. Consequently, the 'how to do' and the 'what to do' were all based on foreign values. Therefore, the behaviours that were alien to Arunachal Pradesh took place; and became the essential tools of knowledge, work ethic, and religion tenants. These values and norms governed everyday life in a new society. Slowly, the ingredients of modern society took place in Arunachal Pradesh; and consequently, a new and modern society was born with all the ills inherent to a modern society.

Finally, the focus on Durkheim and Max Weber's analyses was on religion, beliefs and moral codes that constitute the basic foundations for knowledge in traditional society. For Durkheim, all knowledge and beliefs are all observable phenomena in society because they constitute a social order. Religion, in that perspective, plays a specific role in providing moral order and maintaining or binding social relations (Mazman, 2008). In the traditional society of Arunachal Pradesh, this was the case. Community or individuals could not transgress societal laws or moral codes without being ostracized from the community. Therefore, it was hardly possible for corruption to take place in the indigenous society of Arunachal Pradesh; although it was not absent in these societies. Simply, it was known as a societal form of the anticipation of the friendship making process. For Max Weber, knowledge deals with ideas or beliefs with respect to their meaning to persons and with respect to the social action that followed (Mazman, 2008). In the context of traditional Arunachal Pradesh, this means each individual person was following exactly the ideas of the community because; the community was not based on individual freedom. Although an individual is a whole person, who has rights, his or her rights were under the supervision of the community. By imposing their religious values on certain indigenous people, Westerners had ultimately created new knowledge, beliefs or ideas to control all the aspects of the conquered societies in Arunachal Pradesh. Therefore, these actions revealed what Weber feared, that ideas or religion can be connected to social forces and may play a role in the constitution of society (Mazman, 2008). Indeed, after colonization, Europeans fostered a new and confused society in Arunachal Pradesh. Consequently, this construction led to many of the modern ills that the state faces today.

Corruption is endemic in all modern societies. It is even acute in developing countries. Many observers believe that social capital theory may constitute a remedy for curbing this phenomenon in many developing countries. This theory generates the notion of civil society, its implication and how it can curb corruption by including many civil associations into the democratic process regarding governing the public and private services. It is mostly recommended for the emerging democracies in the global South, notably in Arunachal Pradesh.

Mouritsen (2003) indicates the importance of civil society participation in fostering good governance, based on the work of Putnam's Making Democracy Work (1993). To understand the role of the civil society, he, first, defines Social Capital as: 'It refers to the rather different idea that political and administrative quality, productivity and responsiveness as well as economic development are outcomes of the civic community'. Further, he indicates that the civic community consists of those networks of trust, norms, and habits of cooperation which, according to Putnam, grow from the microcosm of society. Basically, this definition implies that social capital is then the result of the combination of forces or synergies that stem from group association or individuals in order to accomplish something good for the community. These kinds of associations were also known across traditional Arunachal Pradesh, before the arrival of the European colonists. In traditional Arunachal Pradesh, trust also was an important social norm, which constitutes the basis of any cooperation and building block of the development of any institutions regarding good governance, community participation, etc. Finally, trust in traditional Arunachal Pradesh creates an obligation for all members of the community, which in turn fosters bonding and builds bridges across ethnic lines. Without these values and norms that were the foundations of the traditional indigenous values, nothing from the outside can create conditions for democracy and good governance in Arunachal Pradesh.

It also shows that combating corruption in the emerging states like Arunachal Pradesh cannot be stemming solely from external interventions or even from the state. Culture and its elements including values, norms, symbols, and languages are the key elements that must be included in the approach when it comes to corruption in Arunachal Pradesh.

Combating Strategies

Combating corruption in Arunachal Pradesh is not a simple thing to do. There are many ways to approach the issue. Concerning the analysis, this chapter presents a few suggestions or strategies that the state government may use in its policy to deal with this phenomenon. Non-Governmental Organizations, researchers, and other policy-makers are also invited to take a look at these strategies and they may include them in their plans concerning the genesis of corruption in Arunachal Pradesh.

One of the most important things can be useful in the approach towards corruption in Arunachal Pradesh is the development of mass education. Arunachal Pradesh is comparatively the least educated state and this situation contributes to the problem of corruption. To curb corruption, this analysis affirms that public sector education is crucial for the success of any anti-corruption initiative in public service and in private business as well. Once people are aware of the danger and the evil character of corruption and its consequences on them, their families and relatives as well as on their own businesses, corruption can be reduced.

For now, the number of illiterates across Arunachal Pradesh is staggering, so the only way to convince people of anti-corruption messages is to the use of the media. First, government and other non-profit organizations must encourage the use of a radio broadcasting system. Through this system (in all languages or dialects across the state), the government can send information, spots, stories and play messages against corruption and corrupted officials. These messages will reach thousands of people even in remote places across the state.

Professionalism, studies on ethical issues, and training of all public and private servants as well must be included in all school curriculums. This cultural change must start in primary school and continue through the university. It must also be a part of curriculums in professional schools and government training schools and academics (police, customs services, justice, etc.) to foster the idea that corruption is bad and is contaminating the entire society including the future generations.

The government must implement a state service of public audit each year, so citizens can hear and see for themselves, each agency's performance, their annual allocations, and spending. This will encourage many public servants to be accountable to the people. The government must regulate and implement tough measures concerning non-profit organizations' funds and they must be audited quarterly, so the citizens know the status of the organization regarding their budgets.

Finally, the Arunachal Pradesh government and other agencies must create jobs and implement a system of social security to avoid rampant joblessness, lack of health coverage, and housing shortages. The immense poverty across Arunachal Pradesh constitutes the foundation for corruption in Arunachal Pradesh. Once these strategies or measures are implemented, corruption may become irrelevant, even though, the phenomenon is not very clear-cut when it comes to its genesis.

Conclusion

Understanding corruption in the socio-cultural context of Arunachal Pradesh is more difficult than actually combating the phenomenon. In traditional societies of Arunachal Pradesh, most of the public services, relations, and other community services were done through strict moral, ethical codes that were enacted for a type of society where the sacred and shared values governed the life of all the community members as one. Most of the indigenous cultural values of people of Arunachal Pradesh did not consider gift-giving as a form of corruption, but as an exchange of gifts and a creation of an anticipation of a new relationship, that will create more harmony, good, and peace between people. With colonization, all these norms and values were replaced by a foreign form of society, which brought new institutions, values, and new organizations, based on individualism, and merit regarding work. This new society, later on, created cultural confusion, and in many instances, disrespect for public services. Corruption results from this strange attitude of disrespect for any public services and institutions that are seen as foreign and illegitimate for many indigenous people of Arunachal Pradesh. This attitude was created in response to foreign-imposed institutions, corruption, and disregard of the government even after independence. With its devastating effects on development, leaders of Arunachal Pradesh must implement strict measures and strategies to overcome this endemic disease that is killing hope for millions in Arunachal Pradesh.

References

Achebe, C 1960, *No longer at ease*, Heinemann Educational Books, London, pp. 87-88.

Alvarez, MR & Hall, TE 2006 'Controlling democracy: the principal-agent problems in election administration', *The Policy Studies Journal*, vol. 34, no. 4, pp. 491-510.

Gauld, R 2007, 'Principal-agent theory and organizational change: lessons from New Zealand health information management', *Policy Studies*, vol. 28, no. 1, pp. 17-34.

Mazman, I 2008, 'Knowledge and religion in society: a comparative perspective', *Ekev Academic Review*, vol. 12, no. 36, pp. 1-14.

Mouritsen, P 2003, 'What's the civil in civil society? Robert Putnam, Italy, and the republican tradition', *Political Studies*, vol. 51, pp. 650-668.

Murdoch, A 2009, 'How much culture is there in corruption? some thoughts on transformation-cum-collective culture shock in post-communist Poland', *Journal of Intercultural Management*, vol. 1, no. 1, pp. 42-63.

Rajiv Gandhi Institute for Contemporary Studies (RGICS) 2012, *Corruption in Arunachal Pradesh* (Issue Brief), RGICS, New Delhi. [08 September 2012].

Sewanta, K 2009, 'Local level perception of corruption: an anthropological inquiry', *Dhaulagiri Journal of Sociology and Anthropology*, vol. 3, pp. 163-174.

Shehu, AUR 2009, 'Democracy, corruption and economic development: evidence from Nigeria', *An Interdisciplinary Journal*, vol. 22, no. 4, pp. 40-64.

Shore, C 2005, 'Culture and corruption in the EU: reflections on fraud, nepotism, and cronyism in the European Commission' in *Corruption: anthropological perspectives*, eds D Haller & C Shore, Pluto Press, London, pp. 131-155.

Sztompka, P 1993, 'Civilizational incompetence: the trap of post-communist societies', *Zeitschrift fur Soziologie*, vol. 22, no.2, pp. 85-95.

Torsello, D 2014, *Corruption as social exchange: the view from anthropology*, University of Bergamo, ANTICORRP.

Transparency International Report 2005, 2006. Available from: www. transparency international. org.

Chapter - 4

Fertility across Generations: A Study of the Minyong Mothers and Daughters

Maitreyee Sharma

Introduction

Recent researches suggest associations of reproductive outcomes and behaviour of the parental generation with their offspring generation in a particular socio-cultural context (Vogl, 2015). The study of such kind of associations may help to shed light on the process of demographic transition and transmission of fertility dynamics across generations. Recent studies in community-based fertility patterns; it is observed that the attitude of the family and a woman's origin-family size are statistically associated with her completed fertility pattern (Booth and Kee, 2009). Intergenerational fertility pattern may show an increase or a decrease and a study of the associated factors may well predict the future population structure. Thus, fertility change across generations forms an important area of research in demography. From the cross-cultural perspective, the educational level of women and the acceptance rate of contraceptive measures have increased in the last few decades (Pouta et al., 2005) and the women in those societies deliberately postpone their conception showing significantly higher age at first conception and relatively lower fertility than the preceding generations of women. In addition to that, the preferred social norms have an influence on women's reproductive performances. In societies where the introduction of contraceptive measures is very recent, we can predict a change in the fertility pattern and desire for pregnancy. Intergenerational patterns of reproduction are vital to the understanding of the association between the socio demographic factors and the fertility transition of a genetically homogenous population.

The aim of this chapter is to assess the intergenerational fertility dynamics between a sample of mothers-daughters in a tribal community: the Minyong. The Minyong is a hill tribe of Arunachal Pradesh, the majority of their villages is concentrated in the East and the West Siang districts of Arunachal Pradesh. The Minyong belongs to the Mongoloid division of mankind and linguistically belongs to the *Tani* speaking Adi group of Arunachal Pradesh (Srivastava, 1990). Through this study, it is tried to assess how the fertility behaviour of the younger generations is influenced by the preferences and desired of the maternal generation as well as changes in certain determinants of fertility.

Sample and Methodology

The sample consisted of 88 mother-daughter pairs. The pairs are selected as such that the mothers' ages at the time of investigation ranged from 55-65 years and this group of mothers has a surviving daughter of aged at least 35 years and above at the time of the investigation. The mothers have attained menopause, showing a mean menopausal age of 46.38±0.20 years. As the mean age at last delivery of these mothers is found to be 37.46±0.14 years so the daughters are so selected that their current age lies close to this mean of last delivery of the mothers. The ages of the daughters ranged from 35-37 years. None of the daughters attained menopause. The data on the intergenerational fertility behaviour patterns of the mother-daughter pairs are assessed in the following parameters: menarche; age at marriage; children ever born; age at first birth, second birth, and third birth; the prevalence of family planning methods across generations and desirability of family size preferences. Fertility behaviour and outcomes are compared between all mother-daughter pairs. The mean age of the mothers is found to be 61.71±0.16 years and that of the daughters is found to be 36.23±0.11 years. The data were collected by a semi-structured interview schedule covering all the information on these parameters including the desirability of family size from the mother-daughter pairs who either reside in the same village or the adjacent Minyong villages under the Alo, Headquarters of West Siang district of Arunachal Pradesh. For household per capita monthly income, an arbitrary classification is generated according to the actual income of the households in the community as follows: above 75th percentile (Rs 2,500) as high-income group (HIG), 50th percentile (Rs 2,000-2,500) as middle-income group (MIG) and below 50th percentile (less than Rs 2,000) as low-income group (LIG). Thc data are analyzed with the help of SPSS software (14.0 versions).

Results

It is observed in the study that the menarche of the daughters occurred slightly early (14.12±0.09 years) than that of the mothers (14.88±0.04 years) and the mean difference between the mother-daughter pairs is not found to be statistically significant (t=2.41, p>0.05). The median age at menarche of the daughters is observed to be 14 years (inter-quartile range 14,15), whereas, the median age at menarche of the mothers is found to be 15 years with the inter-quartile range of 14,15. On analyzing the intergenerational pattern of menarcheal age, there is a significant correlation between the daughters' and their mother's age at menarche (r = 0.262, p<0.001). An increasing monotonic trend is noticed between the age at onset of menarche of the mothers and the daughters (Table 4.1). A positive correlation suggests that the age at onset of pubertal development and maturation is partly determined by the genetics of the individual for which there is an association between the age at onset of menarche of the mother and the daughter. When the age at onset of menarche of the mother is low, the chance of onset of menarche of her daughter is also low and vice-versa.

Table 4.1 Mean age at menarche across the two generations

Generations	*Age at menarche (years)*	*95% CI*
Mother	14.88±0.04	15.39, 15.51
Daughter	14.12±0.09	14.61, 14.48
Spearman Correlation Coefficient (r)=0.262, p<0.001		

The age at consummation of marriage is a significant variable which affects the fertility behaviour of the woman because it is the time when a woman enters into cohabitation. If the age at marriage varies across generations, fertility behaviour may also change across generations. The mean age at marriage has increased in the daughters than their mothers, though the age at menarche of the daughters has gone down comparatively than their preceding generation. The mean age at marriage is 16.21±0.31 years among the mothers compared to 17.57±0.23 years among the daughters (Table 4.2). On analyzing the association between age at marriage of the mothers and their daughters, a positive and significant association (Spearman Correlation Coefficient (r) =0.201, p<0.001) is observed. This indicates

Table 4.2 Mean age at marriage across the two generations

Generations	*Age at marriage (years)*	*95% CI*
Mother	16.21±0.31	15.39, 15.51
Daughter	17.57±0.23	14.61, 14.48
Spearman Correlation Coefficient (r)=0.262, p<0.001		

that when the age at marriage of the mother is low, the chances of age at marriage of her daughter are also low and vice-versa. This trend shows the transmission of age at marriage across generations.

Table 4.3 shows the results of Univariate and Multivariate analyses of the adjusted effect of daughters' age at marriage with some background characteristics of the mothers. The results of Univariate analysis suggest that the educational level of the daughter, per capita household income of their mothers and the literacy level of the mothers, have significant and positive association on the age at marriage of the daughter. It is clearly observed from the table that the daughters, who studied up to secondary standard and above, show later age at marriage than the daughters who studied up to the primary standard. The coefficient of age at marriage among the secondary educated is 1.76 ($p<0.01$) and amongst the most educated is 2.67 ($p<0.01$). Thus, it refers that as the level of education goes higher, the age at marriage is likely to go higher. It is interesting that the daughters from the high-income household group (HIG) are likely to marry later in age than that of the low income (LIG) and middle-income household groups (MIG) (0.31, $p>0.01$). Here, it is pertinent to highlight the fact that the daughters of mothers who are educated up to secondary level are likely to marry later. A similar trend is noticed when the Multivariate analysis is done to know the effects of the confounding variables associated with mothers (occupational status, family type, family composition and clan affiliation of the mothers). Here, daughters' own educational level and their mothers' educational level appeared as significant influencing factors on the age at marriage of the daughters. When the level of education of the mothers is high, the age at marriage of the daughters may increase. Thus, the intergenerational increase in the level of education may be a significant factor in decreasing generations.

Table 4.3 Univariate and multivariate analyses of daughters' age at marriage with some background characteristics of the mothers

Characteristics	*Univariate analysis*	*95.0% CI*	*Multivariate analysis*	*95.0% CI*
Daughters' literacy level				
Illiterate				
Primary standard	0.34	-0.10, 1.18	0.24	-0.32, 1.01
Secondary standard	1.76[a]	1.26, 2.38	0.87[b]	0.37, 1.36
Matriculation and above	2.67[a]	1.42, 3.07	1.67[a]	0.44, 1.48
Type of family				
Nuclear (Ref)				
Joint	-0.28	-0.71, 0.46	-0.07	-0.41, 0.32

(Contd...)

Household per capita income				
LIG (Ref)				
MIG	0.31	0.06, 1.15	0.21	-0.31, 0.52
HIG	1.87^{a}	1.37, 2.13	0.47	0.26, 1.21
Mothers' literacy level				
Illiterate				
Primary standard	0.43^{c}	-0.22, 1.27	0.20	-0.51, 0.68
Up to secondary standard	1.63^{a}	1.16, 1.06	0.41^{b}	0.18, 0.87

$^{a}p<0.01$; $^{b}p<0.05$; $^{c}p<0.10$; Ref- Reference category

Table 4.4 indicates the mean number of children ever born to the daughters (to the time of the survey) and the mothers. This is obvious that the mothers show the higher mean number of children ever born with a minimum number of children ever born is 4 and maximum 9, whereas the daughters show the lesser mean number of children ever born with a minimum number of children ever born is 3 and maximum 6. Here, it is pertinent to note that as the mean age at last delivery of these mothers is found to be 37.46±0.14 years and we can assume that the daughter's current age lies near to this mean of last delivery of the mothers. Thus, from this, it can be assumed that there is a reduction in the fertility level in the daughter's generation. However, it is interesting that there exists an association between the number of children ever born to the mothers and the daughters. When the mothers' show a higher number of children ever born, there is a higher probability of their daughters to have comparatively higher children.

Table 4.4 Mean children ever born across the two generations

Children ever born	*Mean*	*Minimum*	*Maximum*
Mother	6.62	4	9
Daughter	4.74	3	6
Spearman Correlation Coefficient (r)=0.216, p<0.001			

As the minimum number of children ever born to the mother and daughter pairs is found to be three (03), so it is intended to study the mean ages at first birth, second birth and third birth across generations (Table 4.5). The age at first birth is an important variable that can predict the probable level of fertility as well as dynamics of the reproductive span of a woman. In societies with lower age at marriage and with natural fertility, lower age at first birth may be an indication of higher fertility (Kumar, 2014). It is observed from the table that the mean ages of all births have increased across generations. The mean age at first birth was 16.08±0. 11 years among the mothers and 17.22±1.01 years among the daughters. Thus, the mean age at first birth has increased by about one year across the generations. It is interesting that the mean difference in the second and third birth increased by about two years and three years respectively in the successive generation. As the first and the second births are delayed, so the birth of the third child is even further delayed among the daughters. The mean age of second birth is 19.11±0.28 years among the mothers and 17.22±1.01 years among the daughters. The mean age of third birth is 22.11±0.31 years among the mothers and 26.41±0.23 years among the daughters.

Table 4.5 Mean ages at first birth, second birth and third birth across generations

Birth order	*Mean*	*Minimum age*	*Maximum age*
Age at first birth			
Mother	16.08±0.11	15	18
Daughter	17.22±1.01	16	19
Age at second birth			
Mother	19.11±0.28	16	20
Daughter	21.62±0.08	16	23
Age at third birth			
Mother	22.11±0.31	20	24
Daughter	26.41±0.23	23	28

Table 4.6 attempts to predict the daughter's family size preferences by their mothers' family size preferences for the daughters. By controlling the effects of mothers' and daughter' level of education, it is revealed that the daughter's family size and their preferences are positively influenced by the mother's preference for them as well as the size of the sib-ship of the daughters. The coefficient of mothers' total children ever born is 0.371 ($p<0.01$) and the coefficient of mothers preferred number of children for the daughters is 0.211 ($p<0.01$). Thus, this clearly suggests that the desire for a preferred number of grandchildren is comparatively less than the effect of the preferred number of children ever born to the mothers. The maternal influence of daughter's fertility is found to be significant in this case. It is also observed that the educational levels of the daughters and their mothers are negatively associated with the desire for family size preferences of the daughters. As the educational level goes higher, the preferred number of children tends to decrease.

Table 4.6 Linear regression analysis for the influence of mother's family size and their preference for the daughter's family size

	Coefficient
Mother's children ever born	0.371[a]
Mother's preferred family size for the daughter	0.211[a]
Controls	
Daughter's education	
Illiterate (Ref)	
Primary	0.572
Secondary	-0.787[a]
Matriculation and above	-0.926[b]
Mother's education	
Illiterate (Ref)	
Primary	0.442
Secondary	-0.267

[a]$p<0.01$; [b]$p<0.05$ Ref- Reference category

Table 4.7 refers to the prevalence of various contraceptive methods among the mother-daughter pairs. Here, it is pertinent to state that the daughters are the first wave of mothers in the area of study who are exposed to various contraceptive methods apart from periodic abstinence (which is known by all the married women and the mother generally make the daughters aware of this method). None of the mothers have been exposed to contraceptive methods (as shown in the table) and they are found to practice periodic abstinence whenever they desired. Total acceptors among the daughters are found to be 23.86 percent, of whom, the highest percentage of daughters has accepted intra-uterine contraceptive device (IUCD/ Copper-T) followed by the oral contraceptive pill (OCP) users. It is known from the daughters that the public health center at the Alo area provides information on the various contraceptive devices and about their utilization. However, the number of non-acceptors of family planning devices is found to exceed the number of acceptors. The non-acceptors stated two reasons for not accepting and practicing any family planning methods and these are: fear of side effects and non-reliability. The investigator encountered three women who abandoned using IUCD (copper-T) due to severe urinary tract infection, occasional bleeding and abdominal pain. The daughters who currently use IUCD are found to be suffering from various types of abdominal pain and they attribute these problems to IUCD. Only 4.55 percent of daughters have undergone tubectomy. Permanent sterilization was not being accepted by the males as well as the females as according to their traditional belief a human should not become permanently sterile as fecundity is a God's blessing.

Table 4.7 Prevalence of contraceptive devices across generations

Contraceptive devices	*Mother*	*Daughter*
IUCD	-	12.50
OCP	-	6.82
Tubectomy	-	4.55
Total acceptors Total non-acceptors	- 88 (100%)	21 (23.86%) 67 (80.62%)

Discussion

Recently the interplay between the dynamics of fertility and intergenerational fertility transmission has received significant attention. The fertility patterns across the generations are responsible for forming the overall population structure and composition at a particular point in time. Most of the empirical studies in fertility dynamics are silent on the fertility transition as well as transmission across generations but in the recent decades, the investigators have diverted their focus of attention to the various factors that are responsible for dictating the fertility pattern of a particular generation during the demographic transition as well as how the socio-cultural milieu of the community implicitly moulds the fertility of a generation. A recent meta-analysis (Murphy, 1999), shows that the predictive power of parental fertility in influencing offspring fertility is significant particularly in developing countries.

The results of this micro-level study show that there exists a notable change in the fertility pattern across generations of the mothers and daughters. The study also finds a positive intergenerational correlation between mother and daughter in the age at onset of menarche and the age at marriage; as well as a significant association between the educational achievement of the mother and the daughter, age at marriage of the daughter with the household income and educational attainment of the mother; and more importantly a significant association between maternal preferences for the number of grandchildren and daughters' preferences for the children. The sib-size of the daughter also influences the preferred number of children of the daughters.

The age at onset of menarche is essentially interplay between the gene and the nutritional status and other environmental factors. The secular trend in declining the age at onset of menarche is well documented in many types of research (Kalarov et al., 2005; Walvoord, 2010; Talma et al., 2013; Pathak et al., 2014). This obviously reflects an improvement in the environmental factors and the nutritional status as for the attainment of menarche a critical weight gain is essential (Frisch, 1985, Laitinen et al.,

2001). However, in the present study, the investigator has found a significant correlation of age at onset of puberty of the mother-daughter pairs. This again shows that the gene also plays an important role in the sexual maturation process of the human. This finding corroborates with the similar findings made by Kalarov et al. (2005) and Pouta et al. (2005). Theoretically, though a woman becomes fecund on the onset of menarche, her reproductive span becomes functional and active when cohabitation starts after the consummation of marriage. In the present study, though the age at marriage has increased in the daughter's generation a significant association is observed between the age at marriage of the mother and her daughter. This indicates that when the age at marriage of the mother is low, the chances of age at marriage of her daughter are also low and vice-versa. This trend shows the transmission of age at marriage across generations. When age at marriage changes over time, the fertility behaviour may change over time. A similar finding is also observed by Axinn et al. (1994).

Various demographic surveys show that the educational level of women has risen up in recent decades across the globe. This is also evident in the present study. A positive intergenerational correlation in the level of education is noticed between the mother and the daughter (Pouta et al., 2005). Not a single mother is found who is educated beyond the secondary standard. When the mother is educated, the daughter is also found to be educated. The illiterate daughters in the study show illiterate mothers. When the level of education of the mothers is high, the age at marriage of the daughters may increase. The daughters of mothers who are educated up to secondary level are likely to marry later. Thus, the intergenerational increase in the level of education may be a significant factor in decreasing the level of fertility in the succeeding generations. Daughters' own educational level, their mothers' educational level, and household per capita income appeared as significant influencing factors of delaying the age at marriage of the daughters.

The age at first birth of all mother-daughter pairs suggests that they were at the adolescent stage of their life when they attained motherhood for the first time. The mean age at first birth of the mother is approximately one year lower than the mean age at first birth of their daughters. The findings also show that the mean spacing between two successive births is higher in the daughters than among the mothers. Of the many reasons, one of the reasons for comparatively higher spacing between successive births among the daughters is acceptance of family planning devices apart from periodic abstinence. Not a single mother is observed who accepted any family planning devices but the majority of mothers are aware of these devices. They preferred periodic abstinence over these methods which they knew from their mothers. It is already been mentioned that the daughters are the first wave of mothers who are exposed to various contraceptive methods. However, the number of daughters who did not accept these devices outnumbers the acceptors. When the overall females of the community are observed, the numbers of acceptors increase gradually in the younger generations from the daughter's generation. Thus, in the daughter's generation, the introduction of family planning devices acts as an important medium for the postponement and limitation of births. The result also suggests that the desire for a preferred number of grandchildren is comparatively less than the effect of the preferred number of children ever born to the mothers. The maternal influence of daughter's fertility is found to be significant in the study. Thus, the pattern of fertility across generations seems to highlight the influence of the parental generation through the socio-cultural context.

References

Axinn, WG, Clarkberg, ME & Thornton, A 1994, 'Family inuences on family size preferences', *Demography*, vol. 3, pp. 65–79.

Booth, AL & Kee, HJ 2009, 'Intergenerational transmission of fertility patterns', *Oxford Bulletin of Economics and Statistics*, vol. 71, no. 2, pp. 0305-9049.

Frisch, RE 1985, 'Body fat, menarche, and reproductive ability', *Seminars in Reproductive Endocrinology*, vol. 3, pp. 45–48.

Kalarov, N, Cerni, M & Jovic, B 2005, 'Correlation of age at menarche of mothers and daughters in Backa Palanka', *Medicinski Pregled*, vol. 58, no. 3-4, pp. 208-210.

Kumar, A 2014, *Intergenerational transmission of fertility behaviour in Rural Bihar*. Ph.D. thesis, International Institute for Population Sciences (IIPS), Mumbai.

Laitinen, J, Power C & Jarvelin, MR 2001, 'Family social status, maternal body mass index (BMI), childhood BMI and age at menarche in predicting adult obesity', *The American Journal of Clinical Nutrition*, vol. 74, pp. 287–294.

Murphy, M 1999, 'Is the relationship between the fertility of parents and children really weak?', *Biodemography and Social Biology*, vol. 46, no. 1-2, pp. 122-145.

Pathak, PK, Tripathi, N & Subramanian, SV 2014, 'Secular trends in menarcheal age in India-evidence from the Indian human development survey', *PLoS ONE*, vol. 9, no. 11.

Pouta, A, Järvelin, MR, Hemminki, E, Sovio, U & Hartikainen, A.L 2005, 'Mothers and daughters: Intergenerational patterns of reproduction', *European Journal of Public Health*, vol. 15, no. 2, pp. 195-199.

Srivastava, LR 1990, *Social organization of the Minyongs,* Directorate of Research, The Government of Arunachal Pradesh.

Talma, H, Schonbeck, Y, Dommelen, PV, Bakker, B, Buuren, SV & HiraSing, RA 2013, 'Trends in menarcheal age between 1955 and 2009 in the Netherlands', *PLoS ONE*, vol. 8, no. 4.

Vogl, TS 2015, 'Intergenerational dynamics, and the fertility transition', *AEA Paper and Proceedings*, Bocconi University.

Walvoord, EC 2010, 'The timing of puberty: is it changing? does it matter?', *Journal of Adolescent Health*, vol. 47, pp. 433–439.

Chapter - 5

Factors Affecting Infant and Child Mortality among two Tribes of Arunachal Pradesh, India

Tiluttoma Baruah

Introduction

Children are loved everywhere in this globe. They occupy a special position in people's life. But a large number of them become a cause of sorrow due to their illness and untimely deaths. Mortality in infancy and childhood is used as a reliable indicator of health status and well-being of children. It is quite well-known that determinants of infant and child mortality vary between geographical regions, between cultural groups and also between the regions of different economic status. Again, among the infants and children, the risk of death is very closely related to the environment in which they grow. The deaths occur for less medical facilities to deal with infections, inadequate food and lack of elementary hygiene (Ko Ko, 1987).

Mortality studies carried out in our country are largely based on data generated through the Census, Sample Registration Scheme, hospital data and National Sample Surveys. Most of these studies were carried out using secondary data. The exception of these is the National Family Health Survey. However, the pioneering work of Chandrasekhar (1972) based on secondary data, covered most of the dimensions of mortality study besides comparing the findings, cross-culturally and internationally. The study of Jain (1974) based on Bombay and Poona secondary data on mortality. Kulkarni (1975) and Agarwala (1975) focused mainly on establishing the relationship between infant and childhood mortality and its influence on fertility.

Some major studies have been carried out in different parts of India, generating primary data on mortality. For example; Simmons et al. (1978) and Smucker et al. (1980) conducted a study in Uttar Pradesh. Mahadevan et al. (1986) conducted a study on nutrition and infant and childhood mortality. The study area was Andhra Pradesh. Side by side, socio-economic and cultural correlates of infant mortality were studied by Sandhya (1991) in Andhra Pradesh. From various studies on infant and child mortality in India, it was noticed that there were significant effects of maternal age on mortality of offspring among women of different age, caste and Muslim population groups of North India (Ara et al., 2008).

Though in Northeast India, as a whole, in comparison to rest of our country very few works have been done on mortality, however, relatively more works on the same are available in the state of Assam in particular (Das and Das, 1982; Das et al., 1989). The present study is an appraisal of factors affecting infant and child mortality among two tribes of Arunachal Pradesh.

Material and Method

The present study was conducted among the Miju Mishmi and Khampti tribes of Lohit district, Arunachal Pradesh. Agriculture is the main occupation of the Miju Mishmi. They have their own animistic religious faith. On the other side, though the Khampti are traditionally cultivators many of them are at present engaged in a business-like timber merchant. They are Buddhist by religion. Necessary information was collected from the Khampti and Miju Mishmi families residing in Chowkham and Hawai Administrative Circle respectively of Lohit district, Arunachal Pradesh.

Altogether 128 Miju Mishmi and 115 Khampti families were covered to collect data on demographic characteristics. To obtain the age of the individuals retrospective method depending on recall has been applied and cross-checked from a number of elderly individuals. In the second phase, 32 Miju and 30 Khampti mothers were specially interviewed who experienced at least one infant or child death (1-4 years) during the last decade. In this connection, the cases of last deaths were only taken into consideration.

The measure of infant mortality used in this study was calculated following the method suggested by Khan (1987). To calculate the index of the infant mortality all births which took place during 12 months prior to interview were excluded from the analysis as they did not have one full year of experience. The index thus obtained is similar to Infant Mortality Rate (IMR) estimated from a cohort but is different from a period (one year) rate. It averages the period IMRs over the entire reproductive period of women included in the sample. A similar approach has been adopted by Garma (1983) in Mexico with quite useful results.

$$\text{Index of infant mortality} = \frac{\Sigma\, Idi}{\Sigma\, Bi} \times 1000$$

Where I_{di} = Total number of infant deaths reported by an ith woman of the sample

B_i = Total number of live births reported by an ith woman of the sample

Following this index of child mortality also derived. This is as follows:

$$\text{Index of child mortality} = \frac{\Sigma\, Cdi}{\Sigma\, Bi} \times 1000$$

Where C_{di}= Total number of child deaths (0-4 years) reported by an ith woman of the sample.

B_i = Total number of live births reported by an ith woman of the sample.

Results

Data on the reproductive history of the two population groups have been furnished in Table 5.1. Out of 128 mothers, 454 children were born of the Miju Mishmi mothers, while among the 115 Khampti mothers 402 children were born. The Khampti show considerably lower level of infant deaths (87.06) than that of the Miju Mishmi (107.93). The same is true in the case of child mortality.

Table 5.1 Reproductive performance

Population	*Total No. of mother*	*Total No. of live births*	*No. of infant died (0-1 year)*	*No. of the child died (0-4 years)*	*Index of infant mortality*	*Index of child mortality*
Miju Mishmi	128	454	49	28	107.93	61.67
Khampti	115	402	35	18	87.06	44.78

Mosley and Chen (1984) proposed in their analytical framework that all social and economic determinants of child mortality necessarily operate through a common set of biological mechanism, or proximate variables, to exert an impact on mortality. It is well established that many biosocial factors are involved in the survival and well-being of a child.

In this section altogether eight biosocial factors were dealt with in relation to infant and child mortality. These are:

1. Medical check-up of the mother during pregnancy,

2. Place of delivery,
3. Medical treatment of the child,
4. Immunization of child,
5. Education of mother,
6. The sense of personal hygiene of mother,
7. Mother's age at marriage and
8. Mother's age at first childbirth.

The data collected in the second phase were taken into consideration in this section i.e. the mother who experienced at least one infant or child death (0-4 years) during the last decade, and the cases of last deaths were only examined. The reason for considering the last deaths was that complete information regarding that particular delivery was available. But if we consider the earlier deaths, we have to depend mainly on the recall method in which there are strong possibilities of recall lapses. So, for the sake of accuracy of data we had restricted our observations only on last deaths. For this purpose, 32 Miju Mishmi and 30 Khampti mothers were specially interviewed.

Table 5.2 shows the frequencies of various biosocial factors in relation to infant and child mortality among the Miju Mishmi and Khampti tribes. It was seen that in respect of each of the factors there exist considerable differences between these two populations. However, since this Table is self-explanatory it needs no further description, but an occasional reference to this Table will be made while dealing with each factor.

Table 5.2 Biosocial factors in relation to infant and child mortality

Factors	*Miju Mishmi (n=32)*		*Khampti (n=30)*	
	No.	*%*	*No.*	*%*
1. Medical check-up of the mother during pregnancy				
Yes	6	18.75	10	33.33
No	26	81.25	20	66.67
2. Place of delivery				
Home	25	78.13	13	43.33
Hospital	7	21.87	17	56.67
3. Medical treatment of child				
Regular	7	21.87	18	60.00
At times	25	7.13	12	40.00

(Contd...)

4. Immunization of child				
Completed	4	12.50	10	33.33
Partly completed	10	31.25	12	40.00
Not taken	18	56.25	8	26.67
5. Education of mother				
Illiterate	19	59.37	7	23.33
Just literate	10	31.25	9	30.00
Primary & above	3	9.38	14	46.67
6. The sense of personal hygiene of mother				
Yes	9	28.12	13	43.33
No	23	71.88	17	56.67
7. Mother's age at marriage				
-17 years	26	81.25	13	43.33
18-22 years	4	12.50	14	46.67
23+year	2	6.25	3	10.00
8. Mother's age at first childbirth				
-18 years	27	84.37	14	46.67
19-23 years	3	9.38	13	43.33
24+years	2	6.25	3	10.00

To find out whether there exist significant differences or not for each of the factors between the Miju Mishmi and Khampti two statistical methods were applied on the basis of the findings of Table 2. These are:

(i) Binomial test of equality of proportion (Table 5.3) and

(ii) Test of significance (Table 5.4).

Table 5.3 A binomial test of equality of proportion

Sl. No.	*Factors*	*Miju Mishmi Vs. Khampti*		
		T_1	T_2	*Inference*
1.	Medical check-up of the mother during pregnancy	0.1458	0.1111	Not significant
2.	Place of delivery	0.3478	0.1238	Significant
3.	Medical treatment of child	0.3800	0.1247	Significant
4.	The sense of personal hygiene of mother	0.1521	0.1216	Not significant

Table 5.4 Test of significance

Sl. No.	*Factors*	*Miju Mishmi Vs. Khampti*	
		χ^2 *value*	*Inference*
1.	Immunization of child	6.54	Significant (p>.001)
2.	Education of mother	12.65	Significant (p>.001)
3.	Mother's age at marriage	10.03	Significant (p>.001)
4.	Mother's age at first childbirth	10.52	Significant (p>.001)

In respect of medical check-up of the mother during pregnancy, it appears that there exists no significant difference between these two populations (Table 5.3). Miju Mishmi and Khampti both show the considerably lower number of mothers who opted for a regular medical check-up during pregnancy (Table 5.2).

More than 56.00 percent of the mothers opted for hospital delivery among the Khampti, while only 21.87 percent of the Miju Mishmi mothers preferred this service (Table 5.2). Two populations differ significantly in this respect (Table 5.3). It may be well assumed that medical care must be much better in the hospital than at home.

From the binomial test of equality of proportion, it appears that in respect of medical treatment of a child (regular or at times) significant difference exists between the Miju Mishmi and Khampti (Table 5.3). It is seen that the Khampti prefer regular treatment of a child by medical doctors more than the Miju Mishmi (Table 5.2). This may be considered as one of the probable reasons for higher infant and child mortality among the Miju Mishmi than the Khampti.

Regarding the sense of personal hygiene of the mother, there exists no significant difference between the two populations (Table 5.3). From Table 5.2 it appears that the Khampti mothers have a comparatively better sense of personal hygiene than the Miju mothers.

In the case of immunization of child, the Khampti differ significantly from the Miju Mishmi (Table 5.4). It is observed from Table 5.2 that considerably more number of Khampti children has completed child immunization than that of the Miju Mishmi.

Table 5.4 indicates that in respect of education of mother the two populations differ significantly (Table 5.4). The Miju Mishmi shows (Table 5.2) higher percentage of illiterate mothers (59.37%) than that of the Khampti (23.33%). It is well known that education of the mother plays an important role in child survival and mortality in a community.

Regarding the mother's age at marriage there exist significant differences between these two tribes (Table 5.4). It appears from Table 5.2 that the Miju Mishmi mothers show lower age at marriage in a higher percentage (81.25%) than the Khampti (43.33%).

Mother's age at first childbirth also shows a similar trend like the earlier factor i.e. in this case also significant result has been found between two tribes (Table 5.4). It reveals that a high percentage of Miju Mishmi mother (84.37%) shows the age at first childbirth in the category of the lower age group of age at first childbirth (i.e. below 18 years). Whereas, the Khampti mothers show considerably a lower percentage (46.67%) in this age group (Table 5.2).

Discussion

Taking into consideration all these biosocial factors it was found that the Khampti significantly differs from the Miju Mishmi in six factors out of eight factors. It has already been stated that both infant and child mortality is considerably lower among the Khampti than the Miju Mishmi. The probable reasons for the lower rate of infant and child mortality among the Khampti may be due to the fact that they largely depend on the regular medical treatment of the child, immunization of child and delivery in hospital rather than at home. Besides, it is found that the Khampti mothers have better education and both age at marriage and age at first child birth are higher than the Miju Mishmi. It is well recognized that biosocial factors play a vital role in infant and child mortality and child's chances of survival in any population. In the present study, the above findings can be considered as the probable reasons for the lower level of infant and child mortality in these populations.

In this connection, it can be mentioned here that the Chowkham and Momong village of Chowkham Administrative Circle, from where the Khampti data were collected, both situated in the plain area, on the roadside and have good communication facilities. Tinsukia town of Assam is nearer to these Khampti villages and well connected by the highway. As a result, the Khampti people in these villages enjoy modern transport facilities and can go for better medical treatment to Tinsukia whenever a problem arises.

But the situations of Changing, Walla, and Watong, from where the Miju Mishmi data were collected, found to be quite different than the Khampti area. These Miju villages are situated at a relatively higher altitude i.e. in the hills. There is no direct bus service from Tinsukia to this place, which cause great inconvenience to the people. The Miju Mishmi are living there permanently since long, depending mainly on shifting cultivation, who hardly come down to reach the nearest urban center Hayuliang for other necessities. The only way to reach their area is a hanging bridge. For crossing the bridge one has to walk the rugged terrain in the upper areas for near about two hours. In this area, communication is cumbrous, difficult and irregular around the year and to reach the district headquarters Tezu one has to depend mainly on defense vehicle which is irregular too. For all the reasons the availability of modern amenities and healthcare facilities are quite poor in this area. Therefore, these may be the reasons that due to the geographical barrier and lack of proper health knowledge the Miju Mishmi of the present study shows a poor status of health than than the Khampti population of Arunachal Pradesh.

References

Agarwala, RD 1975, 'Influence of infant and child mortality on fertility in India'. Paper presented at the seminar on *Infant mortality in relation to the level of fertility*, CICRED Series, Bangkok, Paris.

Ara, G, Siddique, YH, Beg, T & Afzal, M 2008, 'Abortion index and mortality of offspring among women of different age, caste and population groups of North Indian Muslims', *Journal of Biosocial Science*, vol. 40, pp. 431-443.

Chandrasekhar, S 1972, *Infant mortality, population growth, and family planning in India*, George Allen and Unwin Ltd., London.

Das, BM & Das, PB 1982, 'Child mortality among rural Assamese', *Anthropological Survey of India*, vol. 31, no. 3-4, pp. 14-29.

Das, BM, Das, PB, Das, R, Walter, H & Hopfe, HD 1989, 'Anthropological studies in Assam, India. 7. Socio-biological observations on Assamese populations', *Anthropologischer Anzeiger*, vol. 47, no. 2, pp. 129-143.

Garma, IOGY 1983, 'Some factors associated with infant mortality in Mexico', *Infant and Child Mortality in the Third World*, Inter-Centre Cooperative Research Programme. Project No. 1: Final Report. CICRED, WHO/OMS, Paris. pp. 91-128.

Jain, SP 1974, 'Some aspects of mortality' in *Population in India's development*, eds A Bose, PB Desai, AK Mitra and JN Sharma, Vikas Publishing House, New Delhi.

Khan, ME 1987, 'Infant mortality in Uttar Pradesh', *Social Change*, vol. 17, no. 3, pp. 52-64.

Ko Ko, U 1987, 'Children health: tomorrow's wealth', *Indian Journal of Paediatrics*, vol. 54, no. 1, pp. 33-34.

Kulkarni, GA 1975, 'Relation between infant mortality and fertility', *Sample Registration Bulletin,* vol. 9, no. 1-2.

Mahadevan, K, Reddy, PR, Murthy, MSR, Reddy, PJ, Gowri, V & Siva Raju, S 1986, 'Culture, nutrition and infant and childhood mortality' in *Fertility and mortality: theory, methodology, and empirical issues*, ed K Mahadevan, Sage Publications, New Delhi.

Mosley, W & Chen, L 1984, 'An analytical framework for the study of child survival in developing countries', *Population and Development Review,* vol. 10, pp. 25-45.

Sandhya, S 1991, *Socio-economic and cultural correlates of infant mortality*, Concept Publishing Company, New Delhi.

Simmons, GB, Smucker, CM, Misra, BD & Majumdar, P 1978, 'Pattern and causes of infant mortality in rural Uttar Pradesh', *Journal of Tropical Paediatrics and Environmental Child Health*, vol. 27, no. 5, pp. 207-216.

Smucker, CM, Simmons, GB, Berustein, S & Misra, BD 1980, 'Neo-natal mortality in South Asia: special role of tetanus', *Population Studies*, vol. 34, no. 2, pp. 321-335.

Chapter - 6

Understanding Life in the Inter-State Borderlands of Assam and Arunachal Pradesh

Ratna Tayeng

Introduction

The present chapter intends to present a brief overview of how the Assam- Arunachal Pradesh border comes into being and how people, who live along and are divided by state borders, have adjusted to the borderland situation. Borders and borderlands as a field of studies is not a recent one, in fact, in the last two decades, many anthropologists, as well as other social scientists, have increasingly turned their attention towards the issues of border and borderlands. Research on Indian borders and borderlands though gradually growing, Willem Van Schendel (2005), the pioneer of borderland research in South Asia is of the opinion that 'South Asia as a whole is poorly represented in borderland studies'. Nevertheless, Chanda's (2003) work on border community of West Bengal and Orissa is an excellent piece of anthropological work. It gives a critical analysis of the network of interaction pattern of a borderland community in an inter-state situation.

So far Northeastern borderlands are concerned, a few political scientists and historians attempted to study the dynamics of these borderlands. Their prime focus revolves around the issues of refugee questions, terrorism, ethnic violence, and national security. First of all, mention may be made of Bhattacharyya's (1995) work '*The Troubled Border*', a commendable pioneering study on the border disputes of Northeast India. Dutta (2002) in his work entitled '*Cross-Border Trade of North-East India: The Arunachal Perspectives*' provide some valuable information on the cross-border trading system of Arunachal Pradesh. Upadhyay's (2009) work '*India's Fragile*

Borderlands: The Dynamics of Terrorism in Northeast India' is a study of terrorism. Mishra's (2011) work '*Becoming a Borderland: The Politics of Space and Identity in Colonial North-eastern India'*, provides a lucid account of the developments in the western borderlands of northeastern India. More recently, McDuie-Ra (2016) work '*Borderland City in New India'* provides an interesting historical as well as ethnographic account of the new northeastern borderland cities - the capital city of Manipur, Imphal, which he calls as a gateway to Southeast Asia. It is a study of the dynamic process of urbanization in one of India's most critical yet little-understood borderlands.

Without any doubt, we can say that there has been little attempt to examine the life and culture of people living in the Northeast borderlands. Therefore, it poses a challenge to the Indian anthropologists and more particularly Northeastern anthropologists to explore and understand these dynamics in this part of the region. As a matter of fact, the field of anthropology of borders and borderlands is still in an incipient stage in India. In Indian Anthropology these issues are rarely discussed in research and it seems that they see the relationship between people and place as natural one. And therefore, attempt must be made to understand the socio-political scenario of Indian borderlands and to find out its interrelatedness with global borderlands and most importantly how people of this region interpret/recognize their borderlands.

Assam-Arunachal Borderland

This borderland is an administrative inter-state borderland dividing the two states of a single nation. Put differently, it is a boundary that divides hill and plain set up by the colonial rulers. However, with the passing of time the political influence of 'dividing line' has grown stronger. It ultimately helps in developing a sense of distinctiveness among the people and a sense of imaginative communion –'Arunachali'. Today, the people of the state argue that peace, development, and prosperity of the state lie in this border. It gives them a sense of security and freedom. According to Wouter (2012: 59), 'The categories hill and plain do not just refer to a natural division of space but are also a reflection of socially constructed images and perceptions'. Berdalh Daphne (1999) aptly noted borders are artifacts of history and are subject to change over time. When borders shift, lands and peoples are subjected to changes.

The history of this borderland begins on June 30, 1947, when The North East Frontier (Assam) Tribal and Excluded Area Sub Committee (popularly known as Bordoloi Committee) was constituted under the leadership of Gopinath Bordoloi and Justice Bijan Kumar Medhi. The Committee was asked to prepare a report on the future pattern of the administration of North East Frontier Tracts (Present day Arunachal Pradesh) and submit it to the President of India before August 25, 1950. The Commission submitted its report on August 22, 1950, to the President of India. The committee recommended that Government of Assam to take over the administration of North East Frontier Tract. However, this recommendation was overlooked and the center continued to administer North East Frontier Tracts as 'excluded area' through the Governor of Assam. Their recommendation for transferring of certain plain areas of the North East Frontier Tracts to Assam on the ground that 'the people of these plain areas should not be denied the advantages of the franchise and regular administration' was accepted. This report was accepted by the Minority Sub Committee of the Constituent Assembly presided over by Late Sardar Ballabh Bhai Patel in 1950. And once the Presidential assent was obtained, Assam, having the authority, formally notified the report on 23.02.1951 that demarcated the 756 km boundary between the then NEFT and Assam[1].

The notification excluding these areas from the North East Frontier Tracts was issued on 23-02-1951. As a result, new territory was produced which three years later became the North Eastern Frontier Agency popularly called NEFA (present Arunachal Pradesh). Presently, the boundary between Assam and Arunachal Pradesh runs from the tri-junction of Assam, Arunachal Pradesh and Bhutan at Bhairab Kundo on the west bank of Dhansiri River to the tri-junction of Assam, Nagaland, and Arunachal Pradesh on the Tiok River on the east. It has a length of about 716 kilometers.

The Socio-economic ties along Assam-Arunachal Borderlands

This borderland is a product of colonial commercial interest, where colonial administration converted large foothills tracts into tea plantations. As a consequence, even today, vast areas of the Arunachal Pradesh-Assam foothills border are covered with tea gardens. Although, historical evidence suggests that trade relations with the Assam plains flourished between almost all the tribal groups of Arunachal Pradesh. According to B.K. Roy Barman (2004:96) '…certain communities played the role of bridge communities and certain others may play the role of buffer communities'. Historically, this commercial relationship was more marked with the Abors (present-day Adis) of the Sadiya Division. This was so because a considerable part of the Sadiya area remained within the boundaries of the Ahom kingdom for quite a long time. Passes (*Duar*) were therefore opened at Sadiya,

Kobo (present day Pasighat) and Dhola for which they used to pay some kind of duty (M'Cosh, 1837: 144; Michell, 1883; Gait, 1906: 321).

Lila Gogoi wrote 'The tribal people inhabiting the NEFA region always have to keep close touch with the neighboring people for the supply of their bare necessaries of life. It is not easy for the NEFA areas to be independent in matters of food and other things of the daily requirement. In order to procure these things, they always have to go to the plains' (Gogoi, 1958). With the advent of time, today, Assam-Arunachal Pradesh border has its own distinctive character of the market in the border. It is distinctive because it is held once a week on Wednesday or on Friday or on Saturday. But there also regular market exists in the region which people regularly visit. People across the border come and visit such a market. In fact, border markets are important economic aspects of people living in this borderland.

The growth of border market centers like Bhalukpong, Banderdewa, Harmutty, Likabali, Jonai, etc. along Assam-Arunachal Pradesh borderlands have been the result of improvements in roads and development in the last two-three decades. Most of the Arunachal Pradesh borderlanders survive on such border markets and equally all border markets are surviving on the people of Arunachal Pradesh. Among the items, household utensils, vegetables, electric appliances, and dress materials are the most important items for people of Arunachal Pradesh whereas for Assam people mostly come to purchase local agricultural products. Along with these, there are also many kinds of traditional healers, medicine vendors, which attract Arunachal Pradesh borderlanders, but what attracts most is that commodities sold in these markets are always cheaper. In all the market, the vendors are mostly from Assam, coming from the far-flung area.

Interestingly, selling and buying of beads is one of the fastest businesses among borderlanders. There are many beads shops at Lakhimpur, Harmutty, Jonai in Assam, from where the tribal communities of neighbouring states are buying beads basically for business purpose. These shops keep all the beads of Arunachal tribes. Some shops are very old while others are newly open. Apart from Arunachal beads they also keep Nagas beads and Manipuri beads. Usually, shops are attached to a small factory (behind the shops) where they do polish, cutting and finishing. Buyers from Arunachal Pradesh are mostly women; some are buying for domestic purpose while most of them are buying for business purpose. These ladies buy beads at wholesale price and selling them in the state at a higher price. Mostly the Nyishis, the Apatanis, and the Adis are the regular customers.

The most interesting feature of the Assam-Arunachal Pradesh border economy is the labour exchange. In many places, people of Arunachal

Pradesh have owned land across the border and annually, these Arunachalee pay land taxes to the Govt. of Assam. Most of the owned lands in Assam are used for agriculture and often people from across the border are employed to look after the land in a share hold basis. For example, in East Siang district of Arunachal Pradesh bordering Dhemaji district of Assam, most of the sharecroppers who are employed to look after the plot are Nepalese and Mishing. The landholders (Arunachalee) provide land and monetary help to the sharecropper and the sharecropper in return gives almost half of the production of the land. The owner visits the land twice or thrice a year during agricultural seasons.

Again, most of the agricultural labours working in the adjoining border areas of Arunachal Pradesh are from bordering villages of Assam. Often these labourers are engaged on contract basis. The contracts range from Rs 3000.00 – Rs.5000.00 per month. Not only in the agricultural field, but they are also invited and engaged in fencing the bamboo garden, kitchen garden, ginger field and cutting of wood, etc. Many are also engaged in in-house and road construction work. Apart from men, womenfolk, especially small girls' age between 10-20 years are also kept as a housemaid in many families of Arunachal Pradesh.

Socio-cultural ties along Assam-Arunachal Borderlands

Lila Gogoi (1958:11, 12) writes that 'The hills and the plains of Assam are not separate identities. Before the advent of the British, except its positional distinction, there was no difference whatsoever in the social and cultural field between the hills and the plains people. There existed an unbreakable friendship with the tribes that surround the boundaries of Assam'. Many borderlanders had strong cultural and kinship ties with their relatives beyond this borderland. The borders, for them, are artificial constructs imposed by colonial and Indian rulers.

There are around 10,000 Nyishis living in Assam, inhabited mainly in the Sonitpur and Lakhimpur border districts of Assam. Some of them were migrated back to mountain terrain of Arunachal Pradesh when the boundary demarcation was made in 1951, but many still remain there. Some of the remaining Nyishi clan of Assam are Welly, Chuku, Techi, Tana, Taw, Sengdo, Wahge, Chiri, Yumlam, Rari, Tachang, Nabam, Taku, etc. They inhabited in the areas of Phuloguri, Rangagarah, Boroli Basti, Dolong Basti, Hodubari, Gormara, Dubea, Soibari, Jorhat, Rangajan of North Lakhimpur district and Rangajan and Charduar of Sonitpur district.

In recent years, Nyishi Elite Society (NES) has shown an interest to hold up their Assam Nyishi brethrens affair as they are being marginalized by the Government of Assam. NES is the apex organization of the Nyishi tribe with the full initiatives of educated people for looking at the welfare activities of the tribe. Dr. Joram Begi, a retired Director of Higher and Technical Education, Government of Arunachal Pradesh was the founder President of Nyishi Elite Society (NES) and also longest-serving President of NES. Presently, Nyishi Elite Society (NES) is headed by Bengia Tulom as the President and Tarh Tabin as General Secretary. In an interview with Vijay Sonam (former General Secretary of Nyishi Elite Society) on April 25, 2013, noted:

'The Nyishi of Assam are the real inhabitant of Sonitpur, they were already there prior to the British and Ahom arrival. In fact, these areas were part of the NEFA territory (Balipara Frontier Tract) which was transferred to Assam in 1951. Till today, Nyishis of Assam is not given ST (Scheduled Tribes) status unlike the Garos, Singhpho, Khampti and Nagas, whom the Assam Government notified the Hills Tribe of Assam. It has caused a lot of hardship and difficulty in the reservation of job and political representation. It is the time that we think afresh for the Nyishi people of Assam who are being deprived of constitutional rights and benefits, such as ST status in their own land of origin and habitat'.

As a matter of fact, the native of this borderland not only contend with their local issues, pan-tribal issues but also with the trans-state political and economic dynamics and with the expression of indigeneity in the trans-state forums. In recent year, a series of cultural exchange programme going along Assam-Arunachal Pradesh borderland. For example, Nyishi-Bodo tribe of Arunachal Pradesh and Assam had a number of cultural exchanges programme conducted in recent years. The first historic summit called 'Bodo-Nyishi Peace Summit' was conducted at Itanagar on 11th April 2002. Nabam Rikam (2005) writing about the Nyishi and Bodo relations noted 'there was a strained relationship between the Bodos of Assam and the Nyishis over a few years. The Nyishis living along the Assam-Arunachal Pradesh border areas were subjected to kidnap, torture and extortion allegedly by Bodo outfits. Consequently, the Nyishis under the banner of Nyishi Elite Society called for a voluntary social boycott of all Bodo communities working in Arunachal Pradesh. After having a number of preliminary talks between the two communities, a historic summit called 'Bodo-Nyishi Peace Summit' was conducted at Itanagar on 11th April 2002. With the signing of this agreement, there is a perceptible change of positive environment along the borders'. The cordial relation between the two communities, in fact, dates back to Assam turmoil of the 70s and 80s when the Nyishi living in the foothills accorded shelter to the Bodo when they were persecuted. So far both the communities have signed two accords on February 11, 2002, at Banquet Hall, Itanagar and February 16, 2012, at Seijosa, East Kameng of Arunachal Pradesh.

Similarly, the relation between Adis and Mishing is worth mentioning. It is an open secret that Mishing of Arunachal Pradesh are attempting to recognize themselves as part of Adis so that they can get the benefits of constitutional incentives reserved for scheduled tribes in the state of Arunachal Pradesh. Consequently, a number of programs and meets were organized between Adi and Mishing in the last few years. On 4th and 5th April 2013, there was two days cultural exchange program between the Adi community of Arunachal Pradesh and Mishings of neighboring Assam and Arunachal Pradesh at Jonai. The chief organizer of the 'Adi-Mising Cultural Exchange Meets' and the President of Adi-Mising Lemo Kebang (AMLK), Raju Medok says:

'The sole purpose of organizing such meet is to exchange our feeling to foster unity and brotherhood…We all are sons and daughters of Abotani…There is no denying fact that Adi-Mishing doesn't have a bio-socio-cultural bond….The Assam-Arunachal Pradesh boundary was created for the administrative convenience of the governments, but the demarcation can never distort the parental relationship between Adi and Mising'.

Adi-Mishing Lemo Kabang (AMLK) is a newly formed organization of Adi and Mishing, formed on 6 February 2013 under the leadership of Okom Yousung and Raju Medok. The objective of forming this organization according to them is to promote brotherhood feeling among Adi and Mising of Arunachal Pradesh and Assam. In another development, Adi Agom Kebang (AAK) and Mising Agom Kebang (MAK) jointly develop a single script for Adi and Mising. There is also an emergence of kinship unions (*Opin Kebang*) among the Mising and Adis. Such meetings are held every year in the month of January and February. In my last fieldwork in January 2014 'Pegu and Megu kin meet (*Opin Kebang*)' was held at Jonai, Assam. At the meeting, many solidarity speeches were given and many proposals were given to strengthen the brotherhood bonds. In fact, such a meeting or kebang does take place every year among various Adi and Mishing kin groups. For instance, between Jerang of Adi and Regon of Mishing, between Pangam of Adi and Bori of Mishing, between Mize and Taye, between Doso, Danggen, and Dang, between Morang and Borang and between Lego and Mili, etc. These kinship groups regard themselves as descendent of the same ancestor. They regard themselves offspring of the same father and mother. At the same time, there are also many clan surnames living on both the sides, for instances Tayeng, Modi, Borang, Taye, Moyong, Dai, etc. of Adi in Assam and Arunachal Pradesh. Similarly, Doye, Riba, Basar, Rina, etc of Galo in Assam and Arunachal Pradesh. Pao, Techi, Welly, Tana, etc. of Nyishi in Assam and Arunachal Pradesh. These equivalences between surnames, which amount to equivalences between descent groups, are commonly found in the Assam-Arunachal Pradesh borderlands.

There is also a dialogue going on to unite the Mishing and Galo especially among Karko Aos, such as Bado, Bam, Basar (Rihar), Geyi, Karbak, Riba, Rike, Rina, Riram, etc. of Galo and Pagro groups of Mishing, such as Pegu and Doley. The reason for their relations is not clear, but it seems that they all lived together at some point in time. In an interview with Gomar Basar at Rajiv Gandhi University on 14/10/2016 noted '…The Pegu and Doley of Mishings are traced to be a direct descendant of the Karko Aos who lost on the way when they migrated from side bordering China. Even older people know the places where ancestors settled before coming to their present place. This is also sung in the folk songs of Karko clan members'. Dr. N. Lego (2005) also mentioned that Doley and Pegu clans come down from a place called Karko wherefrom Karko groups of Galo migrated.

One can also identify a trend of identity construction among the Tani tribes of this borderland. The identity construction among Nyishi, Adi, Apatani, Galo, Tagin, Hill Miris and Mishing of Assam, etc or so-called the sons of Abotani. Abotani is the mythical ancestor of the Adis, Apatanis, Galos, Hill-Miris, Nyishis, Mishing and the Tagins tribes of Arunachal Pradesh and Assam. Literally, Abo-means father and Tani mean human, so etymologically it means father of humankind or ancestor of Tani tribes. This Pan-Tani movement is based on the basis of commonalities in cultural traits and more importantly, on the basis of the genealogy of origin, which illustrate their brotherhood.

This identity consciousness is stimulated by some educated youths to promote their language and identity. The key issue of their movement is to develop a common dialect for Tani groups. Taba Taku, one of the leading cultural activists and President of Arunachal Pradesh Abotani Community Confederation (APACC) is of the opinion that: '…The aim of our group is to create a sense of nationalism inside the hearts and minds of every single Tanis…It is our duty to let the whole world know that Tani Clans is one of the existing strong and not just a myth and stories'. Arunachal Pradesh Abotani Community Confederation (APACCC) is a newly formed organization, active in Arunachal Pradesh headed by Taba Taku as the President and Subu Kechi as General Secretary.

There is also a dialogue going on between the members of Tani tribes in the states of Arunachal Pradesh and Assam to form a Taniland. It is often told that there has planned to form a Taniland province comprising of the northern Mishing tribe bordering Arunachal Pradesh of the Brahmaputra valley. In an Interview with Taba Taku on 23/04/2013 at Itanagar, he noted, '...Abotani Community Confederation of Arunachal Pradesh was launched by me. We are Tanis at first and then we are Mishings, Nyishi, Apatani, Tagin, Adi, or Galo or even Lhoba. Let call our state as Taniland. Moreover, the majority of our population is of the Tani group with almost 10 plus districts covering a geographical area. It will be more like a tribal identity to us, which we as a tribal-state lack. People think we are tribals from Andhra Pradesh, Madhya Pradesh or Nepalis from Uttaranchal or Uttrakhand when we say we are from Arunachal Pradesh. They never asked it to Nagas or Mizo. We as a state lack our identity. We are only known when China asserts their claim on Tawang; else we are just a bunch of Chinki Dajus.

'...When we can have our country name as 'Hindustan' with so much diversity, the same way we all can it Taniland. When we can have so much 'Gandhi' in the state, why not something closer to us? Perhaps, we are so much indoctrinated not to accept our own, but gracefully accept names like 'Madhuri Lake', without actually remembering or respecting its original name. For that to happen, there should be an Annual Tani meet fest every year...'Top of Form.

Again, there is also a forum called the Tani Federation Forum, which claims to work to revive indigenous culture and language across Assam-Arunachal Pradesh borderland. It is a Guwahati based forum. The organization was formed on 16 June 2007 at Lakhimpur, Assam. J. K. Riba is the President, Dheeraj Pao as Secretary-General and Tagam Nabam as Convener. Apart from Pan-Tani Movement, there is also a movement of Pan Nagas or Greater Nagalim[2] active in bordering areas of Changlang, Longding and Tirap district of Arunachal Pradesh. Interestingly, it has been observed that recently, Nagas of Arunachal Pradesh like Nocte, Wancho, Ollo, Tangsa, Tutsa now did not want to identify themselves as Nagas. Recently, on February 20, 2014, thousand of Nocte, Wancho, Ollo, Tangsa, Tutsa, took out a procession against the NSCN's demand to integrate Naga areas in its proposed 'Greater Nagalim'.

Conclusion

The history of this inter-state borderland began with the expansion of the British Empire in the early 18th century. It was a product of colonial commercial interest (Barpujari 1981: 255). And after independence, considering the need to administer the areas, the Government of India created the present-day inter-state boundary following British legacy. Historically, this borderland used to be the meeting place of India and China, what Zou and Kumar (2011:141) called 'contact zone' between peripheral civilizations of Inner Asia.

Edmund Leach (1960: 54) noted, 'Every society in South-East Asia of which we have knowledge which has possessed even a modest degree of cultural sophistication has been quite emphatically subject to Indian or Chinese influence; usually to both'. Obviously, it is one of the migration routes of many races. Remnants of Itaport at Itanagar, the temple of Malinithan at Likabali and Bhismaknagar Fort at Roing speak volumes about how peoples of different races and cultures and at a different time come to this part of the region and contributed to the formation and enrichment of the local culture throughout the centuries.

Unfortunately, with the drawing of boundaries after India's independence, uncertainty and insecurity overwhelm the region. Gellner (2013: 7) noted, 'It is quite disheartening that the post-colonial state has become more of a problem than a blessing in most of Northeast India. The question that begs for an answer is whether a borderless Northeast as a replacement for the multiplicity of unviable states that currently dot the Northeast landscape will necessarily make a positive meaning to the long-suffering people'. Nonetheless, the narratives of the people reside at Assam-Arunachal Pradesh borderland indicates boundary matter little for all practical reasons. This is more so because the people who have been living along the boundary engage in the individual occasion, influences cultures, the exchange between people. In fact, it is the place where mixed people share memories together, and these memories can be identified in the form of a festival like Bihu, Ali-Aye Ligang, Diwali, Durga Puja, where lots of cultural exchange takes place by participating in the festivals.

Notes

1. Pradeep Kumar, One-man Bordoloi Commission: Boundary row haunts people, Cong wields BC, *Arunachal Front*, 12/06/2013.
2. Greater Nagalim is the purported objective of the National Socialist Council of Nagaland-Isak-Muivah (NSCN-IM) to establish Greater Nagaland, consisting of all the Naga-inhabited areas of Assam, Manipur, Arunachal Pradesh, and some portions Myanmar, which it considers to be the rightful homeland of the Nagas.

References

Barpujari, HK 1981, *Problem of the hill tribes; North-East frontier, the inner line to the Mc Mohan Line*, United Publishers, Guwahati.

Bhattacharyya, B 1995, *The troubled border*, Lawyer's Book Stall, Guwahati.

Chanda, S 2003, *The border society: a study of network and linkage*, Anthropological Survey of India, Kolkata.

Daphne, B 1999, *Where the world ended: re-unification and identity in the German borderland*, University of California Press, London.

Dutta, S (ed.) 2002, *Cross-border trade of North-East India: the Arunachal perspective,* Hope India Publications, and Greenwich Millenium, London.

Gait, EA 1906, *A history of Assam*, Thacker, Spink, and Co, Calcutta.

Gellner, DN (ed.) 2013, *Borderland lives in northern South Asia*, Duke University Press, London.

Gogoi, L 1958, 'The Age-old amity of the hills and the plains' in *The outlook*, ed P Chaliha, Assam Sahitya Sabha, Jorhat, Assam.

Leach, ER 1960, *The frontiers of Burma, comparative studies in society and history*, vol. 3, no. 1, pp. 49-68.

Lego, N 2005, *History of the Mishings of Arunachal Pradesh and Assam*, Mrs. Ponung Lego, Peregrine Graphics, Itanagar.

M'Cosh, J 1837, *Topography of Assam*, G. H. Huttmann, Bengal Military Orphan Press, Calcutta.

McDuie-Ra, D 2016, *Borderland city in New India: frontier to gateway*, Amsterdam University Press, Amsterdam.

Michell, JF 1883 (1973), *The north-east frontier of India; a topographical, political and military report*, Vivek Publishing House, New Delhi.

Mishra, S 2011, *Becoming a borderland: the politics of space and identity and in colonial Northeastern India*, Routledge, New Delhi.

Rikam, NT, 2005, *Emerging religious identities of Arunachal Pradesh: a study of Nyishi tribe*, Mittal Publication, New Delhi.

Roy Barman, BK 2004, 'Structure of bridge and buffer communities in the border areas' in *Anthropology for North-East India: a reader*, eds A Basu, BK Das Gupta & J Sarkar, Indian National Confederation and Academy of Anthropologists, Indian Anthropological Society and National Museum of Mankind, Calcutta, pp. 96-99.

Schendel, WV 2005, *The Bengal borderland; beyond state and nation in South Asia*, Anthem South Asian Studies, London.

Upadhyay, A 2009, *India's fragile borderlands: the dynamics of terrorism in Northeast India,* I.B. Taurus, London.

Wouters, Jelle JP 2012, 'Keeping the hill tribes at bay: a critique from India's Northeast of James C. Scott's paradigm of state evasion', *European Bulletin of Himalayan Research*, vol. 39, pp. 41-65.

Zou, DV & Kumar, MS 2011, 'Mapping a colonial borderland: objectifying the geo-body of India's Northeast', *The Journal of Asian Studies*, vol. 70, pp. 141-170.

Chapter - 7

Changing Trends in Living Megalithic Practices in Pamohi, Guwahati

Garima Thakuria and Manoj Kumar Singh

Introduction

Megaliths, referred to large stones, either stand singly or in rows or are found in clusters forming definite structures or monuments. The word megalith has been derived from two ancient Greek words, *Megas* meaning big or large or great, and *lithos* meaning stones. These stones were collected from river beds or from hills and put up in memory of the deceased or to commemorate important places or institutions like markets or youth dormitories, clubs, etc. Megaliths provide insights into the socio-political, economic and ideological attribute of life of prehistoric men and thus showcase varied meanings, viz., funerary, commemorative, religious and ceremonial (Marak, 2015: 31). In Neolithic Europe, as revealed by Chapman in 1981, the megalithic structures functioned as territorial markers which were under control of kinship-based corporate groups. The distribution of great stone graves among the Neolithic population in Western and Northern Europe has been most plausibly explained by repercussions of the beliefs then formulated in the Ancient East (Childe, 1936: 99). Megalithic construction as memorial stones and burial chambers has been a prehistoric tradition in the Mediterranean nations and in Western Europe. This custom dated to the New Stone Age and the Bronze Age.

Megaliths found across the world from prehistoric times exhibited varied distinctive characteristics, viz., representation of an elite class of individuals or groups (Haimendorf, 1946; Flemming, 1973; Sherrat, 1990; Nelson, 1999), focus on inherent symbolism (Hodder, 1990; Bradley, 1998), used for astronomical observations (cited in Marak, 2015: 31), enhancement of fertility cult in a magical way (Haimendorf, 1946; Bloch, 1906-07) and to depict commonness and authoritative quality (Marak, 2015: 41). Moreover, the megalithic structures show similarity as well as dissimilarity at different places worldwide. These may range from Menhirs to Dolmens, Stone hinges, Cairns, etc.

Megalith and the Practice of its Erection across the Indian Sub-continent

The oldest megaliths in India, found in the form of stone circles and dated to about 3000 BC, are discovered from the westernmost part of the country. These large stone structures are now in Afghanistan in the upper Indus Valley. Megaliths encountered from the Deccan region in the southern part of India vary from those of the other Indian regions including central, southern and eastern India where they are a part of continuing traditions. These stone structures show definite characters and are found to belong to the Iron Age that is from 1000 BC to 1000 AD. Also, a broad time evolution with the megaliths in central India dated to be in-between 1000 BC and 500 BC is found while those in the east are much later and are dated till 900 AD (Vahia et al., 2010).

Considering the complexity of Indian megaliths, Haimendorf (1945) combined both the archaeological and ethnographical data and classified megalithic cultures in India into two distinct parts –

(a) a living tradition in Eastern and Central India, and

(b) a tradition in South India documented using the archaeological leftovers. These two were independent of each other (Marak, 2015: 31).

Thus, megaliths are significant stone structures that can reveal a great deal of information not only about the lifestyle of the people who made them but can also disclose details about their faiths and beliefs. Some of these have even been suspected of being astronomical observatories and as objects spread over space and constructed in order to keep track of time! Thus, in the past megaliths were regarded as the most curious of objects in that these connect concrete experiences of movement of time and space, its periodicity and its relation to nature and environment (Vahia et al., 2010).

The practice of erecting megalithic monuments has been found in European and Asian countries including India. In the year 1823, Babington reported about megaliths for the first time in India. Megaliths of all kinds are found in the subcontinent of India. The tradition of constructing megalithic structures has been a prehistoric as well as a recent phenomenon prevalent in the eastern, central and Northeastern region of India, viz.,

Madhya Pradesh, Orissa, Chotanagpur, Meghalaya, Nagaland, Manipur, and Assam (Sharma, 1998: 30). Stone repositories, in the form of megalithic burial chambers belonging to the Iron Age, were established from the South Indian states of Andhra Pradesh, Karnataka, and Tamil Nadu. These dated between 1000 and 300 BC. While in some regions of the country, these stone structures are traditionally a living phenomenon, yet in some other areas, these are only erected archaic structures. The megalithic monuments of peninsular India, believed to have been erected during the Iron Age (1500 BC – 200 AD), can broadly (potentially overlapping) be classified into two varieties on the basis of their function (Moorti, 1994, 2008):

1. Sepulchral (containing remains of the dead) in which memorial stones with mortal remains may not be present but clearly seem to be associated with human life, and
2. Non-sepulchral including largely patterned placement of stones over a wide area. (Vahia et al., 2010)

While considering the stylistic aspects, the megaliths are uniform in typology, unlike the megaliths in southern India which tend to be menhirs, dolmens and other non-sepulchral structures as well as sepulchral megaliths including the stone circle typology. Dalton has mentioned about memorial stones in the shape of menhirs and dolmens located in Ho and Munda villages in Chotanagpur. As many as eighty-nine megalithic sites have been catalogued in Suvrathan (2010) in Vidarbha region out of which 51 are around Nagpur region. Out of the total of eighty-nine sites, 54 sites have only stone circles, four sites have a dolmen while one has a dolmen and a stone circle. Among these, forty sites are purely habitation sites. Khairwada is the largest megalithic site comprising about 1400 stone circles, cairns and habitation deposits spanning from megalithic to the early historical period (Jamkhedkar, 1981). Junapani, the second largest site with the presence of 150 stone circles of similar period, was excavated by Thapar (1961). The most common amongst the non-sepulchral megaliths are the Menhirs, stone alignments and avenues (Moorti, 1994, 2008; cited in Vahia et al., 2010). At present, the practice of erecting megaliths in South India has become obsolete. However, it is still an ongoing tradition among some of the tribes in Northeast India, which is carried on from one generation to the next. The megalith building practices are undoubted of prehistoric origin. Haimendorf had observed that the recent practices of the tribal communities of Northeast India have close parallels with the Godabas and the Bondos of Orissa and Southeast Asia (Sharma, 1998: 32).

The Department of Archaeology and Museums Officials of Andhra Pradesh have found about 200 megalithic burial sites on the Nagarjuna

Sagar reservoir bed. This was a rare archaeological find which surfaced after the water level in the dam receded below the Minimum Draw Down Level (MDDL) and which the officials believe to have been used as a community burial site because a large number of stone circle burials were found at one spot (Reddy, 2015).

Megaliths in Northeast India

The Northeastern region of India is a pocket in the whole world where the megalithic culture has been found to survive to date. Taking into consideration the undivided Assam, it was Godwin Austen (1871-72) who for the first time found uniqueness in the Khasi megaliths during his geographical surveys across Assam. Dalton also provided an account of megaliths, specifically monoliths, erected by various tribal communities of Northeast India. In 1933, Mills pinpointed the living tradition of erecting megaliths and regarded the remains as one of the archaeological wealth presents in the world. Gurdon surmised that the prehistoric people of Northeast India were represented by a common cultural development as observed from the megalithic tradition and quoted on the Khasi and Jaintia Hills's megalithic monuments as, 'probably one of the first objects which strikes the eyes of a visitor to the Khasi hills is the very large number of monoliths and table-stones, and cromlechs that are to be met with almost everywhere in that country' (Gurdon, 1914: 13-45; cited in Sharma, 1998: 30). He recorded the megaliths or the monoliths as Khasi memorial stones and classified these into menhirs or vertical stones; dolmens or table stones; and cairns or stone cromlechs. Gurdon further made comparisons among the Khasi monuments, the stones erected by the Mikirs (or Karbi) and the monoliths erected by the Nagas of Manipur and Ho-Mundas. Lyall reported about the prevalence of the system of the erection of monoliths by the hill Karbis. McCalls provided information about the erection of megaliths by the Lushai (presently known as Mizo, Saikia, 2007: 432-433). Besides stone, monuments of wood are found to be raised occasionally in memory of the deceased by their kin. This practice of raising memorial monuments is accompanied by elaborate sacrificial rituals (Rao, 1991: 106). During the prehistoric time when the megalithic culture prevailed, monoliths like menhirs were erected in the memory of the dead (Sharma, 1998: 13). The Khasis, Nagas, Karbis and other tribes who erect megalithic monuments have distinct ethno-lingual terms for the large stone or wooden structures.

In Meghalaya, the raising of lithic structures was a living tradition until recent times. Thus, such huge structures are found abundantly in the form of dolmens, cists, table-top stones, menhirs, stone slabs or capstones from Nartiang, Umstow, Laitkar and Laitlyngkot in the Khasi and Jaintia Hills, which exhibit different socio-religious functions. Moreover, Godwin Austen (1872) reported megaliths to be concentrated at Cherrapunji, Maoflong, Lailong, Kote, Laitkhor, Jowai and Nartiang. The menhirs erected at Nartiang are peculiar among the Indian megaliths such that these are as tall as 27 feet and 2.5 feet in thickness. These erections have been basically to commemorate the deceased ancestors. Gurdon (1975) has classified these stones of various dimensions into -

(a) Menhirs or vertical stones,

(b) Table-stones or dolmens, and

(c) Stone cromlechs or chamber tombs or cairns.

The huge stones in Nartiang have been clustered in an uneven number. Since the disposal of the dead was usually by cremation, the ashes and the uncalcified bones were collected and then deposited in the clan chamber tombs or cromlechs (Rao, 1977: 194).

Further to understand the significance of the megaliths, Rao (Rao, 1991: 109-115) classified these stone structures into two groups based on function, structure and socio-ideological meaning attached to the megaliths:

A. Funerary stone, which is directly associated with post-cremation ritual including disposal of the mortal remains of the deceased; and

B. A memorial stone, erected by clansmen or any other to commemorate an event of public interest – social, political, ideological, etc.

Mawlong (1996) gave a classification of the megalithic monuments of the Khasi and Jaintia Hills in her Ph.D. thesis, wherein she classed these structures into five groups based on morphology, namely,

Group A- Menhirs, Alignments, Avenues

Group B- Dolmens

Group C- Cists, Cairns and Cairn-cists

Group D- Stone circles

Group E- Stone Cremation Platforms; and functionally into two groups, viz.,

Group A- Funerary stones or Mawbynna Niam, and

Group B- Memorial stones or Mawbynna Nam, which are further subdivided into a few more groups.

All these megalithic monuments signify important aspects of ways of life like linking concepts of unity of maternal ancestry and social continuity; concepts of fertility and social merit; rank and status of dominant groups in societies over others etc. (Mitri, 2009: 9-10). In an article in 2005, Mawlong noted about the association of megalithic structures with the establishment of markets at important centers like Nongsksch, Laitlngkot, Nongkrem, Mylliem, Cherrapunji, Sutnga, Raliang, Nangbah, Shangpung, Nartiang, Jowai; at intra-tribal boundaries such as Shillong and Jowai; and at ecological boundaries, viz., Mawsmai, Cherrapunji, Jaintiapur etc. (Marak, 2015: 41). Works on megaliths of the Khasis were also undertaken by Lyngdoh (1937), David Roy (1963), Bareh (1967), Shadap Sen (1981), Bareh (1981) among others (Rao, 1991: 107-108). Playfair (1909) has recorded about the memorial posts or *Kima* raised by the Garos against the deceased in his monograph *The Garos*. Basically, these were decorated bamboo posts. *Asong* was another type of monolith used for the purpose of sacrificing animals; decorated on the day of sacrifice and erected at the entrance of every village. *Kosi* was yet another type of stone used by the Garos to mark a spot where a man is killed in war or for the sake of revenge. Deb Roy recorded about the tradition of erecting megaliths behind a deceased among the Jaintias which has become obsolete and at times erection of small tombs or tombstones have been observed (Saikia, 2007: 434).

Besides, tribes of Manipur, Nagaland, and Assam have been practicing the raising of megaliths from time immemorial as has been depicted by the age-old large stones found from different sites across the states and also from various ethnographic studies conducted on them by several scholars. For instance, Mate in his book *A Mate Tribe of Manipur (A Case Study on Twisomjang)* provided an account of the presence of megalithic practice among the Mates, who erect a post carved with varied pictures on the center of a grave (Saikia, 2007: 435). Among others, Haimendorf (1945) has observed that megalithic monuments scattered over the areas inhabited by the Angami population described the 'Feast of Merit' or the 'Stone-dragging Feast' and regarded these stones as 'a living and vital part of Naga culture'.

Megaliths of Assam

Assam, the frontier state of Northeast India, has been populated with numerous tribes of different ethnic origins speaking different languages and dialects and possesses diverse socio-cultural traditions besides a host of the non-tribal populace. Besides stone tools and pottery, the other significant archaeological attribute of the region is the presence of megaliths and the continued tradition associated with these large stones. Megaliths are found to be widely dispersed in the North Cachar Hills and Karbi Anglong districts (Mills and Hutton, 1929; Medhi, 1999, 2002; Bezbaruah, 2004; Sarma, 2010) and also in Kamrup district (Choudhury, 2004) of Assam. These have been a common sight in the Karbi dominated pockets of the state and found abundantly in Karbi Anglong district. Bezbaruah in the year 2005 has recorded megalithic remains from Kamarpha, Rongali, Nongjrong, Mukhrow, Umcherra, Bowlagog, Habang, Umteli, Opthernala, Jorshala, Locrew and Mauslai in Karbi Anglong (Bezbaruah, 2012: 307).

In Assam, these stones are erected by the Karbi population residing both in the hills and the plains. It is one of the ongoing cultural practices found among the Karbi population living across the state. These large stones are erected in the specific site allotted for the erection after the death of an individual. Generally, this type of site is located by the side of the paths leading to the paddy fields from the village or at the fringe of the villages. The corpse is either buried or burnt by this tribal community. Baruah has carried out extensive studies on the megalithic tradition of the plain Karbis and megalithism. The Lalungs or Tiwas were also used to erecting megaliths in the past. Gohain (1993) has observed engraving of an image of Mohan Pator, an ancestor of the Hill Lalungs, on the upper part of the tall upright megalith (Saikia, 2007: 434-435).

In the earlier times, megalithic structures were reported by Gurdon from the Mikir Hills (presently Karbi Anglong), the Naga Hills and parts of Manipur inhabited by the Nagas. Mills and Hutton (1929: 285-300) also revealed numerous megalithic sites in Ndunglo, Bolasan, Derebora, Kobak, and Kartong of North Cachar Hills, which were located in the hill tracts joining Nagaland with the Khasi and Jaintia Hills. The structures ranged from stone cists, some at Derebora containing human remains and referred to as megalithic burial cists.

The megaliths of Dimoria have been classified into several types by Medhi and Choudhury (2009) on the basis of morphology and function. These types included menhir, table stone, dolmen, a stone seat, and a stone pillar. Nevertheless, the Karbis of Dimoria classed these erected stones into three types, viz.,

(a) *Long-e*, which included menhir and stone pillar,

(b) *Cheng-e*, including dolmen and table stone, and

(c) *Along-kangni-anglong*, which included a stone seat.

Again, on the basis of structure, they have pertinently categorized the megaliths as male and female menhirs. Here, the male menhirs have been represented by megaliths with a more or less pointed tip, whereas the top of the menhirs erected in the memory of dead women has been invariably broken down. The Karbis of Dimoria erect megaliths in the memory of dead persons who die of natural death and not due to unnatural deaths or deaths caused by accidents, suicide attack of animals and whatsoever, which is considered a taboo for them (Medhi and Choudhury, 2009: 218).

The megalithic structures of Dimoria have been categorized into two broad divisions to depict their significance. These classes are:

(a) Memorial and commemorative or menhir of social status;

(b) Funerary and ritualistic megaliths.

The Karbis of different villages of Dimoria set up menhirs in order to commemorate the dead and as monuments of social achievements of the living. In the name of the dead individual, a feast of merit is arranged by relatives to honour him/her. This tribal community residing in the villages of this area erects series of stone related to funerary and ritualistic purposes. Along with the *long-e* or menhirs, flat stone is put up in front of each menhir to offer food to the dead. This additional flat stone has been named as *cheng-e* by the Karbis (Medhi and Choudhury, 2009: 222-225).

The Karbis

Previously known as the Mikirs by the Assamese and other communities, the Karbis constitute an important ethnic group of the hill regions of the state of Assam though its origin is unknown. They are the principal tribal community residing in the hilly Karbi Anglong district of Assam and the North Cachar Hills besides other plain areas like Dimoria, Marakdola, Garchuk etc. of Kamrup district and the districts of Jorhat, Morigaon, Nagaon, Golaghat, Karimganj, Lakhimpur and Sonitpur of Assam, and the Khasi Hills district of Meghalaya (Sarma, 1993:20-21; Sahu, 2002: 86). The word 'Mikir' is believed to have been derived from the word 'Mengkiri' meaning 'in search of a cat' (Choudhury, 2003: 133). Whereas, the term Karbi has been derived from *Me Aakar Bi* (*Me Aakar* = to light a fire; *Bi* = to leave) with *Me* and *Aa* being given up in due course of time (Sahu, 2002: 86). According to Census of India, 2001, there are 419,534 Karbi people living in Assam (www.censusindia.gov.in).

Racially, these people belong to the Mongoloid group. The Karbi tribe inhabiting the Karbi Anglong district of Assam belongs to the Assam-Burma group of the linguistic family but the people can neither be put under Bodo nor any other linguistic group (Kar, 1986: 135). On the basis of language, Grierson (1904) classed this population as an intermediate group between the Bodo and the Western Naga. Again, other scholars want to suggest that Karbi language shows a mixture of Austric and Bodo languages, though the group undoubtedly belongs to the Tibeto-Burman linguistic family. However, Lyall (1881) mentioned that the Karbis are more akin to the Bodo than the Khasis. The Karbis are believed to arrive from the north (Kar, 1986:135), especially Central Asia (Bordoloi et al., 1987: 57) in one of the waves of migration. Ethnically the Karbis belong to the great Mongoloid group and linguistically they belong to the Tibeto-Burman branch of the Sino-Tibetan group of Southeast Asia. The ballad prevalent among the Karbis reveals that the Karbis are closely related to the Kuki-Chins and the Karbi language belongs to the Kuki-Chin sub-group.

Constituting the third largest tribal community in Assam after the Bodos and the Mishings, the Karbis sometimes call themselves *Arleng* which literally means ‘a man’ (Lyall, 1908: 4; Bordoloi et al., 1987: 57) though actually *Manit* or *Munet* is the proper term used by the Karbis to denote a person. Gogoi (1962) and Medhi (1988) pointed out that the term *Arleng* means ‘slanting place near a hill’ and thus it denotes the people living in the slopes of the hills. In fact, the word *Arleng* is confined to the men of the Karbi tribe only. Nowadays they identify themselves as Karbi, though the origin of the term is uncertain (Medhi, 1988: 8) because of lack of their own script and hence the absence of written records. For learning about their origin, migration, and development, one should take the assistance of Karbi folklore, mythological tales, and recent anthropological and linguistic findings of the scholars (Choudhury, 2012: 32-33). Kalaguru Bishnu Prasad Rabha called the Mikirs as the ‘Discoverer of Assam’ as they were among the earliest inhabitants of Assam tracing their origin and existence in China and Southeast Asia.

The Karbis living in the hills are divided into Chinthong, Ronghang and Amri groups, on the other hand, the Karbis living in the plain districts of the state are called Dumrali or Dumurali or Thalua. Basically, the Dumurali Karbis are found to inhabit the plains of Kamrup district (Kathar, 2014: 9). They have five clans or *Kur*, i.e. Terang, Teron, Enghee, Ingti and Timung, and each clan is again divided into several sub-clans, viz. Ingti (5), Teron (6), Terang (6), Enghee (30) and Timung (30). The clans are equal in status. Marriage among the same clan is strictly prohibited. Monogamy is the prevailing practice among the people. Cross-cousin marriage is highly preferred. Divorce and remarriage are permissible. The Karbis are a patrilocal, patrilineal and patripotestal tribe. They worship numerous deities known as *Arnam-atum* in the local language. Ancestor worship has also been observed commonly (Sahu, 2002: 91). *Chojun* or

Swarag is the most important household religious festival of the people. *Birkilut* is an important occasion among the Karbis. But the most expensive religious ceremony prevalent among them is the *Chomangkan* i.e. final death ceremony. The Karbis cremate the dead bodies in the specific place allotted against each clan in the crematorium (*Thiri* or *Tipit*; Bordoloi et al., 1987: 62; Das, 2000: 42-45). They also practice the tradition of erecting megaliths. *Jambeli Athon*, a designed and decorated wooden pole, carved by artisans is required during *Chomangkan* and other important ceremonies. They believe in rebirth as human beings. The traditional institutions are *Me* (the village council), *Jirkedam* or *Farla* (the bachelor's dormitory) and *Kerung Amei* (the grain bank). The settlement pattern of the Karbis is in the form of a village. The village headman or *Gaonbura* or *Sarthe* or *Sarbura* is appointed by the authority of Karbi Anglong Autonomous Council (Bordoloi et al., 1987: 60; Das, 2011: 16-19).

In the hills, the Karbis live in huts made on bamboo platforms using timber posts for the superstructure, whereas the plain Karbis live in houses constructed on the ground. The primary occupation of the Karbi tribe is agriculture. They mainly cultivate paddy. The hill Karbis practice shifting cultivation where they cultivate other crops and vegetables as mixed crops besides paddy. They practice *jhum* cultivation in the hills in a traditional way (Das, 2011: 16-19). The residents of Marakdola, Sarutaru, and Pamohi practice the wet cultivation of paddy as well as grow paddy and other vegetables in the *jhum* fields in a limited quantity. Rice is their staple food. Besides, they consume vegetables like brinjal, cabbage, chilie, fern, etc.; fish and meat of cock, hen, pig, and goat. They also prepare rice beer (called locally as *Horlang*). All Karbi women are expert in weaving and spinning. *Rikong*, *choilok,* and *poncho* (headgear) are male attires whereas women tie *pinicamflak* around their waist, *jar-ek* over their upper body, *ringkok* (a long cloth or *chadar*) and *wankok* (waistband) (Kathar, 2014: 16).

Megalithic Tradition among the Karbi Population

The practice of erecting megaliths is found only in a few isolated pockets among the tribal communities of Northeast India (Jamir, 2014: 333), particularly in Assam, Manipur, Meghalaya, and Nagaland in the same pristine way or in a modified form (Choudhury, 2012: 311). Among the tribes of Assam, the Karbis are still practicing it since time immemorial. The tradition is seen among the Karbi villagers of Pamohi, Datalpara, and Maghoapara near Guwahati.

Though some differences are observed in the practice of erection of megaliths among the hill and the plain Karbis, yet the 'feast of merit' exists as the common feature integral to both the communities (Choudhury, 2012: 311). One of the differences is that the plain Karbis perform this ritual after the death of each and every individual whereas the hill-Karbis perform the same ritual collectively, usually after the death of 10-15 persons (Sarma, 2014: 353-354). The nature of the feast decides the power, property, and position of the deceased in the society and it is held by the dead person's kith and kin to entertain the villagers at the time of erecting the megalith. Among the Karbis, a megalith is erected only when an individual die of natural death. No megaliths are erected for the person who dies an unnatural death caused by accident, suicide, attack of animals like tiger and elephant, etc. and is considered inauspicious.

The Karbi megaliths have been categorized into two broad groups based on their structures. These are (Choudhury, 2012: 314):

1. Memorial or Commemorative: This type of megalith is generally erected to commemorate the demise of an individual or the members of a clan; or at times commemorate events of public interest - social, political or ideological. This commemoration signifies status, prestige or social eminence of an individual. Typologically, this type of memorial has been identified as menhir or *long-e*, in the local dialect and may remain erected near village path(s) leading to *jhum* fields or habitation areas.
2. Funerary and Ritualistic: These are megaliths erected in series and related to funerary and ritualistic purposes. These may be menhir or dolmen. The dolmen is locally known as *cheng-e*.

Hard, consistent, harmonious and durable rocks, viz., igneous, sandstone, granite and their metamorphic varieties are preferred for the construction of these megalithic monuments. The Karbis of Dimoria raises megalithic structures in their own names while the performer is still alive or after death or in loving memory of their parents or any dead member of the family. Numerous kinds of sacrifices accompanied by a grand feast of merit with their pristine beliefs are performed by the Karbi community. These feasts require lots of wealth in the form of pigs, fowls, rice-beer and rice (Choudhury, 2012: 315-316).

The Process of Erecting the Megaliths

Numerous steps are involved in the raising of megaliths by the Karbis. These are discussed below:

1. Selection of stone: The selection of stone to erect as megalith or monolith depends on the availability of the specific rocks and their closeness to the village. After the death of a person, a few villagers go to the nearby hill in search of a rock which might be erected as a megalith in the memory of the deceased person. These people carry along with them a pair of betel nuts, a pair of betel leaf, a handful of rice, a pot full of rice beer (*Harlong*), a few matches and a hammer. The Karbis use only the 'living stone', which is un-weathered, uneroded and is fresh, as megaliths. They test the required rock by striking with the hammer and carry it subsequently back to the site meant for the erection. At times, if the rock is too big, the people break it as per requirement and carry it to the specified spot.
2. Performance of rituals: The villagers with the help of the priest or *karkun* purify the selected stone. Then the stone is shifted to the specific ground meant for the erection which is purified by sprinkling basil dipped in water. The stone is also washed and purified after which the erection takes place amidst incantations by the priest addressing the stone.
3. Ritual after the erection of megalith: Pigs and hens are sacrificed after the megalith is erected and then the stone is sprinkled with the blood of the sacrificed animals. Chanting of hymns continue during this performance. Then the stone is wrapped by a *fail* (a loin cloth) or *gamocha* (handwoven towel) if it represents a dead male person. Whereas a megalith meant for a dead female is wrapped by a cotton thread that is not hardened with starch. Sometimes, the cloth is taken away on the last day of the funeral. This is followed by a feast of boiled rice and curries of sacrificed pigs and fowls served to the villagers. The deceased is given his/her share of the feast on the flat stone or *cheng-e* meant for such purposes laid close-by to the *long-e*. The people present during the feast are then entertained with songs and dances after which they move to the house of the deceased person and console the bereaved family members. People sing and dance the whole night in order to console the grieved family and then without uttering a parting word move out of the dead person's house. Parting word during this time is regarded inauspicious by the community members. The bereaved family members are not allowed to consume any bitter food or prepare rice beer from the first day of a person's death to the last day of the funeral.

Changes and Continuity in the Tradition of the Erection of Megaliths

The monoliths found from Pamohi have been raised in the memory of the dead people by the Dumurali Karbi population residing in the vicinity. These are usually of contemporary period and small in size. These are erected with traditional fervour as memorial stones in fond memory of the dead individuals of the family or clan, the death being natural in an occurrence like that due to old age or suffering from sickness. Although there are similarities observed in the cultural practice viz., to commemorate the death in the Karbi community, no such ritual for the unnatural deaths and the selection of the ground for the erection of these stones to be different from the burial ground, yet there exist some changes that have occurred in the present day practice in Pamohi. These are underlined below (Thakuria, 2017: 203-204):

1. Generally, two types of stones were erected by the villagers of Pamohi. One big stone act as the menhir and another flat stone put up on two smaller stones like that of a table in order to offer food and other ritualistic offerings. But, at present, flat stone is laid in front of the upright menhir to offer betel nut and leaf to the deceased person.
2. Out of the two stones put up, the upright menhir is in the memory of the dead individual and the other one is in the name of the maternal uncle of the deceased.
3. In the early days, the size of the monoliths or menhirs was big but nowadays the ritual is performed using comparatively small to medium sized stones, with the Karbis believing that the stone will grow with time depending on the character or good deeds of the dead individual during his lifetime.
4. A gender difference has been observed in the erection of the megaliths or monoliths. In case of it being raised for a dead male Karbi, a piece of white loin cloth is tied to the upper part of the stone, which depicts the headgear used by menfolk. Whereas, in case of a woman, the loin white cloth is tied towards the lower part of the monolith depicting a traditional wrapper worn by the female folk. Previously, these clothes used to be of the colour that the male and the female cloth generally happen to be.
5. Due to lack of time among the present generation of people, some of the rituals observed during and after death is cut short. Previously, a gap of fifteen days occurred between the ritual of calling the spirit of the dead (*jiulimata*) and the erection of

monolith or megalith, which is not observed today (personal communication, Kathar, 2014-2015)

6. Nowadays, the erection of the stones takes place for some important individual(s) of the Karbi community residing in the village or among their clan members. It is not for every dead individual of the community or the clan, unlike the ancient time.
7. Previously, the big stones required to raise as monolith or megalith were brought from the hills or the bed of the rivers chanting hymns by the priest or *karkun* as well as assisted by villagers. But due to factors like unavailability of time and raw material, people bring in any rock or piece of a bigger rock from the vicinity to perform the ritual of erecting the monolith in the memory of the deceased.

Summary and Conclusion

Megaliths are prevalent in Assam along with a few other Northeast states from the remote past. In Assam, a distinct practice of the raising up of large stones has been found from time immemorial with evidence of these stones erected at different locales of the Karbis and Khasis. Since no proper date has been provided yet, the exact time period of these stones is not found. The Karbis maintain the megalithic tradition as a commemorative ritual of the deceased members of the family or the village or the clan. This erecting of megaliths has been observed as a living tradition, i.e. a cultural practice which has taken the form of a tradition till the present time. Though the contemporary stone structures erected in Pamohi are not too big in size yet the Dumurali Karbis living in this village have kept up with the age-old tradition in memory of the deceased members of the family or clan.

References

Bezbaruah, D 2004, *Megalithic ruins in Karbi Anglong district, Assam: a study in the context of Karbi culture*. Ph.D. thesis, Gauhati University, Guwahati.

Bezbaruah, D 2012, 'The megalithic tradition of Northeast India: a critical assessment' in *People of contemporary North-East India*, ed T Baruah, Pratisruti Publication, Guwahati, pp. 306-310.

Bordoloi, BN, Sharma Thakur, GC & Saikia, MC 1987, *Tribes of Assam*, part-I, Tribal Research Institute, Guwahati.

Census of India 2001. Available from: www.censusindia.gov.in at 14.20. [14 May 2018].

Childe, VG 1936, *Man makes himself*, Watts and Co., London.

Choudhury, K 2004, *Megaliths and their associated remains in Dimoria area of Kamrup district, Assam*. Ph.D. thesis, Gauhati University, Guwahati.

Choudhury, K 2012, 'Megalithic culture, a living tradition of the Karbis of Assam' in *People of contemporary North-East India*, ed T Baruah, Pratisruti Publication, Guwahati, pp. 311-319.

Das, GN 2000, 'Socio-economic profile of the Karbis: a case study', *Bulletin of the Department of Anthropology, Dibrugarh University*, vol. 28, pp. 42-58.

Das, K 2011, 'Socio-economic features of Karbi tribes in Karbi Anglong district of Assam', *Vanyajati,* vol. LIV, no. 1, pp. 16-19.

Flemming, A 1973, 'Tombs for the living', *Man*, vol. 8, no. 2, pp. 178-193.

Furer-Haimendorf, C 1945, 'The problem of megalithic cultures in middle India', *Man in India*, vol. 25, no. 2, pp. 73-86.

Gogoi, J 1962, 'Mikir' in *Asamar Janajati*, ed PC Bhattacharya, Assam Sahitya Sabha, Jorhat.

Gurdon, PRT 1914, *The Khasis*, Macmillan, London.

Hodder, I 1990 *The domestication of Europe: structure and contingency in Neolithic societies,* Basil Blackwood, Oxford.

Jamir, W 2014, 'Affinities of Naga megaliths: an ethnoarchaeological study' in *50 years after Daojali-Hading: emerging perspectives in the archaeology of Northeast India*, eds T Jamir & M Hazarika, Research India Press, New Delhi, pp. 333.

Jamkhedkar, AP 1981, *Indian archaeology 1981-1982 - a review*, pp. 51, Archaeological Survey of India, Government of India (1984), New Delhi.

Kar, RK 1986, 'The people of North-East India: an appraisal', *Bulletin of the Department of Anthropology, Dibrugarh University*, vol.15, pp. 128-139.

Kathar, D 2014, *Dumurali Karbi lok-sanskriti*, Wo-Ram Publication, Guwahati.

Lyall, CJ 1908, *The Mikirs,* Spectrum Publications, Guwahati, Delhi.

Marak, Q 2015, 'Megaliths and living cultural traditions' in *Explorations in anthropology of Northeast India,* ed S Sengupta, Gyan Publishing House, New Delhi, pp. 31-51.

Mawlong, CA 1996. *Megalithic monuments of the Khasi Jaintia hills; an ethno-archaeological study*. Unpublished Ph.D thesis, North Eastern Hill University, Shillong, Meghalaya.

Medhi, BK & Choudhury, K 2009, 'Types, distribution and religious significance of the megaliths of the Karbis of Dimoria, Assam' in *Tribes of North-East India: issues and challenges*, eds BK Medhi, RP Athparia & K Jose, Omsons Publications, New Delhi, pp. 217-226.

Medhi, DK 2002 (1999), *Man and environment in Northeast India*, vol II, Omsons Publications, New Delhi.

Medhi, DK 2002, 'Archaeological research in Karbi Anglong, Assam' in *Man and environment in Northeast India*, vol II, Omsons Publications, New Delhi, pp. 48-64.

Mills, JP & Hutton, TH 1929, 'Ancient monoliths of North Cachar', *Journal of Asiatic Society of Bengal,* vol. XXV, pp. 285-300.

Mitri, M 2009, *An outline of the Neolithic culture of the Khasi-Jaintia Hills of Meghalaya, India: an archaeological investigation*, BAR International Series 2013, Oxford.

Moorti, US 1994, *Megalithic culture of South India: socio-economic perspectives*, Ganga Kaveri Publishing House, Varanasi.

Moorti, US 2008, 'Megaliths' in *Encyclopedia of archaeology*, ed DM Pearsall, Academic Press, New York.

Rao, SN 1977, 'Continuity and survival of Neolithic traditions in Northeastern India', *Asian Perspectives*, vol. XX, no. 2, pp. 191-205.

Rao, SN 1991, 'Megalithic practices among the Khasis and Nagas' in *Archaeology of North-east India*, eds JP Singh & G Sengupta, Vikas Publishing House, New Delhi, pp. 106-125.

Sahu, C 2002, *Tribes of Northeast India,* Sarup and Sons, New Delhi.

Saikia, SY 2007, 'Trends of megalithic culture in Northeast India – an observation', *Man in India*, vol. 87, no. 3 and 4, pp. 431-436.

Sarma, M 1993, 'Techniques and workmanship associated with different artifacts used by the Hill Karbis: an account', *Bulletin of Department of Anthropology, Gauhati University*, vol. VII, pp. 20-24.

Sharma, S 1998, 'A study on the Dimapur ruins of Nagaland', *Bulletin of Assam State Museum*, no. XIV, pp. 9-14.

Sharma, TC 1998, 'Prehistoric and archaeological sources for the history of Nagaland', *Bulletin of the Assam State Museum*, no. XIV, pp.19-35.

Sherratt, A 1990, 'The genesis of megaliths: monumentality, ethnicity and social complexity in neolithic north-west Europe', *World Archaeology*, vol. 22, no. 1, pp. 147-167.

Suvrathan, U 2010, 'Landscape of life and death: considering the region of Vidarbha' in *Ancient India new research*, eds U Singh & N Lahiri, Oxford University Press, pp. 124-173.

Thakuria, G 2017, *Neolithic culture of Assam*. Ph.D. thesis, The University of Delhi, Delhi.

Thapar, BK 1961, *Indian archaeology,* 1961-1962 – a review, pp. 32, Archaeological Survey of India, Government of India (1964), New Delhi.

Vahia, MN, Srikumar, MM, Abbas, R & Yadav, N 2010, *Megaliths in Ancient India and their possible association of astronomy*. Inaugural review talk presented at the *7th International Conference on Oriental Astronomy*, Japan.

Chapter - 8

Administration of Village Council among the Dimasas of Assam in a Rural Context

Arifur Zaman

Introduction

Administration in human society is based on healthy life and progress of that society. Any deviation from the path of justice brings about disorder in any society. India is a classic land of villages and village form the one exclusive social and political institution which housed a variety of subsystem of justice within it. The tribal villages in India stand as an administrative unit where traditional laws control their lifeways and it is intricately knitted with the value system of the community. Kullu (1994) mentioned that for the tribal their village means everything. It is in their village that they live out their family, economic, religious and political life. In the villages, the tribals have their altar, their place of government, their court of justice, in a nutshell, a mini world within it.

Every village is an independent unit and it is under the jurisdiction of a traditional council headed by one elderly elected person assisted by a council of elders. These elderly persons are responsible for the maintenance of law and order of the village. Disputes arise out among the inhabitants are settled by the perjury of the council in accordance with their customary law and justices are dispensed by it which are collectively honoured by the inhabitants of the village. It stands as one of the integral parts of the organization of the village. In the age-old traditional system of the tribes, every aspect of the people's life is regulated by the customary system. Their family, marriage, divorce, kinship, guardianship, descent, inheritance, succession, right over land, forest right, fishing authority, and transfer of land, sale, lease and civil and criminal cases, etc., are all governed and trialed according to their customary laws. Breach of customary law is considered a punishable offense for which village council acts as a traditional court with a definite name and function exists in every tribal society. The regulatory mechanism is controlled by the village council through customary laws. The procedure of the trial in the village council varies from tribe to tribe. Most of the disputes are settled in a single sitting. Customary laws thus include those rules, which are acknowledged and approved by the public opinion in the society and sanctioned by the will of the community. It is thus apparent that customary laws existed even prior to the emergence of the nation or the state and which continue to exist along with the change of time.

Village council is a socio-political organization that is the connection between people who relates themselves to each other creates an arrangement of persons that make a unit. It is a part of the large social organization which refers to the institution which maintains rules and regulation of the society. For instance, the stability of every social structure there is needed to have some system or organization in it. This is to be found in civilized as well as uncivilized societies. The connection between the people relates themselves to each other creates an arrangement of persons that make a unit. The organization stands for juridical rights of the people are safeguard and these juridical obligations are inferred in them. Village organization coincides in most cases villages act as territorial social as well as a political unit.

Village council is a social organization which bears an important role in the broad social organization. It refers to the institution as well as social structures and machinery through human activities required to satisfy human needs are monitored. The word organization does not mean only the aggregates of individuals, but it must have a common interest or aim to full fill human needs of society. The individual interest thus mixed or hidden with a common interest and different social structures under these circumstances operate itself as an organization. In a broad sense, a village itself is an organization. In a village, there is a fine relationship among each family or each number of families by one or another means. Village organization is actually a mirror image of social organization which forms through social relations. Village organization is the voluntary organization of society. It has been included among human society from the long part. But its forms and structure have always been changing with time.

Every indigenous community of Assam has its own system of administration of justice carried out by the concerned village council in accordance with their customary laws. Law and justice are an integral element of each culture and it has an indispensable relation with the social, cultural and political life of the community. Elaborate ethnographic study of a particular community regarding the customs, rituals, taboos, etc., related with traditional law and justice were carried out by different researchers like Thaosen (1962), Pospisil (1963), Stack and Lyall (1973), Danda (1978), Majumder (1980), Mills (1980), Bordoloi (1984), Bordoloi et al. (1987), Das (1987), Roy and Rizvi (1990), Dutta (1991), Nakha (1993), Singh (1993;1995), Kilikder (1998), Playfair (1998), Gurdon (2002), Mitkong (2002), Vitso (2003), Medhi and Barpujari (2006-2007), Barooah (2007), Endle (2007), Barpujari (2011), Zaman and Upadhaya (2015), and others and they also focus on the correlation of customary rules and practices regarding justice dispensation with social life. In this chapter, an attempt has been made to examine the traditional village council, its role in conflict resolution along with administration of justice among the Dimasa Kacharis of Dakshin Kumurakata village in Hojai district of Assam.

The Dimasa Kacharis

The Dimasa Kacharis are one of the scheduled tribes of Assam. They belong to the great Bodo groups of people; ethno-linguistically who are Tibeto-Burman. The main abode of the Dimasa Kacharis is the Dima Hasao District of Assam. They are also found in Karbi Anglong, Nagaon, and Hojai districts of Assam and Dimapur of Nagaland. Bordoloi (1984: 6) mention that 'the term Dimasa literally means the children or descendants of a big river, meaning the Brahmaputra. 'Di' means water, 'Ma' means big and 'Sa' means children'. According to Thaosen (1962: 44), the Dimasas were known as Bodosa prior to their settlement in Dimapur. When the Bodosas migrated to Dimapur region and started living on the bank of Dhansiri, they came to be known as Dimasa. He refers to Dimasa as the son of the big river (Brahmaputra). The Dimasas are Hindu by religion but traces of animism are also observed among them. They have their own parochial gods and goddesses known as *Madai*. The Dimasas believe that they are the descendants of Bangla Raja, the god of earthquake and Arikhidima, the great divine bird. Arikhidima laid seven eggs amongst whom from the first six benevolent ancestral gods (*Madai*) were born namely- Sibrai, Doo Raja, Naikhu Raja, Waa Raja, Ganyung-Braiyung, and Hamidao. From the seventh egg evil spirits were born who are considered as responsible for all diseases and natural calamities. Amongst the six ancestral gods, Sibrai is considered as supreme and he is equated with Lord Siva of Hindu Pantheon and his wife Ranchandi/Hedemdi with Goddess Parvati or

Kali. There are forty male clans known as *Sengphong* and forty-two female clans *Julu* or *Jaddi* among the Dimasas. They are exogamous with each other and presence of female clan among them is one of the unique features found only among the Dimasas which is very rare within the other tribes of Northeast India. The main economy of the Dimasas is agriculture and they are also engaged in government jobs, petty trades, wage earners, etc. The main festivals observed by the Dimasas are Bishu, Rajini Garba, and Harni Garba amongst which the Bishu is a most elaborate one. During the festival, various type of dances like baidima, baimajai, etc. was performed by the Dimasa people. *Fangsla*, a special decorative gate erected during the Bishu festival is worth mentioning.

Objectives

The main objectives of the present study are

(i) To study about the village council among the Dimasas of the study area;

(ii) to know about the administration of justice of the village council; and

(iii) the present scenario of the role of the village council.

Methodology

The present study is an empirical one and standard anthropological methods like non-participant observation, household survey schedule, unstructured interview, and case studies were used during the field investigation. Data gathered from one individual/informant is cross-checked with another individual/informant in order to verify the authenticity of the information.

Findings

Administration of justice is unique in its function and structure among the Dimasas and governed by the age-old customs and tradition that is unique from the rest of the communities of Assam. Kumurakata is one of the oldest Dimasa villages. The village has its own traditional council, headed by the *gaonburah* (*khunang*) who is the head of the village council and other 10-12 elderly members who help the *gaonburah* solving the village disputes are known as *barikah*. The disputes are settled within the village by them. Whenever any dispute or crime takes place in the village the villagers should immediately inform the *gaonburah* and accordingly *gaonburah* orders the *barikah* to investigate the case. The village council headed by the *gaonburah* review the case and settled it by pronouncing a fresh judgment, which is mandatory for both the parties.

Village Leadership and Administration

The village system of the Dimasas in their own language is called *nolai* and the whole inhabitants of the village are known as *raji*. The village council among the Dimasas is *hosom* which is no other than a council for the entire administration of the village. It is headed by a headman appointed by the government known as *Sarkari gaonburha* to assist in the administration of the village. Below this government appointed headman there is the traditionally elected headman who assists him in the maintenance of law and order of the village.

The village headman who is at the top of the village administration is called *khunang*. He has both executive and judiciary powers. He is appointed by the government through the Deputy Commissioner of Hojai district and is selected through his educational qualification. He is the second authority of the village after the Deputy Commissioner. He had six villages under his jurisdiction: Dakshin Kumurakata, Uttar Kumurakata, Mainapathar, Raikota, Chandanpur, Raikota Islampur, and Raikota Kachari *gaon*. In each of these villages, one traditional *gaonburah* is appointed to assist him. The traditional *gaonburah* is elected through open selection by the villagers. All the official works are done by the *Sarkari gaonburha*. Both of them have different duties and responsibilities towards their office. They have both executive and judicial powers.

Sarkari Gaonbura

The *Sarkari gaonbura* is well educated and takes care of the village administration. The tenure for the *gaonburah* is up to 60 years. He should be a politically neutral person who is selected on the basis of his impartiality, knowledge about traditional custom and educational qualification. In the earlier days, the *gaonburah* used to be elected through the hereditary process but nowadays it is through educational qualification. The minimum qualification for a government-appointed *gaonburah* post is Higher Secondary passed with good command in the Hindi language. His powers and functions are as follows:

(a) To solve the problems of the village people like disputes, crisis, etc.

(b) The *gaonburah* is mainly involved with the Revenue Branch. He has to represent as a Circle Officer and conduct the revenue administration. He appoints meetings and gives information regarding the local land development schemes. Moreover, he also organizes awareness campaigns through the V.L.M.C.C. (Village Land Management and Conservation Committee) for flood-affected areas, landslide and other natural calamities. The circle officer or the *gaonburah* also check about the land production used in the village. He assembles the people in a particular place and collects land revenue. Here, agendas are also made on how the tax should be collected or paid.

(c) The *gaonburah* also plays a major role in the events of birth and death. He issues the birth and death certificates. In case of home delivery of a child, the *gaonburha* writes an application to the Birth and Death Registration Office.

(d) The *gaonburha* organize and supervise village meetings. He organized the meetings in a community center named *Devosthan.*

(e) During the time of elections held at the government level, the Deputy Commissioner selects the polling center and the circle officer i.e. the *gaonburha* have to look after it. He has to provide facilities and protection to the duty officers and it is his duty to protect the ballot boxes (or voting machine) and safely transfer them to the designated office.

(f) The *gaonburha* also summon and settle civil and criminal disputes to the villagers. In case of murder, the villagers have to inform the *gaonburha.*

(g) The *gaonburha* also played a major role in oaths and ordeals, to control society, to unite the society for mutual understanding and binding each other in the village.

(h) If an unknown people from other places come to the village, then the *gaonburha* have to inform the police station through written application. It is formal and mandatory for the *gaonburha* to inform the police.

(i) If in a cultivated area or a government property land, a house is built then the owner of the house has to inform the *gaonburha* and take permission from Deputy Commissioner.

(j) As Kumurakata is a flood affected area along with frequent attack and encroachment of wild elephants, the *gaonburha* provide relief camps to the villagers and advised them to shift to the unaffected areas.

(k) If a *gaonburha* dies, then his land will be registered under his son's name as a nominee.

(l) The *gaonburha* also issues marriage certificates and verify it.

Traditional *Gaonburha*

In Dakshin Kumurakata village, there are three divisions viz., *Nolai Khro* (southern part), *Nolai Hagjer* (middle part) and *Nolai Yaphang* (northern part). For administration of the whole village, there is one elected local *gaonburha* who is under the control of the *sarkari gaonburah*, the chief head of the village. He has both executive and judiciary powers. His executive powers consist of giving guidance in respect of celebration of community festivals in the village. While his judiciary powers consist of a trail of cases, maintenance of law and order in the village. According to their tradition, the *gaonburha* (*khunang*) is to be elected by the village elders in a formal meeting. From the point of view of age and experience, *khunang* should be the senior most elderly person in the village. Thus, in the traditional village council setup, the Dimasas have four officials, viz., the traditional *gaonburha* (*khunang*), next to him is the *barikah* (informer), and then *kharao* (council members) and the subjects (*raji*). The role played by them is as follows:

(a) *Khunang* or the *gaonburah* is the traditional headman of the village. The traditional village council with the four officials headed by *khunang* settles disputes, tries cases of thefts, incest, elopements, etc.

(b) Next to the *khunang* is the *barikah*. He is the informer to the villagers. He acts as an assistant to the *gaonburah*. Any information or notice from the *gaonburah* is informed to the villagers through him.

(c) *Kharao* or the council members consist of 10-12 council members. Their roles are attending the village meetings, and other programmes in the villages. They assist the *gaonburah* in solving disputes.

(d) The subjects (*raji*) also play an important role in the traditional village council. In case of any disputes and problems in the village, they give their opinions to the *gaonburah*.

Powers and functions of the traditional *Gaonbura*

(a) To solve the disputes in the village.

(b) If a boy marries a girl of another tribe or community, a *gaonburah* is called to attend the ceremony. Without his permission, marriage is illegal.

(c) In case of robbery or crime, the *gaonburah* will call meeting along with the council of members and as a punishment, the accused have to offer five numbers of *tamul paan* (beetle nut and beetle vine leaves), banana and 100/- rupees cash as a mark of *rahi* (fine).

(d) If a married couple gives birth to a child, the owner of that house has to inform the *gaonburah.*

(e) In case of robbery, the victim should have an oath-taking before the *gaonburah* saying that he would not commit any more mistakes.

(f) If any person from other places visits the village, then he/she has to inform the *gaonburah.*

Selection of the *Gaonburha* and the Members of the Village Council

Selection of *gaonburha* is the most vital event in the Dimasa village. *Gaonburha* is generally selected from among the active members only. Wise, cool tempered, impartial and well versed in pristine customs and traditions are the essential qualities of a *gaonburha*. Therefore, *gaonburah* and other village council members are selected by the villagers. No females are elected as the members of village council but sometimes headman (*gaonburha*) seek advice from some elderly women of the village in some women related cases. The village council settles most of the disputes under their jurisdiction. As the village council is responsible for the village peace, so the council tries a variety of cases for peaceful settlement. The civil and criminal cases such as boundary disputes, disobeying or breaking the village rules, theft, assault, adultery, illicit relation, divorce, etc., are settled by the council.

After receiving suit, the village council fixed the date in consultation with *gaonburha* and venue for the settlement of the dispute. Accordingly, the *barikah* announced the message to the villagers at evening when he patrols the village regarding the meeting and venue. On the appointed date all the council members, village elders and *gaonburhas* of different villages attend the meeting. The village council has its unique systems of sitting arrangement. The *gaonburhas* and elderly members constitute one bench and the members of the council constitute the other bench. Before the council, the complainant and accused arbitrate on the subject matter. Then the council heard the witnesses. After hearing both the disputant parties and their witnesses the members arrived into a consensus judgment, which they sent to the higher bench constituted by the *gaonburhas* and elderly persons for approval. Normally the bench approved the judgment, but in some cases, if the bench is not satisfied with the judgment, they may send it back to the member's bench for review. After reviewing the judgment, again sent to the *gaonburhas* bench for approval. After getting the approval the verdict is passed and pronounced for public and is mandatory for both. The guilty may offer a prayer for pardon and minimize the fine, as he cannot afford the prescribed fine. The *gaonburhas* have the power to minimize the fine if found necessary looking at the economic ground of the guilty person. This is the most important part of the council system. This flexibility nature of the council makes it more convenient and participatory in the Dimasa society. Before minimizing the imposed fine, they consult the future consequences on similar cases. Thereafter the person found guilty has to pay a *daisumaiba* (fine) to make him free from all allegations.

On the other hand, if the case is complex, to avoid any conflict between both the parties, the council does not permit to attend the meeting. The disputed parties are asked to stay in relative's house near the venue of the meeting. The council chooses a mediator to mediate between the two parties. As per tradition, they choose a mediator from the third clan to avoid any partiality, i.e., neither from the complainant clan nor from the accused clan. The mediator is sent to the complainant to hear the grievances and he directly comes to the council meeting and conveyed the same. Again, he is sent to the convicted person to hear the defensive statement and the mediator conveys the same to the council. On the basis of the information of the mediator, the council alters prolong discussion arrive into a unanimous judgment which is binding for the both. The guilty person has to pay the fine imposed by the council on the spot.

Nature of Offence

Divorce (*Garlaiba*)

Customarily divorce is permissible among the Dimasa tribe. Both male and female have equal right to divorce their partner. The practice of divorce is very rare in society because of their strong social bondage and social cohesion. The village council approves divorce on sufficient reasonable ground. The grounds of divorce are maladjustment, extramarital relation, disobedient nature, and so on.

As per the customary law of the Dimasa in divorce cases, the following fines are imposed:

a. When a husband wants to divorce his wife, the divorce proposal is not immediately accepted and the couple is given a period of one month to resolve their matter to avoid divorce. But when even after one month the husband wants a divorce then the couple has to sign in a paper before the *raji* (community) and the husbands have to give half of his property to the wife.
b. On the other hand, if the wife proposed to divorce her husband then also a period of one month is given to her to resolve the conflict between them. But even after one month, she wants to take divorce and if she has a valid reason then she will get a divorce by signing a divorce form by her and her husband in front of the *gaonburah* and the whole community. She would also get half of his husband's property as per customary law.

Here it is interesting to note that, this is applicable if the divorced woman has her child. On the other hand, if the woman is adamant on divorce without any genuine reason as a judge by the council, this clause is not applicable. Sometimes the woman herself pardons her husband from this clause. *Dai sumaiba* (fine payable to the Village Council) of Rs. 1,000/- has to pay by the husband for this purpose.

Illegitimate Child

In case of an illegitimate child born out of illegal sexual relation, the woman has to pay a fine amounting Rs. 501/- to the village council. If the man responsible is identified then he has to pay the fine of Rs.1001/- on behalf of the woman.

Adultery

The case of adultery is not very uncommon among the Dimasa society. If a Dimasa woman is indulged in adultery and caught red-handed, then her husband would divorce her and she would not get anything from her husband property. On the other hand, if a man caught red-handed then it depends upon his wife whether she wants to divorce her husband or not because mostly Dimasa woman tends to forgive their husbands. But he has to pay a *daisumaiba* of Rs.1001/- to the *gaonburah*.

Illicit Relation

Illicit relation i.e., clan incest or illegal sexual offense within the prohibited categories, are considered as a punishable offense. The accused male or female who is indulged in this type of offense are directly excommunicated from the community.

Law of Marriage

In the Dimasa society, marriage is endogamous but they follow strict clan exogamy. Dimasa people have very unique clan system. In Dimasa tribe both male and female have different clans. The male clan is known as *Sengphong* and the female clan is known as *Julu*. There are about forty male clans and forty-two female clans. The male clan is inherited by the sons and the female clan is passed to their daughters. There are different types of fine and punishment when a Dimasa girl or a boy marries by violating the pristine rule. They are:

(a) Marriage within the clan: Violation of clan exogamy leads to severe punishment. Whenever marriage within the clan takes place they are excommunicated from the village. They are not allowed to take participate in any public ceremonies. For twelve years the couple has to reside outside of their community and after completion of the period they can return into their tribe and village, but for that couple has to invite the whole village or tribe members for a feast arranged by them, special invitation is given to the *khunang (gaonburah)* with *tamul pan* (betel nut and betel vine leaf), banana and Rs.101/-. After the success of the feast with due consent of the *khunang* and other elderly members of the village, the couple is permitted to stay in the village. But in spite of all these the woman who had married within the clan loses her *Julu* and she cannot further pass her clan to her daughters.

(b) Marriage outside of the tribe: Marriage outside of the tribe is also prohibited. When a girl marries a boy of another tribe, she is bound to lose her *Julu* and when a boy marries a girl of any other tribe then the boy's family has to arrange a feast and offer beetle nut and leaf with Rs.501/- to the *khunang (gaonburah).* The females who come from other tribes as a daughter in law are conferred a new *Julu* (female clan).

(c) Marriage by elopement: When a boy and a girl elope to marry each other then it is called *khaolanglaiba* in their local term. The boy's father should immediately inform the *khunang* about the matter with bettlenut-leaf along with Rs.101/-. Then they have to arrange a community feast for the whole village and the eloped couple has to bow down before the elderly invited guest, beg pardon for their misdeeds and seek blessing for their happy married life.

(d) Marriage outside of the religion: Marriage outside of the religion is strictly prohibited in Dimasa society. Anybody marrying outside their own religion is excommunicated from the village. Their family members have to pay the *dai sumaiba* to the *khunang* (*gaonburah*). The estimated fine is Rs.1000/-.

Violation of the Customary Law

If anyone in the Dimasa community of this village violates any kind of customary law he/she is liable to get punished by the *gaonburah*. The intensity of the punishment is depending on the intensity of the law. When someone breaks a law in the village, he has to pays the fine of Rs.1005/-. But sometimes if anyone violates a law which is also regarded as taboo then he/she might get excommunicated.

Theft (*Makhau*)

The theft cases are very rare among the Dimasas. It has been observed that the village people do not lock their door while working in the field. Even though the cases of theft are not reported, the thefts cases are considered as a minor offense for which a minimum fine is imposed on the offender. The fine is decided depending on the value of the things being taken by the thief. A single fine is not fixed in case of theft.

Transfer of Land

(a) According to the customary law, the restriction is imposed on the transfer of land to the non-tribal and outside their own community.

(b) The Dimasa are the absolute owners of their permanent plots, which they can transfer through sale, gift, etc. But the owner is expected to discuss with his clan members before disposing of the land.

(c) The agricultural plots belong to an individual and the owner exercises absolute right over the land. So, individual can transfer this plot if the owner of the plot abandons it, it will remain fallow and no other person can cultivate there without the owner's permission. On the other hand, the agricultural plots are heritable and it is transferred to the sons of the owner.

(d) The transfer of land is very rare in Dimasa society.

(e) Exchanging of the land among Dimasa society is also rare due to variation in the value of the land; exchange is done only after judging the value of the land to be exchanged by the parties' concern.

Mode of Inheritance

Certain customary laws of the Dimasas, which are followed since time immemorial, govern the transmission of property. The Dimasas are patriarchal and follow the patrilineal system i.e., the descent is traced through the male line only but their mode of inheritance of property is unique.

(a) Among the Dimasa tribe, all movable and immovable properties are heritable. The movable property consists of livestock, household belonging, clothes, ornaments, domestic utensils, agricultural implements, and so on. The immovable property includes the house, cultivable land, and the areas reserved for fishing, a collection of honey, etc.

(b) For the distribution of property, the clan members are informed and distribution is done in the presence of the witness.

(c) According to customary laws, equigeniture is the method, where father's properties are equally distributed among the sons called *basa han riba* in their local term and mothers' properties are equally distributed among the daughters called *busu han riba*. Here equal does not imply the partition of land by measuring it but by the number of plots owned by an individual.

(d) At the time of distribution of property among the sons and daughters, valuable property is kept in the name of the parents. This is perhaps to make the parent's life secure in their old age.

(e) The son who lives with the parents in their old age and performs the last rite entitled to inherit the parents remaining property and the house.

(f) The household belongings, agricultural equipment, cooking utensils, and ornaments are equally divided among the sons and daughters.

(g) The practice of will for the distribution of properties is not practiced. A declaration of parents in front of the relatives is the only method of distribution of property.

(h) In the family where there are no sons, the order of inheritance goes to the paternal uncle, then to the paternal cousins and to the distant clan relatives.

(i) In the sonless family, both fathers and mother's property is inherited by the daughters equally.

(j) In case if a couple is childless then their property is inherited by any close paternal relative whom they want to give their property or the one who will perform their last rites.

(k) Personal garments are generally disposed along with the dead body. Any surplus garments that the deceased may leave behind are divided among the sons and daughters.

(l) In Dimasa tribe if any childless couple wants then they can donate their property to any tribal organization within their village.

(m) A widow can enjoy the husband's estate as long as she lives without remarriage with any outsider. Among the Dimasa, a marriageable widow is allowed to remarry her deceased husband's brother and thereby he becomes the father of children born out of his deceased brother.

The adopted son is entitled to inherit his parent's properties provided the adoption is done on the basis of the customs. Adoption is allowed only within the clan and preferably within the lineage.

Conclusion

The traditional village council of Kumurakata is still functioning actively and they have great faith in their customary laws. The judgment of the village council is very much respected in society. Therefore, the people have good faith in their traditional justice delivery system. Justice is based on customary laws, which are established and followed since time immemorial. Therefore, the Dimasa people do not approach the modern court of law. The justice delivery system among the Dimasas is not burdened with cumbersome formalities, as it is in case of the modern court of law, which is expensive and time-consuming. There is a common saying that justice delayed is justice denied, but it is not applicable in the justice delivery system of Kumurakata village council. It is because justice is quick, cheap and perceptible. Moreover, due to the flexibility nature, the advantage lies in its economic consideration, by minimizing the fine as deem fit for the offender. The villagers become confused while approaching the Modern Court of Law, due to its formalities, time span and moreover they cannot afford the expenses required to suit a case. However, when serious crimes like murder, homicide, rape, etc., is committed, the matter is referred to and decided by the modern statutory law court. In this case, they approached the nearby Police Station, located at Hojai. There is an interpreter preferably from their own community or a person belongs to Dimasa tribe, who has an adequate knowledge regarding the customary rules of the land as well as their dialect intervenes between the government authority and the aggrieved party. The cases related to disputes are therefore settled in accordance with the customary rules of the community.

References

Barooah, J 2007, *Customary laws of the Adis of Arunachal Pradesh with special reference to their land holding system,* Law Research Institute, Gauhati High Court.

Barpujari, I 2011, *Customary laws among the Tiwas of Assam.* Ph.D. thesis, Department of Anthropology, Gauhati University, Guwahati.

Bordoloi, BN 1984, *The Dimasa Kacharis of Assam*, Tribal Research Institute, Guwahati.

Bordoloi, BN, Sharma Thakur, GC & Saikia, MC 1987, *Tribes of Assam*, part I, Guwahati, Tribal Research Institute, Assam.

Danda, DG 1978, *Among the Dimasa of Assam: an ethnographic study*, Sterling Publisher, New Delhi.

Das, JN 1987, *A study of administration of justice among the races and tribes of Northeastern region*, Law Research Institute, Gauhati High Court.

Dutta, P 1991, *The Tangas of Namchick and Tirap valleys,* Directorate of Research, Govt. of Arunachal Pradesh, Itanagar.

Endle, S 2007, *The Kacharis,* Bina Library, Guwahati.

Gurdon, PRT 2002 (1907), *The Khasis*, Macmillan, London.

Kilikder, BB 1998, *Customary laws, and practices: Reangs of Tripura*, Tribal Research Institute, Govt. of Tripura, Agartala.

Kullu, P 1994, 'Tribal religion and culture', *Jeevandhara*, vol. 24, no. 140, pp. 98.

Majumder, DN 1980, *A study of culture change in two Garo villages of Meghalaya*, Registrar, Gauhati University, The Department of Publication, Guwahati.

Medhi, BK & Barpujari, I 2006-07, 'Changing dynamics of customary laws, traditional institutions in the Tiwa village of Assam', *Bulletin of the Department of Anthropology, Gauhati University*, vol. 10, pp. 25-34.

Mills, JP 1980 (1922), *The Lotha Nagas*, Directorate of Art and Culture, Government of Nagaland.

Mitkong, N 2002, *Customary laws of the Adis of Arunachal Pradesh on succession and property inheritance*, Department of Cultural Affairs, Director of Research, Government of Arunachal Pradesh, Itanagar.

Nakha, HN 1993, *Customary laws of Nyishi tribe of Arunachal Pradesh,* Majestic Book, London.

Playfair, A 1975 (1909), *The Garos*, David and Nutt, London.

Pospisil, L 1963, *The Kapauku Papuans,* Holt, Rinehart, and Winston, New York.

Roy, S & Rizvi, SHM 1990, *Tribal customary laws of Northeast India,* B.R. Publishing Corporation, Delhi.

Singh, KS (ed.) 1993, *Tribal ethnography, customary law and change*, Concept Publishing Company, New Delhi.

Singh, KS (ed.) 1995, *People of Arunachal Pradesh*, vol. xiv, Anthropological Survey of India, Seagull Book, Calcutta.

Stack, E & Lyall, SC 1973, *The Mikirs*, United Publisher, Guwahati.

Thaosen, SR 1962, 'The Dimasa Kacharis', in *Asomor Janajati*, ed M. Neog, Assam Sahitya Sabha, Guwahati.

Vitso, A 2003, *Customary law, and women: the Chakhesang Nagas*, Regency Publication, New Delhi.

Zaman, A & Upadhaya, BP 2015, 'Customary law of the Mossangs of Arunachal Pradesh', *Man and Life,* vol. 41, no. 1 and 2, pp. 51-60.

Chapter - 9

Reproductive Life of Khamti Women of Assam

Juri Borah and Sarthak Sengupta

Introduction

The reproductive life of a woman begins after the commencement of menstruation, which is terminated with the attainment of menopause. Hence, both menstruation and menopause are the vital and imperative events of each and every normal woman's life. Age at marriage, age at first conception and age at first childbirth also represent some vital events which are closely interlinked with each other.

The age at menarche is known to be influenced by a combination of factors such as genetic, environmental condition, body stature, and socio-economic status (Tanner and Keeffe, 1967; Johnson, 1974; Barry, 1988; Thomas et al., 2001; Aryal, 2004 and Ku et al., 2006). Improvement in health and environmental conditions is interpreted as influencing factor for advancing the age at menarche, although the reason remains as unclear (Sengupta et al., 1995; Vaidya et al., 1998; Padmadas et al., 1999 and Garg et al., 2001). Similarly, early and late menopause are also assumed to be allied with bio-social variables like menarcheal age, mother's age at first childbirth, parity, education, socio-economic status, dietary habits, body size and shape, blood pressure, etc. Lower educational attainment (Luoto, 1994 and Gold, 2011), lower socioeconomic status (McKinlay et al., 1972; Magursky et al., 1975; Randhawa et al., 1987; Stanford et al. 1987; Whelan et al., 1990; Luoto et al., 1994; Togerson et al., 1994; Sethi et al., 1996 and Van Noord et al., 1997), nonemployment (Luoto, 1994 and Gold, 2011), earlier age at menarche (Ginsburg, 1991; Cramer and Xu, 1996; Gonzales and Villena, 1997 and Reynolds et al., 2003), lower Body Mass Index (Shreman et al., 1981; Aloysio et al., 1988 and Nagata et al., 1998) and null parity/low parity (Willet et al., 1983; Stanford et al. 1987 and Whelan et al., 1990) are reported as significantly associated factors for early age at menopause. According to Dasgupta and her colleagues (2015), reproductive characteristics including reproductive ageing or menopause show variation among diverse ethnic groups since every ethnic group maintains some biological and cultural identity in terms of marriage and social tradition. However, the inconsistency in the average for other reproductive episodes like age at marriage, age at first conception and age at first childbirth among the masses according to religion, caste, and geographic location is also mentioned by various other studies. The scholars namely, Caldwell et al., 1983; Choudhary and Devi, 1997 and Maheo, 2004 have reported the age at menarche, educational qualification, socio-economic status, cultural beliefs and practices, urbanization and employment status, etc. as the responsible factors behind the variation of age at marriage in different population groups. Similarly, couples' educational and occupational status, age at marriage, etc. are reported to have a relationship with age at first childbirth by the study of Bloom and Trussel, 1984 and Brien and Lilliard, 1994.

All these reproductive phases of a woman's life play their respective role for maintaining the fertility and mortality level of society in particular and a country in general. Age at marriage and age at first childbirth are the two main factors which influence waiting time to motherhood after menarche among women (Tiwari et al., 2005). The age at first childbirth determines the active reproductive period and fertility rate. After overcoming the adolescent sterility period after menarche, a girl becomes biologically fit for reproduction which is also to some extent indomitably regulated by age at marriage. Marriage determines the reproductive span between menarche and menopause because in Indian society marriage permits a woman for getting access into motherhood. Thus, delay in age at marriage shorter the reproductive span and reverse situation is observed in the case of early age at marriage (Agarwala, 1970 and Sharma and Abdul, 1990). Hence, variation exists in reproductive performance among women by community wise, village wise as well as nation wise. Fertility represents the appearance of evidence in one's life; on the other hand, mortality brings declination. Differential fertility signifies disparity in the reproductive performance of a woman. Likewise, mortality differentials also denote the varied mortality rate of individuals of different ages.

Keeping in view the wide variations in reproductive phases and fertility performance and mortality differentials of different regions, the present study was planned with an objective of studying some aspects of reproductive life of Khamti women of Assam and to compare the data with several other population groups of Assam reported so far.

Materials and Methods

The data were collected from both primary and secondary sources. Primary data were collected from 62 ever married Khamti women inhabiting exclusively in four villages namely, Sri Bhuyan Khamti *Gaon,* Gosaibari Khamti *Gaon*, Borpathar Khamti *Gaon*, and Bor Khamti *Gaon* of Lakhimpur district, Assam. No statistical sampling was applied in the selection of the informants. The women who have a minimum of one surviving child and whose husbands are alive are only interviewed. The investigation was carried out in the year 2012 with the help of a specially designed pretested schedule. In the present study, spontaneous abortion cases are only taken into consideration.

Among various Tai speaking population groups of Northeast India, Khamtis is one of them. They are concentrated in Namsai subdivision of Lohit district, Arunachal Pradesh and also in Assam, they are scattered scantily in Lakhimpur, Tinsukia and Dibrugarh district. The Khamti people in Assam are said to have immigrated from Muang Khamti Long in Myanmar (Gogoi, 1971). They profess Buddhism and observed many festivals in connection with their religious belief.

Results and Discussion

The menarcheal age of the Khamti mothers (Table 9.1) ranges from 10 years (3.23%) to 16 years (1.61%). Quite a good number of the respondents had experienced menarche at the age of 12 years (32.26%), followed by the age of 13 years (24.19%) and 14 years (22.58%). The mean age at menarche is calculated as 12.92 ± 0.16 years. The population groups like Telugu (13.30 years) and Rajasthani (13.19 years) reported by Majumder nee Paul (2000), Oraon (13.19 years; Ahmed Das and Konwar, 2002), Christian Oraon (13.19 years) and Savar (13.15 years) reported by Gogoi (2006), Munda both Hindu (13.09 years) and Christian (12.80 years) reported by Gogoi (2006), Kaibarta (12.43 years; Saikia and Boruah, 2009), Mishing (12.97 years; Baruah and Sengupta, 2009), Assamese Muslim (12.16 years; Haloi, 2011), Khamyang (12.91 years; Dutta and Sengupta, 2012), Ahom (12.60 years; Dutta and Sengupta, 2012 and 12.83 years; Gogoi, 2016) and working Assamese women (12.24 years; Sarma, 2015) of Assam show statistically insignificant difference with the present Khamti population. Among the population groups of Assam showed statistically significant difference from the present population, the Bihari (13.28 years) and Punjabi (13.43 years) reported by Majumder nee Paul (2000), Hindu Oraon (13.09 years; Gogoi, 2006), Mishing (13.51 years; Das, 2009 and 14.78 years; Sarma, 2014), Phake (13.81 years; Gogoi, 2016) and rural Dibongiya Deori (13.70 years; Borah, 2017) have higher mean menarcheal age. On the contrary, the Bengali (12.26 years) and Assamese (12.37 years) reported by Chakravarti (2001), Sonowal Kachari (12.45 years; Sengupta and Kalita, 2001; 12.5 years; Baruah and Sengupta, 2009 and 11.88 years; Saikia, 2015), Ahom (12.43 years; Gogoi, 2001 and 12.24 years; Baruah and Sengupta, 2009), Khamyang (12.30 years; Ahmed Das et al., 2008), Savara from Mancotta (11.92 years), Sesa (11.92 years) and Rangchali (12.12 years) tea garden reported by Saikia (2012), non-working Assamese women (12.40 years; Sarma, 2015), Kalita (11.80 years; Sharma and Dutta, 2016), Mishing (11.51 years; Patir, 2017) and Kaibarta from Sonapur (11.73 years) and Deodubi (11.87 years) reported by Hazarika and Sengupta (2017) have lower mean age at menarche. A decreasing trend in the mean menarcheal age among the population groups is observed. Barring few exceptions, statistical affinity is observed more with tribal populations than the Indid population groups considered in the present study.

Table 9.1: Age at menarche among the ever-married Khamti women and some other population groups of Assam

Population group	*No.*	*Mean ± S.E. (in years)*	*t-value*	*Source*
Khamti	62	12.92 ± 0.16	-	Present study
Sonowal Kachari	200	12.45 ± 0.10	2.49*	Sengupta and Kalita, 2001
Sonowal Kachari	185	12.50 ± 0.08	2.35*	Baruah and Sengupta, 2009
Sonowal Kachari	1230	11.88 ± 0.04	6.31*	Saikia, 2015
Dibongiya Deori (rural)	405	13.70 ± 0.09	4.25*	Borah, 2017
Mishing	165	12.97 ± 0.08	0.28	Baruah and Sengupta, 2009
Mishing	159	13.51 ± 0.09	3.21*	Das, 2009
Mishing	95	11.51 ± 0.10	7.47*	Patir, 2017
Mishing	400	14.78 ± 0.12	9.3*	Sarma, 2014
Phake	145	13.81 ± 0.01	5.55*	Gogoi, 2016
Ahom	176	12.83 ± 0.01	0.56	Gogoi, 2016
Ahom	162	12.43 ± 0.01	3.06*	Gogoi, 2001
Ahom	164	12.24 ± 0.09	3.70*	Baruah and Sengupta, 2009
Ahom	415	12.60 ± 0.07	1.83	Dutta and Sengupta, 2012
Khamyang	75	12.30 ± 0.16	2.74*	Ahmed Das et al., 2008
Khamyang	212	12.91 ± 0.10	0.05	Dutta and sengupta, 2012
Bengali	400	12.26 ± 0.07	3.78*	Chakravarti, 2001
Munda (Hindu)	100	13.09 ± 0.09	0.93	Gogoi, 2006
Munda (Christian)	100	12.80 ± 0.07	0.69	Gogoi, 2006
Oraon	70	13.19 ± 0.17	1.16	Ahmed Das and Konwar, 2002
Oraon (Hindu)	124	13.42 ± 0.11	2.58*	Gogoi, 2006
Oraon (Christian)	101	13.19 ± 0.08	1.51	Gogoi, 2006
Savar	101	13.15 ± 0.07	1.32	Gogoi, 2006
Savara (Mancotta)	226	11.92 ± 0.04	6.06*	Saikia, 2012

(*Contd...*)

Savara (Sesa)	198	11.92 ± 0.04	6.06*	Saikia, 2012
Savara (Rangchali)	78	12.12 ± 0.02	4.96*	Saikia, 2012
Assamese (Working)	307	12.24 ± 0.65	1.02	Sarma, 2015
Assamese (Non-Working)	250	12.40 ± 0.08	2.91*	Sarma, 2015
Assamese	427	12.37 ± 0.07	3.15*	Chakravarti, 2001
Assamese Muslim	1034	12.16 ± 1.25	0.60	Haloi, 2011
Kalita	50	11.80 ± 0.13	5.43*	Sharma and Dutta, 2016
Bihari	240	13.28 ± 0.04	2.18*	Majumder (Paul), 2000
Punjabi	205	13.43 ± 0.05	3.04*	Majumder (Paul), 2000
Telugu	227	13.30 ± 0.36	0.96	Majumder (Paul), 2000
Rajasthani	198	13.19 ± 0.27	0.86	Majumder (Paul), 2000
Kaibarta	81	12.43 ± 0.61	0.78	Saikia and Boruah, 2009
Kaibarta (Sonapur)	102	11.73 ± 0.11	6.13*	Hazarika and Sengupta, 2017
Kaibarta (Deodubi)	116	11.87 ± 0.09	5.72*	Hazarika and Sengupta, 2017

It is apparent from the present study that considerable numbers of the Khamti women have entered into the conjugal life at the age of 18 years (14.52%) and 20 years (14.52%). Their marital age ranges from 12 years (1.61%) to 29 years (1.61%). A sizeable number (19.35%) of the Khamti women got married even before attaining 18 years of age, the minimum marital age determined by the government. The mean age at marriage of the Khamti women is 20.19 ± 0.46 years. The mean age at marriage in population groups from Assam is found to range from the 15.32 years among the Telugu (Majumder nee Paul, 2000) to 24.49 years among the Dibongiya Deori (Gogoi, 2006). The t-test on the existing data shows nonsignificant differences from the Assamese (20.27 years) and Bengali (20.75 years) reported by Chakravarti (2001), Oraon (20.5 years; Ahmed Das and Konwar, 2002), Hindu Oraon (19.34 years; Gogoi, 2006), Hindu (19.70 years) and Christian (19.71 years) Munda reported by Gogoi (2006), Khamyang (19.48 years; Ahmed Das et al., 2008 and 21.49 years; Dutta and Sengupta, 2017), Sonowal Kachari (20.17 years; Baruah and Sengupta, 2009), Mishing (19.88 years; Das, 2009; 20.98 years; Baruah and Sengupta, 2009; 20.18 years; Patir, 2017), Ahom (20.09 years; Baruah and Sengupta, 2009), Kaibarta (18.83 years; Saikia and Boruah, 2009), Assamese Muslim (19.40 years; Haloi, 2011), and non-working Assamese women (20.37 years; Sarma, 2015). Contrary, the mean value of the present Khamti population markedly deviates from a number of population groups of Assam. Among these population groups, the Sonowal Kachari (23.66 years; Sengupta and Kalita, 2001; 24.30 years; Saikia, 2015), Tengaponiya (24.33 years), Borgonya (23.7 years) and Dibongiya Deori (24.49 years) studied by Gogoi (2006), working Assamese women (Sarma, 2015), Phake (21.73 years; Gogoi, 2016) and rural Dibongiya Deori (21.52 years; Borah, 2017) have considerably higher mean marital age than the present population. However, lower mean age at marriage than the present population is observed among the Bihari

(14.83 years), Punjabi (16.46 years), Telugu (15.32 years) and Rajasthani (15.95 years) reported by Majumder nee Paul (2000), Tangsa (19.14 years; Saikia and Dutta Das, 2006), Christian Oraon (19.16 years) and Savar (19.19 years) reported by Gogoi (2006), Savara from Mancotta (17.0 years), Sesa (15.75 years) and Rangchali (17.77 years) reported by Saikia (2012), Ahom (18.77 years; Gogoi, 2016), Kaibarta from Sonapur (16.00 years) and Deodubi (16.48 years) reported by Hazarika and Sengupta (2017). The mean age at marriage is found to increase appreciably among the population groups of Assam. However, the different tribal populations have relatively late mean age at marriage in comparison to the caste population as well as other communities of the region (Table 9.2).

Table 9.2: Age at marriage among the ever-married Khamti women and some other population groups of Assam

Population group	*No.*	*Mean ± S.E. (in years)*	*t-value*	*Source*
Khamti	62	20.19 ± 0.46	-	Present study
Sonowal Kachari	1230	24.30 ± 0.14	8.55*	Saikia, 2015
Sonowal Kachari	200	23.66 ± 0.25	6.63*	Sengupta and Kalita, 2001
Sonowal Kachari	185	20.17 ± 0.24	0.04	Baruah and Sengupta, 2009
Tengaponiya Deori	135	24.33 ± 0.47	6.30*	Gogoi, 2006
Borgonya Deori	62	23.71 ± 0.81	3.78*	Gogoi, 2006
Dibongiya Deori	85	24.49 ± 0.63	5.51*	Gogoi, 2006
Dibongiya Deori (rural)	405	21.52 ± 0.22	2.61*	Borah, 2017
Mishing	95	20.18 ± 0.41	0.02	Patir, 2017
Mishing	165	20.98 ± 0.27	1.48	Baruah and Sengupta, 2009
Mishing	159	19.88 ± 0.26	0.59	Das, 2009
Tangsa	129	19.14 ± 0.03	2.28*	Saikia and Dutta Das, 2006
Ahom	164	20.09 ± 0.27	0.19	Baruah and Sengupta, 2009
Ahom	213	18.77 ± 0.01	3.09*	Gogoi, 2016
Phake	163	21.73 ± 0.05	3.33*	Gogoi, 2016
Khamyang	75	19.48 ± 0.45	1.10	Ahmed Das et al., 2008
Munda (Hindu)	100	19.70 ± 0.17	1.00	Gogoi, 2006
Munda (Christian)	100	19.71 ± 0.15	0.99	Gogoi, 2006
Oraon (Hindu)	124	19.34 ± 0.18	1.72	Gogoi, 2006
Oraon (Christian)	101	19.16 ± 0.20	2.05*	Gogoi, 2006
Oraon	70	20.50 ± 0.23	0.60	Ahmed Das and Konwar, 2002
Savar	101	19.19 ± 0.12	2.10*	Gogoi, 2006
Savara (Mancotta)	226	17.00 ± 0.03	6.92*	Saikia, 2012
Savara (Sesa)	198	15.75 ± 0.04	9.62*	Saikia, 2012
Savara (Rangchali)	78	17.77 ± 0.05	5.23*	Saikia, 2012
Kaibarta	81	18.83 ± 0.52	1.96	Saikia and Boruah, 2009
Kaibarta (Sonapur)	102	16.00 ± 0.31	7.55*	Hazarika and Sengupta, 2017
Kaibarta (Deodubi)	116	16.48 ± 0.30	6.76*	Hazarika and Sengupta, 2017
Bengali	400	20.75 ± 0.23	1.09	Chakravarti, 2001
Assamese (Working)	307	22.47 ± 0.24	4.39*	Sarma, 2015
Assamese (Non-Working)	250	20.37 ± 0.23	0.35	Sarma, 2015

(Contd...)

Assamese (Non-Working)	250	20.37 ± 0.23	0.35	Sarma, 2015
Assamese	427	20.27 ± 0.19	0.16	Chakravarti, 2001
Assamese Muslim	1034	19.40 ± 0.04	1.71	Haloi, 2011
Khamyang	212	21.49 ± 0.49	1.93	Dutta and Sengupta, 2017
Bihari	240	14.83 ± 0.09	11.44*	Majumder (Paul), 2000
Punjabi	205	16.46 ± 0.15	7.71*	Majumder (Paul), 2000
Telugu	227	15.32 ± 0.12	10.24*	Majumder (Paul), 2000
Rajasthani	198	15.95 ± 0.13	8.87*	Majumder (Paul), 2000

The age at first conception ranges from 14 years (1.61%) to 33 years (1.61%). Maximum numbers of women conceived first at the age of 19 years (12.90%). However, only a very nominal fraction of women had the experience of the first conception after the age of 27 years (3.23%). Their mean age at first conception is 20.73 ± 0.49 years. The present finding is compared with some other population groups of Assam reported so far (Table 9.3). In this regard statistically marked deviation is observed with each and every population groups considered except non-working Assamese women (20.96 years; Sarma, 2015) and Dibongiya Deori population (21.49 years; Borah and Sengupta, 2016). All the communities are found to have a lower mean age at first conception except working (23.17 years) and non-working Assamese women (20.96 years) reported by Sarma (2015) and Dibongiya Deori (21.49 years). Most of the population groups considered in the present study have earlier mean age at first conception though the Indian constitution has determined the age 18 years as the minimum age for girls to enter into the conjugal life (Table 9.3).

Table 9.3: Age at first conception among the ever-married Khamti women and some other population groups of Assam

Population group	*No.*	*Mean ± S.E. (in years)*	*t-value*	*Source*
Khamti	62	20.73 ± 0.49	-	Present study
Bihari	240	17.51 ± 0.16	6.25*	Majumder (Paul), 2000
Dibongiya Deori	147	21.49 ± 0.35	1.26	Borah and Sengupta, 2016
Punjabi	205	18.42 ± 0.20	4.36*	Majumder (Paul), 2000
Telugu	227	17.48 ± 0.18	6.23*	Majumder (Paul), 2000
Rajasthani	198	17.16 ± 0.14	7.01*	Majumder (Paul), 2000
Savara (Mancotta)	226	17.37 ± 0.03	6.84*	Saikia, 2012
Savara (Sesa)	198	17.64 ± 0.04	6.29*	Saikia, 2012
Savara (Rangchali)	78	18.04 ± 0.06	5.45*	Saikia, 2012
Assamese (Working)	307	23.17 ± 0.22	4.54*	Sarma, 2015
Assamese (Non-Working)	250	20.96 ± 0.22	0.43	Sarma, 2015
Kaibarta (Sonapur)	102	17.58 ± 0.35	5.23*	Hazarika and Sengupta, 2017
Kaibarta (Deodubi)	116	17.39 ± 0.3	5.81*	Hazarika and Sengupta, 2017

The age of the mother at first childbirth is found to range from 15 years to 34 years. A maximum number of women deliver their first baby at the age of 19 years (12.90%). Their mean age at first childbirth is 21.73±0.49 years. Statistically insignificant differences from the present population is observed among the Bengali (22.66 years) and Assamese (22.10 years) reported by Chakravarti (2001), Hindu (21.18 years) and Christian Munda (21.00 years) and Hindu Oraon (20.75 years) reported by Gogoi (2006), Ahom (21.48 years; Baruah and Sengupta, 2009), Mishing (22.25 years; Baruah and Sengupta, 2009 and 21.21 years; Patir, 2017), Sonowal Kachari (21.80 years; Baruah and Sengupta, 2009), non-working Assamese women (22.00 years; Sarma, 2015), Dibongiya Deori (22.41 years; Borah and Sengupta, 2016) and Khamyang (22.69 years; Dutta and Sengupta, 2017). The population groups like Tengaponiya (25.36 years), Borgonya (24.71 years) and Dibongiya Deori (25.49 years) reported by Gogoi (2006), Mishing (23.98 years; Sarma, 2014), Sonowal Kachari (25.89 years; Saikia, 2015) and working Assamese women (24.16 years; Sarma, 2015) have higher mean age at first childbirth than the present population. Contrary, comparatively lower mean value than the Khamti population is observed among the Telugu (18.25 years), Rajasthani (19.91 years), Bihari (18.18 years) and Punjabi reported by Majumder nee Paul (2000), Savar (20.21 years) and Christian Munda (20.49 years) reported by Gogoi (2006), Kaibarta (19.96 years; Saikia and Boruah, 2009), Ahom (20.09 years; Gogoi, 2014), Savara from Mancotta (17.64 years), Sesa (18.12 years) and Rangachali (18.37 years) tea gardens as reported by Saikia (2012) and Kaibarta from Sonapur (17.94 years) and Deodubi (18.11 years) reported by Hazarika and Sengupta (2017). Mean age at first childbirth is found to increase among the population groups reported so far. However, the population groups belong to tribe have later mean age at first childbirth in comparison to other caste population and communities (Table 9.4).

Table 9.4: Age at first childbirth among the ever-married Khamti women and some other population groups of Assam

Population	*No*	*Mean ± S.E. (in years)*	*t-value*	*Source*
Khamti	62	21.73 ± 0.49	-	Present study
Dibongiya Deori	147	22.41 ± 0.35	1.13	Borah and Sengupta, 2016
Sonowal Kachari	1230	25.89 ± 0.13	8.21*	Saikia, 2015
Sonowal Kachari	185	21.80 ± 0.25	0.13	Baruah and Sengupta, 2009
Tengaponiya Deori	135	25.36 ± 0.45	5.46*	Gogoi, 2006
Borgonya Deori	62	24.71 ± 0.81	3.15*	Gogoi, 2006
Dibongiya Deori	85	25.49 ± 0.63	4.71*	Gogoi, 2006
Mishing	165	22.25 ± 0.27	0.93	Baruah and Sengupta, 2009
Mishing	95	21.21 ± 0.42	0.81	Patir, 2017

(Contd...)

Mishing	400	23.98 ± 0.12	4.46*	Sarma, 2014
Khamyang	212	22.69 ± 0.54	1.32	Dutta and Sengupta, 2017
Ahom	164	21.48 ± 0.26	0.45	Baruah and Sengupta, 2009
Ahom	176	20.09 ± 0.02	3.34*	Gogoi, 2014
Kaibarta	81	19.96 ± 0.50	2.53*	Saikia and Boruah, 2009
Kaibarta (Sonapur)	102	17.94 ± 0.34	6.35*	Hazarika and Sengupta, 2017
Kaibarta (Deodubi)	116	18.11 ± 0.33	6.13*	Hazarika and Sengupta, 2017
Bengali	390	22.66 ± 0.22	1.73	Chakravarti, 2001
Telugu	227	18.25 ± 0.18	6.67*	Majumder (Paul), 2000
Rajasthani	198	19.91 ± 0.21	3.41*	Majumder (Paul), 2000
Bihari	240	18.18 ± 0.18	6.80*	Majumder (Paul), 2000
Punjabi	205	19.07 ± 0.21	4.99*	Majumder (Paul), 2000
Munda (Hindu)	100	21.18 ± 0.18	1.05	Gogoi, 2006
Munda (Christian)	100	21.00 ± 0.26	1.32	Gogoi, 2006
Oraon (Hindu)	124	20.75 ± 0.22	1.82	Gogoi, 2006
Munda (Christian)	101	20.49 ± 0.22	2.31*	Gogoi, 2006
Savar	101	20.21 ± 0.10	3.04*	Gogoi, 2006
Savara (Mancotta)	226	17.64 ± 0.02	8.34*	Saikia, 2012
Savara (Sesa)	198	18.12 ± 0.04	7.34*	Saikia, 2012
Savara (Rangchali)	78	18.37 ± 0.04	6.83*	Saikia, 2012
Assamese (Working)	307	24.16 ± 0.22	4.52*	Sarma, 2015
Assamese (Non-Working)	250	22.00 ± 0.21	0.51	Sarma, 2015
Assamese	425	22.10 ± 0.20	0.70	Chakravarti, 2001

Findings of the present study show that majority of the Khamti women have attained menopause at the age of 48 years (26.09%), which is immediately followed by the age of 50 years (21.74%). Their menopausal age ranges from 43 years (4.35%) to 50 years (21.74%). However, mean menopausal age is calculated to be 46.5 ± 0.51 years. The data on mean menopausal age of the present Khamti population has also been compared with the other population groups of Assam (Table 9.5). In Assam, the higher mean age at menopause is observed among the Mishing (48.44 years; Sarma 2014 and 48.40 years, Baruah and Sengupta, 2009) and the very low mean value is recorded among the Telugu (40.93 years; Majumder nee Paul, 2000). From the t-test of analysis it is evident that the Khamti is much closer to Khamyang (47.75 years; Dutta and Sengupta, 2012), Ahom (46.80 years) and Mishing (48.40 years) reported by Baruah and Sengupta (2009), Sonowal Kachari (47.22 years; Sengupta and Kalita, 2001 and 47.12 years; Baruah and Sengupta, 2009), Assamese Muslim (48.30 years; Haloi, 2011), Kalita (47.33 years; Sharma and Dutta, 2016) and rural Dibongiya Deori (46.70 years; Borah, 2017). On the other hand, statistically significant differences with lower mean value than the Khamti population is observed among the Bihari (41.03 years), Punjabi (41.86 years), Telugu (40.93 years) and Rajasthani (41.86 years) reported by Majumder nee Paul (2000), Assamese 45.13 years) and Bengali (44.78 years) reported by Chakravarti

(2001), Hindu (42.78 years) and Christian Munda (42.89 years), Hindu (42.33 years) and Christian Oraon (42.41 years) and Savar (42.39 years) reported by Gogoi (2006), Tangsa (40.98 years; Saikia and Dutta Das, 2006), Khamyang (44.60 years; Ahmed Das et al., 2008), Ahom (46.16 years; Dutta and Sengupta, 2012), Savara from Mancotta (43.20 years), Sesa (43.76 years) and Rangachali (40.0 years) tea gardens as reported by Saikia (2012) and non-working Assamese women (46.04 years; Sarma, 2015). The Mishing (48.44 years) reported by Sarma (2014) with higher mean value stands statistically apart from the mean menopausal age of the present population. The tea garden communities are found to experience menopause much earlier than many other population groups of Assam (Table 9.5).

Table 9.5: Age at menopause among the ever-married Khamti women and some other population groups of Assam

Population	*No*	*Mean ± S.E. (in years)*	*t-value*	*Source*
Khamti	62	47.52 ± 0.41	-	Present study
Dibongiya Deori (rural)	61	46.70 ± 0.52	1.24	Borah, 2017
Sonowal Kachari	66	47.22 ± 0.29	0.60	Sengupta and Kalita, 2001
Sonowal Kachari	68	47.12 ± 0.50	0.62	Baruah and Sengupta, 2009
Mishing	40	48.40 ± 0.60	1.21	Baruah and Sengupta, 2009
Mishing	150	48.44 ± 0.10	2.18*	Sarma 2014
Tangsa	32	40.98 ± 0.69	8.15*	Saikia and Dutta Das, 2006
Ahom	55	46.80 ± 0.63	0.96	Baruah and Sengupta, 2009
Ahom	140	46.16 ± 0.31	2.65*	Dutta and Sengupta, 2012
Khamyang	23	44.60 ± 0.49	4.57*	Ahmed Das et al., 2008
Khamyang	60	47.75 ± 0.31	0.45	Dutta and Sengupta, 2012
Assamese (Working)	307	47.17 ± 0.22	0.75	Sarma, 2015
Assamese (Non-Working)	250	46.04 ± 0.21	3.21*	Sarma, 2015
Assamese	79	45.13 ± 0.40	4.17*	Chakravarti, 2001
Assamese Muslim	111	48.30 ± 1.33	0.56	Haloi, 2011
Kalita	18	47.33 ± 0.45	0.31	Sharma and Dutta, 2016
Bengali	115	44.78 ± 0.32	5.27*	Chakravarti, 2001
Bihari	240	41.03 ± 0.17	14.62*	Majumder (Paul), 2000
Punjabi	205	41.86 ± 0.67	7.21*	Majumder (Paul), 2000
Telugu	227	40.93 ± 0.15	15.09*	Majumder (Paul), 2000
Rajasthani	198	41.86 ± 0.27	11.53*	Majumder (Paul), 2000
Munda (Hindu)	84	42.78 ± 0.14	10.94*	Gogoi, 2006
Munda (Christian)	81	42.89 ± 0.15	10.61*	Gogoi, 2006
Oraon (Hindu)	98	42.33 ± 0.14	11.98*	Gogoi, 2006
Munda (Christian)	91	42.41 ± 0.12	11.96*	Gogoi, 2006
Savar	93	42.39 ± 0.08	12.28*	Gogoi, 2006
Savara (Mancotta)	64	43.20 ± 0.03	10.51*	Saikia, 2012
Savara (Sesa)	49	43.76 ± 0.04	9.13*	Saikia, 2012
Savara (Rangchali)	24	45.00 ± 0.04	6.12*	Saikia, 2012

Table 9.6 shows the number of conceptions per ever-married women. The maximum number of conceptions experienced by Khamti women is eight (8). Most of the women have 1 (22.58%) and 2 (22.58%) conceptions, followed by 3 number of conception (20.97%). Gradually the number of mothers with higher conception is found to decrease. The mean number of conceptions per mother is 3.16 ± 0.25. Similar mean conception with the present population is also observed among Assamese (3.32) and Bengali (3.01) reported by Chakravarti (2001), non-working (3.09) and working (2.87) Assamese women reported by Sarma (2015) and rural Dibongiya Deori (2.91; Borah, 2017). Relatively lower mean conception than the Khamti population is reported among the Bodo (2.36; Dutta Das and Saikia, 2010 and 2.22; Das, 2014), Assamese Sikh (2.52; Kaur, 2010), Pati Rabha (2.64) and Hajong (2.76) reported by Bhuyan (2013), Rabha (2.65; Das, 2014) and Khamyang (2.55; Dutta and Sengupta, 2017). However, the Semsa (4.72; Limbu and Khongsdier, 2000), Mishing (5.57; Sengupta and Dutta, 2000; 4.32; Baruah and Sengupta, 2009), Sonowal Kachari (4.01; Sengupta and Kalita, 2001 and 3.63; Baruah and Sengupta, 2009), Ahom (3.65; Gogoi, 2001; 3.83; Baruah and Sengupta, 2009 and 3.66; Gogoi, 2016), Oraon (5.0; Ahmed Das and Konwar, 2002), Rengma Naga (4.13; Rengma, 2014) have higher mean conception than the present studied population.

Table 9.6: Number of conceptions per ever-married Khamti women

Number of conceptions	*No of mothers (%)*	*Total conceptions*
1	14 (22.58)	14
2	14 (22.58)	28
3	13 (20.97)	39
4	7 (11.29)	28
5	4 (6.45)	20
6	5 (8.06)	30
7	3 (4.84)	21
8	2 (3.23)	16
Total Mean ± SE	62 (100.00)	196 3.16 ± 0.25

A number of live births per ever-married women by total sibship size are shown in Table 9.7. Like conception, a maximum number of live births among the Khamti women is also eight (8). Most of the women have two live born babies (25.81%), followed by 1 (24.19%). The mean number of live births per mother is 3.02 ± 0.24. The present findings is in conformity with the Ahom (3.00; Gogoi, 2001), Assamese (2.95; Chakravarti, 2001),

Khamyang (3.01; Ahmed Das et al., 2008), Sonowal Kachari (3.21; Baruah and Sengupta, 2009), working (2.79) and non-working (3.04) Assamese women (Sarma, 2015). The Bengali (2.61; Chakravarti, 2001), Bodo (2.25; Dutta Das and Saikia, 2010; 2.10; Das, 2014), Assamese Sikh (2.45; Kaur, 2010), Sonowal Kachari (2.47; Saikia and Dutta Das, 2012), Pati Rabha (2.33) and Hajong (2.21) reported by Bhuyan (2013; calculated by JB), Rabha (2.42; Das, 2014), Khamyang (2.37; Dutta and Sengupta, 2017) and rural Dibongiya Deori (2.72; Borah, 2017) have considerably lower mean live birth than the present population. The mean live birth of Khamti population is lower than that of Semsa (4.28; Limbu and Khongsdier, 2000), Mishing (4.98; Sengupta and Dutta, 2000; 3.99; Baruah and Sengupta, 2009), Pnar (3.35; Khongsdier et al., 2001), Sonowal Kachari (3.76; Sengupta and Kalita, 2001), Oraon (4.7; Ahmed Das and Konwar, 2002), Tangsa (3.51; Saikia and Dutta Das, 2006), Ahom (3.32; Baruah and Sengupta, 2009 and 3.44; Gogoi, 2016), Assamese Muslim (4.13; Haloi, 2011), Mishing (4.78; Sarma, 2014) and Rengma Naga (3.60; Rengma, 2014).

Table 9.7: Number of live births per ever-married Khamti women by total sibship size

Number of live birth	*No of mothers (%)*	*Number of children*
1	15 (24.19)	15
2	16 (25.81)	32
3	11 (17.74)	33
4	8 (12.90)	32
5	3 (4.84)	15
6	5 (8.06)	30
7	2 (3.23)	14
8	2 (3.23)	16
Total Mean ± SE	62 (100.00)	187 3.02 ± 0.24

Table 9.8 shows the incidence of prenatal wastages and postnatal mortality among ever-married women. The proportion of miscarriage and stillbirth is recorded as 5.10 percent and 0.53 percent respectively. In regards to the cases of miscarriage, it shows closer approximation with the rural Dibongiya Deori (5.18%; Borah, 2017) in Assam. The proportion of miscarriage in the considered sample is comparatively higher than the Semsa (3.34%; Limbu and Khongsdier, 2000), Sonowal Kachari (1.35%; Sengupta and Kalita, 2001), Pnar (4.63%; Khongsdier et al., 2001), Khamyang (3.39%; Ahmed Das et al., 2008), Bodo (3.88%; Dutta Das and Saikia, 2010 and 4.73%; Das, 2014), Pati Rabha (2.5%) and Hajong (1.98%)

reported by Bhuyan (2013), and Rengma Naga (0.30%; Rengma, 2014). Higher proportion of miscarriage than the Khamti population is recorded among the Mishing (6.62%; Sengupta and Dutta, 2000), Sonowal Kachari (9.84%; Baruah and Sengupta, 2009 and 5.69%; Saikia, 2015), Ahom (12.26%; Baruah and Sengupta, 2009 and 5.58%; Gogoi, 2016), Rabha (6.80%; Das, 2014) and Khamyang (2.37%; Dutta and Sengupta, 2017).

Comparatively similar finding on stillbirth among the present population is observed with the Bodo population (0.65%; Dutta Das and Saikia, 2010) and Pati Rabha (0.71%; Bhuyan, 2013) in Assam. The Rengma Naga (0.22%; Rengma, 2014) have a relatively lower proportion of stillbirth than the Khamti population. On the other hand, higher incidences of stillbirth in comparison to the present population is reported among the Semsa (2.56%; Limbu and Khongsdier, 2000), Mishing (4.07%; Sengupta and Dutta, 2000; 2.10%; Baruah and Sengupta, 2009), Pnar (1.54%; Khongsdier et al., 2001), Sonowal Kachari (1.17%; Sengupta and Kalita, 2001 and 2.09%; Baruah and Sengupta, 2009), Ahom (1.11%; Baruah and Sengupta, 2009 and 1.09%; Gogoi, 2016), Khamyang (0.84%; Ahmed Das et al., 2008 and 2.37%; Dutta and Sengupta, 2017), Hajong (0.79%; Bhuyan, 2013), Bodo (0.95%) and Rabha (1.96%) reported by Das (2014) and rural Dibongiya Deori (2.29%; Borah, 2017).

The incidence of mortality at infancy is calculated as 3.21 percent. Out of the total infant mortality, the incidence of neonatal mortality is relatively higher (2.67%) than the postneonatal mortality (0.53%). No incidence of mortality at childhood and the juvenile stage is recorded. The causes of death of infants are reported as pneumonia (16.67%), fever (16.67%), stomach problem (16.67%), pox (16.67%) and asthma (16.67%). However, the cause of the death of 16.67 percent of the infant is reported as unknown. The similarity in the incidence of death at infant stage among the Khamti population is observed with that of Rengma Naga (3.25%; Rengma, 2014) of Assam. The Ahom (2.39%; Baruah and Sengupta, 2009) and Khamyang (2.19%; Dutta and Sengupta, 2017) have a comparatively lower incidence of infant mortality than the Khamti population. In contrast, markedly higher incidence of mortality at infancy than the Khamti is found among the Mishing (7.26%; Sengupta and Dutta, 2000 and 3.80%; Baruah and Sengupta, 2009), Semsa (7.55%; Limbu and Khongsdier, 2000), Pnar (4.20%; Khongsdier et al., 2001), Sonowal Kachari (4.38%; Sengupta and Kalita, 2001; 4.04%; Baruah and Sengupta, 2009), Oraon (4.56%; Ahmed Das and Konwar, 2002), Bodo (9.89%; Das, 2014 and 4.75%; Dutta Das and Saikia, 2010), Rabha (11.76%; Das, 2014), Ahom (5.45%; Gogoi, 2016), and rural Dibongiya Deori (4.35%; Borah, 2017).

Table 9.8: Prenatal wastages and postnatal mortality among the ever-married Khamti women

Parameter	*Frequency / Proportion*
Total number of conceptions	196
Total number of live births	187*
Miscarriage	10 (5.10%)
Stillbirth	1 (0.51%)
Infant mortality	6 (3.21%)
Neonatal mortality	5 (2.67%)
Post neonatal mortality	1(0.53%)
Child mortality	0
Juvenile mortality	0

*indicates twin

Conclusion

A good deal of variation in reproductive phases and reproductive performance among various population groups of Assam is observed. The mean age at menarche is in the median range among the population groups reported so far. The mean menopausal age is found towards the higher value which shows close approximation with many other tribal population groups of Assam. Though the instances of early marriage are also recorded, the mean age at marriage is above the minimum marriage age for a girl that is certain by the Indian government. The Khamti have relatively lower mean conception and live birth in comparison to many other tribal population groups of Assam. The proportion of miscarriage is markedly higher as compared to stillbirth. The present study fails to record any incidence of child and juvenile mortality that indicates good child care and awareness among the mothers in particular and family in general.

Acknowledgement

The authors are very much thankful to the inhabitants of the Sri Bhuyan Khamti *Gaon,* Gosaibari Khamti *Gaon*, Borpathar Khamti *Gaon*, and Bor Khamti *Gaon*, Lakhimpur district, Assam for their positive response and immense help during the period of field investigation. The authors also extend their gratitude to the researchers whose data are taken into consideration in the present study.

References

Agarwala, SN 1970, *A demographic study of six urbanized village*, Asia Publishing House, Bombay.

Ahmed Das, F & Konwar, J 2002, 'A note on some demographic features of the Oraon of Tingkong Tea Estate of Tingkhong, Dibrugarh, Assam', *Bulletin of the Department of Anthropology, Dibrugarh University*, vol. 30, pp. 113-122.

Ahmed Das, F, Dutta Das, D & Barua, R 2008, 'A note on the fertility performance of the Khamyang of Margherita, Assam', *Bulletin of the Department of Anthropology, Dibrugarh University,* vol. 36, pp. 17-24.

Aloysio, D, Villecco, AS, Fabiani AG, Mauloni, M, Altieri, P, Miloffi, L & Bologna, F 1988, 'Body mass index distribution in climacteric women', *Maturitas*, vol. 9, pp. 359-366.

Aryal, TR 2004, 'Age at menarche: differentials and determinants', *Journal of Nepal Medical Association*, vol. 43, no. 152, pp. 71-75.

Barry, B 1988, *Patterns of human growth*, Cambridge University Press, New York.

Baruah, P & Sengupta, S 2009, 'A study on demographic variables in three ethnic groups of upper Assam', *Bulletin of the Department of Anthropology, Dibrugarh University*, vol. 37, pp. 9-30.

Bhuyan, J 2013, *A demogenetic study of the Pati Rabha and the Hajong of Kamrup district, Assam*. Ph.D. thesis, Department of Anthropology, Gauhati University.

Bloom, ED & Trussel, J 1984, 'What are the determinants of delayed childbearing and permanent childlessness in the United States', *Demography*, vol. 21, no. 4, pp. 591 - 611.

Borah, J & Sengupta, S 2016, 'Fertility and mortality differential among the Dibongiya Deori of Lakhimpur district, Assam', *North Bengal Anthropologist*, vol. 4, pp. 170-176.

Borah, J 2017, *A study on reproductive health of the Dibongiya Deori women of Assam*. Ph.D. thesis, Department of Anthropology, Dibrugarh University.

Brien, JM & Lilliard, LA 1994, 'Education, marriage and first conception in Malaysia', *The Journal of Human Resources*, vol. 29, no. 4, pp. 1167 - 1204.

Caldwell, JC, Reddy, PH & Caldwell, P 1983, 'The causes of marriage change in South India', *Population Studies*, vol. 37, pp. 343.

Chakravarti, K 2001, *A study on differential fertility among two population groups in Guwahati*. Ph.D. thesis, Department of Anthropology, Gauhati University.

Choudhury, B & Devi, M 1997, 'Fertility differentials in Manipur: a study on the Meities and the Muslims', *Journal of Human Ecology*, vol. 8, no. 1, pp. 51-59.

Cramer, DW & Xu, H 1996, 'Predicting age at menopause', *Maturitas*, vol. 23, pp. 319-326.

Das, B 2009, *A study on Haemoglobin E among two ethnic groups of Northeast India*. Ph.D. thesis, Department of Anthropology, Dibrugarh University.

Das, NB 2014, *Child mortality and morbidity among the Bodos and the Rabhas of Udalguri district, BTAD, Assam*. Ph.D. thesis, Department of Anthropology, Gauhati University.

Dasgupta, D, Karar, P, Ray, S & Ganguly, N 2015, 'Menopausal symptoms and its correlates: a study on tribe and caste population of East India', *Current Gerontology and Geriatrics Research*, Article ID 984767.

Dutta Das, D & Saikia, A 2010, 'Demographic profile of the Bodo Kacharis of Lakhimpur district, Assam', *Bulletin of the Department of Anthropology, Dibrugarh University,* vol. 38, pp. 65-72.

Dutta, D & Sengupta, S 2012, 'Mean age at menarche and menopause in two Tai Mongoloid population groups of Assam', *Bulletin of the Department of Anthropology, Dibrugarh University*, vol. 40, pp. 1-12.

Dutta, D & Sengupta, S 2017, 'A study on the reproductive history and mortality of the Khamyangs: a Tai-Mongoloid population group of upper Assam', *Journal of Indian Anthropological Society*, vol. 52, pp. 127-140.

Garg, S, Meenakshi, Singh, MMC & Mehra, M 2001, 'Perceived reproductive morbidity and health care seeking behaviour among women in an urban slum', *Health and Population-Perspectives and Issues,* vol. 24, no. 4, pp. 178-188.

Ginsburg, J 1991, 'What determines the age at menopause?', *British Medical Journal*, vol. 302, pp. 1288-1289.

Gogoi Konwar, J 2001, *Reproductive health of women: a case study in an Ahom village in upper Assam.* Ph.D. thesis, Department of Anthropology, Dibrugarh University.

Gogoi, G 2006, *A study on population genetics among the Deori of Assam.* Ph.D. thesis, Department of Anthropology, Dibrugarh University.

Gogoi, L 1971, *The Tai Khamtis*, North East Frontier Agency, Chowkam.

Gogoi, Y 2014, 'Demographic study among the Ahom of Assam', *Bulletin of the Department of Anthropology, Dibrugarh University*, vol. 42, pp. 197-202.

Gogoi, Y 2016, *Differential fertility and infant mortality in three Tai Mongoloid population groups of North-East India: a study of bio-social correlates*. Ph.D. thesis, Department of Anthropology, Dibrugarh University.

Gold, EB 2001, 'Factors associated with age at natural menopause in a multiethnic sample of midlife women', *American Journal of Epidemiology*, vol. 153, no. 9, pp. 865-873.

Gonzales, GF & Villena, A 1997, 'Age at menopause in central Andean Peruvian women', *Menopause*, vol. 4, pp. 32-38.

Haloi, A 2011, *A study on fertility and maternal health of the Assamese Muslims of Kamrup district, Assam.* Ph.D. thesis, Department of Anthropology, North Eastern Hill University.

Hazarika, J & Sengupta, J 2017, 'Fertility performance among the Kaibarta women of Assam', *Bulletin of the Department of Anthropology, Dibrugarh University*, vol. 44&45, PP. 125-132.

Johnston, FE 1974, 'Control of age at menarche', *Human Biology*, vol. 46, pp. 159-171.

Kaur, S 2010, *A study on fertility performance and nutritional status among the Assamese Sikh women of Assam*. Ph.D. thesis, Department of Anthropology, Dibrugarh University.

Khongsdier, R, Nsarangbe, A & Phimu, A 2001, 'A bio-anthropological study of the Pnar of Jatinga in North Cachar Hills of Assam', *Journal of Indian Anthropological Society,* vol. 36, pp. 213-222.

Ku, SY, Kang, JW, Kim, H, Kim, YD & Jee, BC 2006, 'Age at menarche and its influencing factors in North Korean female refugees', *Human Reproduction*, vol. 21, no. 3, pp. 833-836.

Limbu, DK & Khongsdier, R 2000, 'The Semsa: a population genetics study' in *Contemporary research in anthropology*, ed R. Khongsdier, Commonwealth Publishers, New Delhi, pp. 39-43.

Luoto, R, Lapiro, J & Uutela, A 1994, 'Age at natural menopause and socio-demographic status in Finland', *American Journal of Epidemiology*, vol. 139, pp. 64-76.

Magursky, V, Mesko, M & Soklik, L 1975, 'Age at menopause and onset of the climacteric in women of Martin district, Czechoslovakia', *International Journal of Fertility and Sterility*, vol. 20, pp. 17-23.

Maheo, LM 2004, *The Mao Tribe of Manipur*, Mittal Publications, New Delhi.

Majumder (Paul), G 2000, *A study on fertility and family planning among the Harijans of Guwahati Kamrup, Assam*. Ph.D. Thesis, Department of Anthropology, Gauhati University.

McKinlay, S, Jefferys, M & Thompson, B 1972, 'An investigation of the age at menopause', *Journal of Biosocial Science*, vol. 4, pp. 161-173.

Nagata, C, Takatsuka, N, Kawakami, N & Shimizu, H 2000, 'Association of the diet with the onset of menopause in Japanese women', *American Journal of Epidemiology*, vol. 152, no. 9, pp. 863–867.

Padmadas, SS, Francis Zavier, AS & Dilip, TR 1999, 'Age at menarche among Indian women: observations from NFHS, 1992-93', *Journal of Family Welfare*, vol. 45, no. 2, pp. 71-79.

Patir, R 2017, *Nutritive value of wild edible insects and plants used in traditional food: an anthropological study among the Mishings of Assam*. Ph.D. thesis, Department of Anthropology, Dibrugarh University.

Randhawa, I, Premi, HK & Gupta, T 1987, 'The age at menopause in the women of Himachal Pradesh, and the factors affecting the menopause', *Indian Journal of Public Health*, vol. 21, no. 1, pp. 40-44.

Rengma, MS 2014, 'A note on fertility performance among the Rengma Nagas of Assam', *Bulletin of the Department of Anthropology, Dibrugarh University*, vol. 42, pp. 191-196.

Reynolds, RF & Obermeyer, CM 2003, 'Correlates of the age at natural menopause in Morocco', *Annals of Human Biology*, vol. 30, pp. 97-108.

Saikia, A 2012, *Some demographic aspects of the Savara, a tea garden community of Dibrugarh, Assam*. Ph.D. thesis, Department of Anthropology, Gauhati University.

Saikia, JR & Boruah, A 2009, 'An anthropo-demographic profile of fertility and mortality of Kaibartas of Dhakuakhana, Assam, a case study', *Bulletin of the Department of Anthropology, Dibrugarh University*, vol. 37, pp. 37-48.

Saikia, N & Dutta Das, D 2006, 'A study on the fertility of the Tangsa women of Ledo of Tinsukia district of upper Assam', *Bulletin of the Department of Anthropology, Dibrugarh University*, vol. 34, pp. 77-84.

Saikia, N 2015, *Fertility performance and blood group incompatibility among the Sonowal Kacharis of Dibrugarh district, Assam*. Ph.D. thesis, Department of Anthropology, Dibrugarh University.

Sarma, J 2015, *A study of completed fertility and postmenopausal health of working and nonworking Assamese women of Guwahati, Assam*. Ph.D. thesis, Department of Anthropology, Gauhati University.

Sengupta, S & Dutta, RK 2000, 'Factor influencing fertility: a case study among the Mishing of Assam', *Bulletin of the Department of Anthropology, Dibrugarh University*, vol. 28, pp. 21-30.

Sengupta, S & Kalita, M 2001, 'Some aspects of reproductive performance of the Sonowal Kachari of Assam', *Bulletin of the Department of Anthropology, Dibrugarh University,* vol. 29, pp. 49-58.

Sengupta, S, Gogoi, G & Chetry, HB 1995, 'Variation in menarcheal age of Assamese girls', *Journal of the Indian Medical Association*, vol. 94, no. 3, pp. 88-90.

Sethi HK, Sidhu, LS & Singal, P 1996, 'Menopausal age and related factors' In *Global development in human biology*, eds LS Sidhu and SP Singh, USE Publishers and Distributors, Ludhiana, pp. 137-155.

Sharma, A & Dutta, P 2016, 'Menarche and menopause among the Kalita of Dhemaji district, Assam', *International Journal of Social Science and Research*, vol. 5, no. 9, pp. 212-213.

Sharma, KNN & Abdul, SK 1990, 'Fertility and mortality trends of Khairwar tribal women of Madhya Pradesh', *Man in India*, vol. 70, no. 4, pp. 446-453.

Shreman, BM, Wallace, RB & Bean, JA 1981, 'The relationship of menopausal hot flushes to medical and reproductive experience', *The Journal of Gerontology*, vol. 36, pp. 306-309.

Stanford, JL, Hartge, P, Briton, LA, Hoover, RN & Brookmeyer, R 1987, 'Factors influencing the age at natural menopause', *Journal of Chronic Diseases*, vol. 40, pp. 995-1002.

Tanner, JM and Keeffe, OB 1967, 'Age at menarche in Nigerian school girls with a note on their height & weight from age 12-19 years,' *Human Biology*, vol. 39, pp.187.

Thomas, F, Renaud, F, Benefice, E, Meeus, TDe & Guegan, J 2001, 'International variability of ages at menarche and menopause: patterns and main determinants', *Human Biology*, vol. 73, no. 2, pp. 271-290.

Togerson, DJ, Avenell, A, Trussel, I & Reid, DM 1994, 'Factors associated with the onset of menopause in women aged 45-49', *Maturitas*, vol. 19, pp. 83-92.

Vaidya, RA, Shringi, MS, Bhatt, MA, Gajjar, M, Joshi, JV, Galvankar, P & Sankari, K 1998, 'Menstrual pattern and growth of school girls in Mumbai', *Journal of Family Welfare*, vol. 44, no. 1, pp. 66-72.

van Noord, PA, Dubas, JS, Dorland, M, Boersma, H & te Velde, E 1997, 'Age at natural menopause in a population-based screening cohort: the role of menarche, fecundity, and lifestyle factors', *Fertility and Sterility*, vol. 68, no. 1, pp. 95–102.

Whelan, EA, Sandler, DP, McConnaughey, DR & Weinberg, CR 1990, 'Menstrual and reproductive characteristics and age at natural menopause', *American Journal of Epidemiology*, vol. 131, no. 4, pp. 625–632.

Willet, W, Stampfer, MJ, Bain, C, Lipnick, R, Speizer, FE, Rosner, B, Cramer, D & Hennekens, CH 1983, 'Cigarette smoking, relative weight and menopause', *American Journal of Epidemiology*, vol. 117, pp. 651-658.

Chapter - 10

The Moria Muslims of the Brahmaputra Valley: A Study on Historical Background and their Distribution

P. K. Guha

The characteristics of any population are usually shaped by the geographic, demographic and socio-economic factors. The geographic factors include climate, soil factors, natural resources, and transport facilities whereas the climate and socio-economic factors play a crucial role in the growth of the human population. The demographic factors are dependent more on the socio-economic and cultural factors. The studies in Northeast India, especially in the Brahmaputra valley, have observed that the geographical factor helped in sustaining various currents of human migration along with its resources (Taher, 1979).

The Brahmaputra valley extends from the easternmost tip of Upper Brahmaputra valley near the syntoxial bend of the Eastern Himalayas to the west of Dhubri on the border of Bangladesh and well demarcated by Eastern Himalayas, Patkoi, and Naga Hills and the Garo-Khasi-Jaintia and the Mikir Hills. The average level of the valley ranges from 130 m. in the east to 30 m. in the west. The Brahmaputra valley is wide in Upper Assam and in Lower Assam but it is narrow at Gauhati because at Gauhati the river flows close to the granite hillocks of Shillong plateau. In the north, innumerable tributaries run down from Arunachal Pradesh and the Bhutan Himalayas.

Three major social groups are found among the Muslim groups in the Brahmaputra valley. They are the Assamese Muslims, the immigrant peasant Muslims from East Bengal and a small group of Urdu speaking Muslims living in the towns and service centers engage in trade and commerce. The

Assamese Muslims are further divided into the Syads, the Sheikhs, and the Morias.

The present study discusses the historical background of Moria Muslims of the Brahmaputra valley of Assam. The early history of Assam is not clearly available. It was only after the coming of the Ahoms in Assam in 1228 A.D. when valuable information was recorded chronologically about the reigning Kings.

The record shows that the first racial migration took place to this area with the Australoids or Austro-Asiatic speaking people from the east during the pre-historic time.

The second group came to Assam from Northeast and east who spoke the Tebeto-Burman group of languages, especially Eastern Himalayan, North Assam Bodo and Naga groups of languages. Racially they belong to Mangoloid and migrated from the east across the Patkoi-Arakan Yoma ranges from Burma.

At the same period, another group of people speaking Indo-Aryan languages started the migration from the plains of northern India with the help of local kings and chieftains in search of their livelihood into the Brahmaputra valley. Originally, they were of the Caucasoid racial group.

While the old Indo-Aryan socio-cultural stream was still trickling in, the migration of a new group of people started with the invasion of Assam by Md. Bin Bakhtiar Khiliji, a Muslim General of Kutubuddin in about A.D. 1205. At that time Mahammedans entered Assam through Goalpara district. Khiliji was defeated and some of the captive soldiers settled in Assam (Taher, 1977). This led to the spread of Islamic influence in Assam. The first Mohammedan invasion took place during Ahom reign in 1527 A.D. In this battle, the Ahoms defeated the Mohammedans. The next invasion made by Turbak in 1532 A.D. and the present Moria Muslims in the Brahmaputra valley are the descendants of the captives during the battle. This battle took place in April 1532 A.D. when a Muslim commander of Bengal named Turbak invaded the Asom territory, with many guns and cannon and other fire weapons and a large battery of artillery. They encamped at Singri (at present in Sonitpur district) opposite to the Ahom Fort on the bank of the river Brahmaputra. On hearing this Suhungmung, the Ahom King sent his son Suklengmung, with a strong force to Singri and himself advance to Sala and after crossing the river Brahmaputra gave a vigorous battle to the enemies. In this battle, Suklengmung defeated and then moved back to Sala and Senglung was made Commander-in-Chief.

As the rain started the Muslim army halted their further advance at Koliabar (Nowgong district) and during this period they captured seven boats of the Ahoms, on the river Brahmaputra. In October, the Muslims advanced to river Ghiladhari (Darrang district) and halted there.

In the meantime, Turbak received reinforcement from Hussain Khan, another Muslim general. Hussain Khan reinforced Turbak with six elephants, one hundred horses, and one thousand infantries. The Ahoms defeated the Muslim invaders in a series of engagements. The final defeat of the Muslims took place in a battle near the river Bharali. Turbak was transfixed by a spear. During the pursuit, Hussain Khan was caught and put to death. The head of Turbak was entombed on the Charaideo Hill (Gait, 1926; Barua, 1966; Acharyya, 1966; Bandopadhyaya, 1982).

Nine hundred Muslim invaders were taken prisoners by the Ahom king during this war and he settled them in different parts of the Brahmaputra valley. According to traditional belief, the Ahom king first ordered them to cut grass for the king's elephants but was found quite unfit for this work. They were next employed as cultivators but it appeared, they were absolutely ignorant about cultivation that once the Ahom King commented, '*Naha Marai Chaha Dhan Pale*' (nine hundred Moria had grown only six hundred paddy grains). Next, they were ordered to construct houses but they failed to do this work also.

After a year the disgusted Ahom King then released the prisoners so that they could earn their livelihood in whatever way possible for themselves without being a burden on the royal exchequer. Some of the mercenaries had knowledge of welding of brass metal as they had used guns which they repaired themselves. However, after the release, some of the Muslim mercenaries had taken to working in brass as an occupation and finally settled down in the Brahmaputra valley. It may be mentioned that, since the Moria Muslims came as invaders in Assam, so they did not bring any females with them. The Ahom king then decided to offer them low caste Hindu ladies. According to a legend, once the king invited all the young Hindu females in his palace. The king presented them *Mekhela-Chaddar* and ordered them to go back by wearing the *Mekhela-Chaddar* presented by him through a marshy path. The king was observing them from behind. He observed that some of the females crossed the road, pulling the *Mekhela-Chaddar* up to their knees to save the new clothes from the mud but some of them crossed the path spoiling their new clothes. The king then decided to offer those who crossed the path, pulling their *Mekhela-Chaddar* up to their knees to the Moria Muslims. Because the king thought that they were born in the low caste and hence were shameless by nature. So, the king picked them and ordered them to marry the Moria Muslims youth. After getting married to the low caste Hindu ladies, the Moria Muslims finally settled down in the different parts of the Brahmaputra Valley[1].

The above-mentioned story indicates that at the beginning of the settlement of the Moria Muslims in this valley they were assimilated with the Assamese Hindu society. However, a new community appeared in the plains of Assam in the 1530s. They started their occupation as braziers but some of them had also taken up rearing of domestic animals like bulls, cows, etc. In a *Zikir* (a type of religious song) it is sung that '*Gariar Garu Marai Bai'* means – cows and bulls of the Garia (another group of Muslims) are reared by the Morias. Slowly their settlements were distributed in different parts of the Brahmaputra valley, from Sibsagar where they were kept in the jail and released from it.

Very little information can be gathered about the Moria Muslims during the British period. W.W. Hunter mentioned in his book, 'A Statistical Account of Assam' that the braziers formed a distinct and separate community and used to depend entirely upon their trade for their livelihood. The brass workers were paid at the rate of six pence per pound of metal worked up. The Marwari traders used to supply metal to the manufacturer and used to sell the finished utensils to the traders (Hunter, 1879).

Another view about the Moria Muslims is that.....'they were looked down upon with detestation by the orthodox followers of Islam. Because of their habit of 'drunkenness' contentious character, they were regarded as a group of degraded Muslims. They participated in Islamic rituals only nominally. The Morias were looked down upon with detestation because of their lowly occupation. But their occupation was not related to the notion of pollution. Because brass utensils produced by them were used in the 'Namghars'. So it can be assumed that they were treated as a group of degraded Muslims because of their profession. In social relationship also, the Syads and Sheikhs tried to keep away from the Morias. Social relations among these groups are guided by a superiority-inferiority attitude among the members. Because of the social distance, maintained by the two 'Elite' groups, the Moria Muslims have become an endogamous group" (Saifun Nessa, 1984).

It is assumed that the word 'Moria' has originated from the beating (*mara* in Assamese) of hot brass metal for making utensils. Another view is that the word 'Moria' originated from the term Marshiya or Murjiiay. Murjiiay was the name of a sect of the Muslim, which came to be first known in the Umayyad age (A.H. 40) in 661 A.D. (Saikia,1978). The group came as invaders and later started their carrier as braziers. They are categorized as Other Backward Classes.

It may be mentioned that, though they had started their livelihood as braziers after the Independence, their original profession has been given up due to the implementation of stainless steel, plastic, etc. At present only 17.59 percent of workers are engaged in the brass industry and the rest of the workers are engaged in other occupational activities.

The Moria Muslim villages are both uni-ethnic and multi-ethnic. The villages are surrounded by Assamese Hindu caste groups like Brahmin, Kalita, Keot, Koch, etc. and the tribes like Mishing, etc. The surrounding communities keep harmony with Moria Muslims which is reflected in their behaviour with their fellow villagers.

The existence of different castes and tribes with Moria Muslims in and around the village shows a relationship of reciprocity and co-operation among the communities. It has also been observed that other communities usually invite Moria Muslim at the time of socio-religious rituals and festivals, which develops a cordial and friendly relation among them. These social and economic relationships have developed between Moria Muslims and other communities through a process of interaction.

They follow Islam by religion but they do not perform the Islamic religious rites fully. They perform all the Islamic religious functions like Id-Ul-Fitr, Id-Uj-Zuha, Muharram, Bakrid-Id, etc. But at the same time, they also go to the pandal of Durga-puja to see the idol. In some villages (Pithakhowa, Kakojan, Becheria, etc.) the executive members of the Durga-puja committee are also selected from this community. They give subscription for the Durga-puja. In Kalipuja also they enjoy bursting firecrackers. Since they are tilting towards the Assamese Hindu religion so the Tablique party - an Islamic missionary people preach Islam among the Morias. The Tabliques don't take food in Moria houses. It may be mentioned that among the Morias only a few observe the Namaz. It is also observed that in Garia *Jamat* (mosque) the attendance usually goes up to sixty, but in the case of Moria *Jamat*, only five or six persons are found to attend it. It shows their lack of interest in the Islamic religion. But now Moulovis and other groups of Muslims are trying to raise the attendance in Moria *Jamat* (mosque) at the time of Namaz.

Distribution

The Moria population is distributed only in nine districts of the valley. They are thus found in northwest and southern part of Dibrugarh district, southern part of Sibsagar district, central and eastern parts of Jorhat district, Golaghat town of Golaghat district, Dhing and Koliabor areas of Nowgong district, Hajo Malara Islampatti and Uzanbazar of the city of Guwahati of Kamrup district, Mongoldai town of Darrang district, Pithakhowa and Bakula areas of Sonitpur district, Dhakuakhana, Lilabari and North-Lakhimpur town of Lakhimpur district. It is, therefore, observed that the Morias settled in and near the urban areas. This is due to the fact that they were mainly braziers so, they liked to settle near the urban areas to avail of the market facilities for purchasing the raw materials and to sell out the finished products.

At village level again, there is a variation in the concentration of Moria Muslim population. From the field survey, it has been observed that they are distributed only in fifty-two villages in the Brahmaputra valley. The highest concentration is found in Chawlkhowa (10.55 percent of the total Moria population) village in Dibrugarh district of Upper Brahmaputra valley (Table 10.1).

Table 10.1 Village wise Moria population

Name of the district	*Name of the village*	*Total population*	*Percentage of population*
Kamrup	Hajo Islampatti	783	3.31
	Malara Islampati	482	2.04
	Uzanbazar	635	2.68
Darrang	Vevarghat	632	2.67
Sonitpur	Pithakhowa	1600	6.76
	Gavorugaon	50	0.21
	Niraiati	150	0.63
	Becheria	1210	5.11
	Bakula	815	3.44
Lakhimpur	Shilabari Balijan	490	2.07
	Balijan Tengabari	81	0.34
	Dhekial	384	1.62
	Nawkari	374	1.58
	Lilabari	382	1.61
	Dhokuakhana	399	1.69
Dibrugarh	Laluka	582	2.46
	Chowlkhowa	2500	10.55
	Sadia	446	1.88
	Bakul	320	1.35
	Margherita	110	0.46
Sibsagar	Demoumukh	581	2.45
	Mothadang	341	1.44
	Bagal	382	1.61

(Contd...)

	Bambari	20	0.08
	Dopdar	16	0.07
	Panidihing	297	1.25
	Khatopahar	20	0.08
	Amguri	360	1.52
	Gauri Sagar	392	1.66
	Nazira	398	1.68
	Geleki	375	1.58
Jorhat	Veleuguri	80	0.34
	Mudoijan	126	0.53
	Jhanji	94	0.40
	Koliapani	200	0.84
	Badulipukhuri	256	1.08
	Neematighat	221	0.93
	Tamulishika	350	1.48
	Fatigasiga	244	1.03
	Naobaisya	286	1.21
	Kakojan	753	3.18
	Gakhirkhowa	209	0.88
	Boloma	56	0.24
Golaghats	Kacharihat	500	2.11
	Kamarbandha	180	0.76
	Moinapar	80	0.34
	Islampatti	800	3.38
Nowgong	Langi	287	1.21
	Jayantipur	925	3.91
	Huntergaon	916	3.87
	Baligaon	801	3.38
	Bilotia	715	3.02

Source: Based on Field Survey, 1988.
(Morias are considered as Assamese Muslims and included in the Census after 1911).

Conclusion

The present study on Moria Muslims of the Brahmaputra Valley provides historical background and their distribution in Assam. Very insignificant research works have been done so far by the historians, anthropologists, and sociologists on this community. The Morias came to the Brahmaputra Valley as invaders and ultimately settled down permanently about four hundred and fifty years ago. The Morias are distributed only in nine districts out of eighteen districts in the valley. It is observed that they generally prefer to settle in or around the urban areas for their profession.

It is urgently required to make systematic plans and policies to improve the economic condition and the spread of higher education among the Morias. Developmental schemes should be based on their present socio-economic situation for their betterment. Emphasis should be given to the development of their economy and education.

The following suggestions may be considered for their economic and educational development:

Their traditional brass industry should be improved by giving loan and subsidy from the State Government at least to those families who are still interested to keep their traditional identity in this industry. At present only a very few families of Hajo Islampatti get this loan irregularly from Gaonlia (rural) Bank. The loan should be given regularly through the Goanlia (rural) Bank. The youths should be given proper training to complete with the machine-made brass utensils. The training centers should be opened at the selected areas or villages, to cater the need through their familiarity with this work and uncultured personal skill. Co-operative societies should be opened among the workers through which they can sell their finished products for their economic enrichment. The price of the finished articles will be fixed according to their quality and craftsmanship and the wages should be determined according to the degree or skills of the artisan and the quantity of the products. If it is done then the following effect may be expected:

(i) The traditional brass industry will survive and revitalize and will be expanded in the villages. Its commercial value also will be increased.

(ii) The illiterate and semiliterate youths may be engaged in their traditional industry in their own villages.

(iii) Their standard of living will be improved.

(iv) Personal interest will grow to develop their own skill. Besides this industry, the weaving cane industry, etc. should be introduced by giving them proper training and financial assistance.

Primary education is available in almost all villages. So middle or secondary schools should be established in or near the villages, such that the guardians can send their children for high school education, without incurring any expenditure. The main focus should be given on their traditional brass industry, other cottage industries, and the higher education. Emphasis should be given to establishing colleges in selected areas in their locality where the youths can avail of opportunity in getting higher education.

Note

1. The legend was narrated by Gausal Ali of Jayantipur village, Koliabor, Nowgong district.

References

Acharyya, NN 1966, *The history of medieval Assam*, 1st edn, Dutta Barua and Company, Gauhati, Assam, pp. 53 and 95-96.

Bandopadhyaya, R 1982, *Banglar itihas*, vol. II, Manmohan Prakashani, Calcutta, pp. 211-212.

Barua, KL 1966, *Early history of Kamrup*, 2nd edn, Dutta Barua, Lawyer's Book Stall, Gauhati, pp.193-194.

Gait, E 1926, *A history of Assam*, 2nd edn, LBS Publication, Gauhati, pp. 92-95.

Hunter, WW 1879, *A statistical account of Assam,* Trubner and Co., London, vol. I, pp. 261.

Nessa, S 1984, *Emergence of the Assamese Muslim society: a social analysis*. M.Phil Dissertation, Northeastern Hill University, Shillong, pp. 109, 118.

Taher, M 1977, 'Tribes in North-East India: a diagnostic survey in a spatial pattern in North-East India', *North- Eastern Geographer*, vol.9, no. 1 and 2, pp. 17-2.

Taher, M 1979, 'Scheduled caste population in Assam: a spatial analysis', *North-Eastern Geographer*, vol. II, no. 1 and 2.

Chapter - 11

Traditional Weekly Markets of Karbi Anglong and Indigenous Numeral System of the Karbis: An Overview

Somenath Bhattacharjee

Introduction

The anthropological study of economic organization is a focal point for discovering the relationship between material and nonmaterial aspects of the environment and human behaviour as well as the social system within which it is exchanged and redistributed as cultural goods and services. The economic organization is treated as a link between the material base to culture and social structure. Economic order in one form or another is a functional prerequisite to societal survival and continuity (Hoebel-Frost, 1976: 247). From the anthropological point of view, the economy is believed as a system of managing the production, distribution, and consumption of goods and services in a society. There is also stress on the fact to the motivations for producing, exchanging and consuming goods and services which are shaped by cultural traditions (Dash, 2004: 123). Piddington (1952) says 'economic system is designated to satisfy material wants of the people to organize production, to control distribution and to determine the rights and claims of ownership within the community' (Dash, 2004: 123). Every society has access to natural resources-land, water, plants, animals, minerals and every society has cultural rules for determining who has access to particular resources and what can be done with them (Ember et al., 2002: 286). All groups are selective choosing to utilize certain resources and to ignore others (Hunter-Whitten, 1976: 237). All societies have customs specifying access to natural resources; customary ways of transforming or converting those resources through labour into necessities and other desired goods and services; and customs for distributing and perhaps exchanging goods and services (Ember et al., 2002: 305). Every society makes use of a technology, which includes tools, constructions, and required skills. The technology and material culture of a people are so intertwined with their economic life that they can be treated as separate only conceptually (Clifton, 1968:187).

Each local economic system represents a more or less unique aggregation of experience built up partly through progressive innovation by the people themselves as they have adjusted to their local setting. Actually, the economic system of any people quickly reveals that behaviours relating to production, exchange, property, and consumption all tie in functionally with social organization and with the political, legal, religious and aesthetic behaviours (Kessing, 1958: 223). The economic behaviour of the people lies in their own cultural terms, focusing on the substantive social and technological processes through which human interactions with one another and with the environment to meet their subsistence needs (Hunter-Whitten, 1976: 251). The study of the relations between cultural patterns and physical conditions is of the greatest importance for an understanding of human society and it is intimately co-related with the economic organization of the concerned society.

In the Indian context, Bose (1971) has discussed different types of traditional occupational practices of the tribal people, in different parts of the country. Vidyarthi (1976) has discussed the utilization of different natural resources in the traditional economic organization by the tribal people of India. In this regard, his study on the barter system among the tribal groups of Niligiri hills described the exchange of indigenous economic productions.

The fundamental requirement of any economic organization is the market, which can cohere, different ethnic groups, irrespective of their social and cultural differences.

The present chapter is focused on the traditional weekly markets or *haat*, in different parts of the Karbi Anglong district of Assam. The Karbis were the numerically dominant tribal group of the said district, whereas Bodo, Dimasa, Naga, Kuki, Khasi, etc. were the other significant tribal groups dwelling there. Although on the Karbis and Karbi Anglong district, studies were done by Lyall (1872) and Phangcho (1956), the relevance of their traditional weekly markets or *haat*, particularly on their barter exchange method, inter-ethnic cultural cohesion, has never been studied.

Background Problems and Relevance of the Study

Related to territorial distribution and several other issues, ethnic conflicts in different parts of Karbi Anglong were noticed in a different period. In 2003, Karbi-Khasi and Karbi-Kuki conflict took place. In 2005, the conflict took place between the Karbis and Dimasas. In Dhansiri, Howraghat and Chokiola region the Dimasa-Naga and Karbi-Naga conflicts related to territorial occupancy was a regular phenomenon. Whatever might be the cause, ultimately poverty and hunger could get resisted under such issues. Amidst ethnic diversity, problems of the poor rural dwellers are quite common to one another. In this regard, could their traditional weekly markets play a vital role to sustain the livelihood of the poor people? Could it bring them closer and depended on one another for livelihood sustainability? Whether it could generate the scope to share their produces with each other and could try to integrate them? Such issues would be studied in detail.

Objectives of the Present Study

The present study is primarily focused

1. To know about the conduction of different traditional weekly markets in the studied areas;
2. to know about the traditional number system of the Karbis;
3. to know about the importance of traditional number systems as practiced in the *haat* by the concerned people; and
4. to know the socio-economic and socio-cultural relevance of traditional markets or *haat* in the studied areas.

Methodology Applied

The study was done in the Karbi Anglong district, one of the two hill districts of Assam and divided into two parts that are East and West Karbi Anglong. The district is situated in the central part of Assam, bounded by Golaghat district in the east, Meghalaya and Morigaon district of Assam in the West, Nagaon and Golaghat district in the north and N.C. Hills district and Nagaland in the south. The district is covered with dense tropical forest covered hills and flat plains are situated between $25^0$33'N to $26^0$35'N Latitude and $92^0$10' to $93^0$50' E Longitude. It is the largest district of Assam with a total geographical area of 10, 434 Sq. Kilometer (Karbi Anglong Autonomous Council, 2016). The Karbis were the earliest settlers and a numerically dominant tribal group of the region. Different other tribal groups like Dimasa, Bodo, Naga, Hmar, Khasi, Kuki, Hajong, Man (Tai), etc. and different other communities were also dwelling in the studied region. The study was conducted in different traditional tribal markets or *haat* organized in different places of Karbi Anglong district. The *haat* which were regularly getting conducted at least for 25 years or more were selected for the purpose of the study. In this regard, a total of 19 *haat* was selected. The total studied population was 7,984 and among them, there were 4,056 males and 3,928 females. The concerned people used to come regularly in the studied *haat* for the sale and purchase of the products. Their ethnic distribution is as follows:

Table 11.1 Ethnic distribution of the studied people

Ethnic groups	*Male*	*Female*	*Total*
Karbi	1,932	1,887	3,819
Dimasa	932	919	1,851
Bodo	342	325	667
Naga	278	257	535
Garo	129	117	246
Khasi	134	127	261
Kuki	117	109	226
Others	192	187	379
Total	4,056	3,928	7,984

The study was conducted during the period of January 2016 to September 2017. During the different phases of field work rapport establishment, observation, preliminary household census schedule, case studies, interviews, key informant interview methods were applied to collect primary data.

Foremostly, the traditional markets or *haat* in different subdivisions and villages were visited. Exchange of different products was observed. The interaction was done with the people of different ethnic groups who assembled there.

Case studies were taken on all the senior most male and female member of the different ethnic groups who was regularly participating in such traditional markets for the selling and purchase of different products. Attempt has been made to know about their different types of productions as well as on their traditional number systems as practiced in the traditional markets. Case studies were also taken on one unmarried old female (aged 71 years) and on one widow female (aged 24 years), who were sustaining their livelihood by themselves through such traditional markets. Data were collected about the barter system of the studied people and the significance of the traditional number system in it.

Interviews were taken on the traditional village headmen, who often used to come to their nearest traditional weekly markets to collect their livelihood requirements. Attempt has been made to find out the socio-economic and socio-cultural relevance of traditional markets or *haat,* which could justify its significance to improve the higher level of ethnic interaction in between them.

The traditional Karbi King dwelling in Hamren and renowned social worker of the district D.S. Teron were the Key Informants. The issues of different ethnic conflicts in the said region as well as their probable solutions were discussed in detail. The relevance of such traditional weekly markets to reduce the ethnic differences as well as to sustain the livelihood of poor people dwelling in the remote villages were tried to find out.

Result and Discussion

Traditional Weekly Markets of East Karbi Anglong

East Karbi Anglong is the major district of Assam and Diphu is the Headquarter of it. Through the National Highways 36NH and 39NH; Railway Station at Diphu is well connected with several other districts of Assam like Silchar, Guwahati, Nagaon, Tezpur, Golaghat, Jorhat, etc and other states like Nagaland and Meghalaya. A number of traditional weekly markets or *haat* were found within Diphu town at Larulangso and in several other places like at Manja, Delai, Desobai, Bakulia, Phuloni, Langhin, Dokmuka, Dangoan, Parokhua market. These weekly traditional markets were connected through NH-36. On the other hand, NH-39 connects the traditional weekly markets or *haat* held at Upper-Deopani, Deopani, Khatkoti, Sarihojan, Silonijan, Japrajan, Balipathar and Daithor. People of different tribal groups like Karbi, Dimasa, Boro, Rengma Naga and other communities like caste Hindu groups, Muslims, Nepalese were regularly coming to those traditional weekly markets from different places and purchasing different organic resources for a daily livelihood at cheaper prices from local people. It was observed that in between the Karbi people even barter exchange method was being practiced. In certain cases, barter exchange has been noticed in between the Karbi people with the Boro and Dimasa people as well. However, with the caste Hindu people and Muslims always the monetary exchange has been practiced. It was observed that particularly the caste Hindu and Muslim people used to come to such traditional markets from outside areas with different products like old used clothes, spices, some attractive items, etc. The local people had a scope to purchase them within their close vicinity, which used to save their cost of transportation instead of going to the markets of town as well as the prices of such objects were much lesser in the *haat* if compared with the regular markets of the town. Here the communication and transportation used to play a vital role in the cultural interaction.

Different Economic Resources

It can be noted that the traditional occupation of the Karbi people was shifting or *jhum* cultivation and on the other hand, they used to collect forest resources for consumption and selling. Along with that, they were associated with traditional weaving, handicrafts, kitchen gardening, and animal husbandry. The traditional occupation of the Dimasa people was also the shifting or *jhum* cultivation. Along with that, they practiced traditional weaving, kitchen gardening, etc. The Bodos were the settled agriculturist mainly. The Nagas were traditionally associated with terrace and *jhum* cultivation. It can be noted that geographically Karbi Anglong is recognized as a hill district and fertile soil is comparatively less in the studied area. On the other hand, it comes under the rain shadow region. Thus, the level or quantity of agricultural production is relatively less. The Karbi people mostly produced paddy, potato, maize through *jhum* cultivation; the Nagas were the prime producers of paddy, pineapple, potato through *jhum* and terrace cultivation; the Bodos were the producers of paddy through settled cultivation and the Dimasas were primarily engaged with *jhum* cultivation to produce ginger, paddy. Different vegetables, leafy vegetables, and fruits were primarily produced through the kitchen garden. Fishes were collected by them from local streams only. However, being the rain shadow region, particularly during summer and winter, the level of water used to get much decreased. In the studied region, although different types of productions were available, the lesser quantity of such produces could hardly satisfy the different requirements for the individual families, related to their food and other essential livelihoods needful. Ultimately, they had to depend and share the productions of each other for their sustenance; in such cases, the traditional weekly markets were the prime platform.

The local Karbi people came down from the hills to sell their organic resources in different traditional weekly markets. They used to carry various local produces, vegetables and natural forest resources. Those were like pumpkin, yam leaf, yam, banana, sugarcane, papaya, chili, beetle nut, betel leaf, banana flower, brinjal, bamboo shoot, mushroom, pumpkin leaf different local leafy vegetables like *Hanrisang, Hansangbi, Hanbipo, Torbob, Dumkek, Tara, Hanjang, Hanthu, Theso-kumbong, Theso-keho, Aantimi, Jokaan, Hendonngdar, Hanserong, Pherklung, Chushot, Hantharvo, Hanche,* etc.

Table 11.2 Traditional weekly markets connected through NH-39

Name of the traditional markets	*People coming from*	*Conducted on*	*Ethnic groups participating*	*Distance from Diphu town*	*Geographical location*
Balipathar market	Dimapur, Bokajan, Borpathar, Sorupathar	Every Monday	Karbi, Dimasa, Naga, Bodo, Assamese	50 km	Foothill region
Upper Deopani market	Bokajan, Borpathar, Silonijan, Golaghat district, Jorhat	Every Wednesday	Karbi, Dimasa, Naga, Bodo, Assamese	40 km	Foothill region
Deopani, Khotkhoti market	Dimapur, Bakajan, Golaghat district, Jorhat, Tinsukia, Borpathar	Every Thursday	Karbi, Dimasa, Naga, Bodo, Nepali, Assamese	37 km	Plainland
Sarihojan, Silonijan market	Bokajan, Dimapur, Manipur, Golaghat district, Jorhat, Tinsukia	Every Friday	Karbi, Dimasa, Bodo, Assamese	35 km	Plainland
Japrajan market	Bokajan, Deithor, Borpathar, Sorupathar, Golaghat district	Every Saturday	Karbi, Dimasa, Naga, Bodo, Assamese	70 km	Foothill region

Source: Field Study.

Table 11.3 Traditional weekly markets connected through NH-39

Name of the traditional markets	*People coming from*	*Conducted on*	*Ethnic groups participating*	*Distance from Diphu town*	*Geographical location*
Langhin market	Nogaon, Doboka	Every Sunday	Karbi, Dimasa, Bodo, Assamese	20 km	Plainland
Center market	Hawraghat, Bakulia	Every Monday	Karbi, Dimasa, Naga, Bodo, Assamese	40 km	Foothill region
Bakulia, Dangaon market	Nagaon, Doboka, Dokmuka, Kothiatuli,	Every Tuesday	Karbi, Dimasa, Assamese	50 km	Foothill region
Dokmoka market	Doboka	Every Wednesday	Karbi, Dimasa, Naga, Assamese	70 km	Foothill region
Phuloni market	Dokmuka, Bakulia	Every Thursday	Karbi, Dimasa, Kuki, Naga, Bodo, Assamese, Bengalee	80 km	Hilly tract
Manja market	Dimapur, Diphu	Every Friday	Karbi, Dimasa, Kuki, Naga, Bodo, Assamese, Bengalee	15 km	Plainland
Dilai, Parokhua market	Dimapur. Kothiatuli, Kampur, Nogaon, Doboka	Every Saturday	Karbi, Dimasa, Kuki, Naga, Bodo, Assamese.	60 km	Foothill region

Source: Field Study.

Further, it was noticed that in the traditional *haat*, different vegetables, leaves, and fruits were sold by the females whereas; the males were dealing with paddy, firewood, fish. The barter exchange was primarily done in between the Karbi people and it was done on the basis of their traditional number system; along with that monetary exchange was also noticed. However, barter exchange was also noticed in between the Karbi people with the Bodos, Dimasas, and Nagas as well as in the between the Nagas, Dimasas, and Bodos. In such cases, balanced reciprocity could be noticed among them.

Traditional Weekly Markets of West Karbi Anglong

The West Karbi Anglong district is a new proposed district formed out of the existing Karbi Anglong district of Assam in 2016. Hamren is the headquarters of the newly formed district. The district is a part of Karbi Anglong Autonomous Council and it is administered according to the Sixth Schedule of the Indian Constitution. Karbi dialect is widely spoken in the district. English, Assamese, and Hindi are the other languages that are spoken in the district. The district is inhabited by many tribes, Karbi being the majority, along with Tiwa, Garo, Bodo, Dimasa tribal groups and caste Hindu, Muslim communities.

The district headquarter is connected by road. Karbi Anglong Autonomous Council Transport buses play at regular interval from the district headquarters to important places like Guwahati, Diphu, Lanka, and Hojai. Also, one Meghalaya Transport runs regularly to and from Hamren to Jowai. The nearest railway station is at Hojai, which is around 47 km from Hamren. In the studied areas, the traditional economic organizations were highly practiced. In those areas, traditional weekly markets or *haat* was organized which made an opportunity for the multi-ethnic cultural and economic interaction, between the concerned people who used to come to such markets from different places.

Different Economic Resources

The tribal communities of the studied region were interacting frequently in terms of economy, various goods, and services, in their traditional weekly markets. Many of the tribal and non-tribal communities could be seen to interact in their traditional markets during the marketing of different productive goods. West Karbi Anglong was the rich zone for the cultivation of various organic resources. The Karbis of those regions cultivated organic ginger; broom grass, pineapple, pumpkin, sugarcane to produce jaggery, pear and organic chilies of different kinds. Apart from this, the Karbi women collected organic herbs and ferns to sell in the traditional weekly markets. Along with that, they used to sell ferns and other natural resources such as bamboo shoot, and different local vegetables like *inglong-a-bobok, inglong-a-behendi, dungkek, bonghom arvo, langdung, tara, henru, hanserong, hippi, hen-up, rui pharkong, plimplam, thichi, ginger, ahan-a-lothe, kolmuk, lang-a-churu, ingki ok, pijo alang, hen dongdar, chosot, hanthu, papaya, birik man, birik losa, birik jangkek, dido, mula arvo, musi, jok-an, Pharklung, hantharvo, hen soksu, henjor, hen kove, inglong kenong ahen, mu-plakplak, mu-arnan, mu-rik, mu-plong, henru, nempo arvo, mora arvo, phi-kangnek, bonghom arvo, mehek, churu, langdun, kove* (battle nut), *bikron* (battle leave), *phinu* (banana), *ahan a lothe* (banana used for cooking) etc. Moreover, different handicrafts like *tar* (mat made up of bamboo), *beleng, hoton* (a kind of basket made up of bamboo and cane) were also sold. *Theng* (firewood) was usually sold by a male.

Tumpreng, Donkamokam, Hamren, Kolonga, Jengkha, Kheroni and Baithalangso were the prime markets where most cultural interaction used to take place. Yeats was mainly sold in Donkamokam weekly market; broom grass and organic ginger were the main sources of the market in Hamren; in Tumpreng market other than the selling of various vegetables and market product, animals like cow, piglet, goat, duck and hen and cock were the main items of marketing. While in the weekly market of Kolonga, Jengkha and Kheroni, organic ginger, organic chili, broom grass, pineapple, pear, and jaggery are the main stuff. However, such sources became variable according to seasonal produce. Mostly different organic products are being supplied from the nearby hilly areas of Jirikindeng.

In those weekly markets traditional ethnic food stalls could also be noticed, mostly ran by the Karbi women, in those food stalls traditional country liquor like *Hor-arak, Hor-lang* and *Hor-po* were also available. In some of the places like Kheroni and Tumpreng, a few food stalls were run by the non-Karbi women with other food items. The people of other ethnic groups coming from the neighboring districts and state used to bring different objects like utensils, dry fish, different vegetables like potato, tomato, onion, garlic, etc., clothes, different kinds of iron implements like knife, a variety of spices, a variety of colourful yarns, etc.

The traditional weekly markets of the studied areas were the prime place of interaction between different ethnic groups like Bodo, Garo, Karbi, Mizo, Khasi, Hmar, Panar, Kuki, Manipuri, Dimasa and other ethnic groups like Bengali, Assamese, Bihari, and Muslims. Such interaction played a vital role in their economic life as well as social life.

Table 11.4 Traditional weekly markets connected through NH-27

Name of the traditional markets	*People coming from*	*Conducted on*	*Ethnic groups participating*	*Distance from Diphu town*	*Geographical location*
Tumpreng	Hojai	Every Monday	Karbi, Garo, Dimasa, Khasi, Bengalee	245 km	Hilly tract
Baithalangso	Hojai, Donkamokam, Hamren.	Every Tuesday	Karbi, Garo, Dimasa, Khasi	232 km	Hilly tract
Jengkha	Lanka, Hojai, Jirikindeng	Every Wednesday	Karbi, Garo, Dimasa, Bodo, Khasi, Assamese, Bengalee	254 km	Hilly tract
Dongkamokam	Hojai, Tumpreng, Baithalangso, Hamren, Kolonga	Every Thursday	Karbi, Garo, Dimasa, Khasi, Bodo, Assamese, Bengalee	230 km	Foothill region
Kheroni	Hojai, Lanka	Every Friday	Karbi, Garo, Khasi, Mizo, Dimasa, Bengalee	220 km	Foothill region
Hamren	Liumphung, Linchika, Rumphung, Rongmandu, Socheng, Taradubi, Umcherra, Hojai	Every Saturday	Karbi, Khasi, Mizo, Bodo, Hmar, Pnar, Kuki, Dimasa, Manipuri, Assamese, Bengalee	215 km	Plain land
Borthol/Kolonga	Hamren, Donkamokam, Tumpreng, Baithalangso, Hojai	Every Sunday	Karbi, Dimasa, Garo, Khasi, Assamese, Bengalee.	210 km	Foothill region

Source: Field Study.

Variation in Commodities in the Traditional Markets

It can be noted that each of the studied *haat* was started in consensus with the local people and the village headmen of adjacent villages. The necessities to sustain a livelihood, by sharing their local products were the prime focus for the conduction of such local markets. The people, who used to come there with their local food produces, did not have to pay any tax or levy to any official source. It was found that the local products were quite variable with geographical locations. In the plain land, there was a better scope of paddy cultivation through settled and *jhum* practices. Along with that, people used to collect fishes from the local streams. Thus, in the *haat* of plain land paddy and fish were mostly found. In the foothill region paddy cultivation could be noticed through *jhum* method; along with that cultivation of vegetables and fruits could be noticed. However, in such locations, it was difficult for concerned people to collect fishes. In the upper hilly tracts, the paddy cultivation through both settled and *jhum* methods were hardly noticed. In such places, kitchen gardening, vegetable cultivation and fruit cultivation were most prevalent. In the *haat* of plain lands, people used to come from foothill and upper hilly tracts to purchase rice, fishes against their fruits and vegetables. On the other hand, the people of plain land used to go to the *haat* of foothills and hilly tracts with fish, ginger, etc. Due to lack of proper transport communication and road construction, it was difficult for the people to take a larger quantity of rice from plain land to upper hilly tracts. Along with the variation of altitude, various natural productions could be noticed, which accordingly determined the exchange of products in different *haat*.

It can be noted that almost every day of the week, in different parts of the district, the traditional weekly markets of the Karbi people used to take place. It used to play the role of a lifeline for the daily livelihood requirements of the concerned people. In this regard, their traditional numeral system plays a very vital role.

The Traditional Number System

The main units of the numeral system of the Karbis are a simple decimal system. The basic units are the tenth and the multiplications follow with hundredth, thousandth and even further multiplication of thousandth. The traditional numbering method of the Karbis represents a unique form till the unit six. Thereafter it represents an addition over six or subtraction from the base of ten. These are as follows:

> 1 = *Isi;* 2 = *Hini;* 3 = *Kethom;* 4 = *Phili or Phli;* 5 = *Pho or Phongo;* 6 = *Throk;* 7 = *Throksi* = *Throk+Isi* = 6+1=7*:* 8 = *Nirkep* = *Ni r Kep* = *Kep – Hini* = 10-2 = 8*;* 9 = *Sirkep* = *Isi r Kep* = *Kep – Isi* = 10-1 = 9*;* 10 = *Kep* [Here the 'r' represents the subtraction as per the original Karbi dialect].

In the feature of compound numbers, unit three is represented in a shortened form. A particular term *'kre'* is prefixed with the unit from 11 to 19 to represent the compound number feature, so the form will be *Kre + unit* = Compound number. Thus, the compound numbers are:

> 11 = *Kre-isi;* 12 = *Kre-hini;* 13 = *Kre-thom;* 14 = *Kre- phli;* 15 = *Kre-pho;* 16 = *Kre-throk;* 17 = *Kre - throksi;* 18 = *Kre- nirkep;* 19 = *Kre-sirkep.*

The multiple of tenth in the compound form represents a significant feature. Barring 20 = *Ingkoi*, 80 and 90, the rest of the multiplication of 10 are formed in the following format: Unit + Ten, thus,

> 30 = *Thom-kep;* 40 = *Phli-kep;* 50 = *Pho-kep;* 60 = *Throk-kep;* 70 = *Throksi-kep.* Meanwhile, in the case of unit 8 *(Nirkep)* and

9 *(Sirkep),* 10 *(Kep)*, the '*Kep'* is already present as a suffix. In such cases, the traditional number system of the Karbi people, have taken the help of 6 *(throk)* by prefixing it to the unit of eight and nine to mean 80 and 90. This means:

80 = *Throk-nirkep;* 90 = *Throk-sirkep.*

The compound numbers from 21 and beyond is termed by having an insertion of 'ra', which may be synonymous with and. It is placed between the tenth unit and the unit. It is represented as:

21 = *Ingkoi-ra-isi;* 22 = *Ingkoi-ra-hini;* 23 = *Ingkoi-ra-thom;......* 91 = *Thorksirkep-ra-isi;* 92 = *Throksirkep-ra-hini;* 99 = *Throksirkep-ra-sirkep.*

Regarding the multiplication of 100, it can be noted that the Karbis consider 100 as *'Pharo'*, thus, the multiple of 100 is the form of Hundred + Unit. It can be represented as:

100 = *Pharo-isi;* 200 = *Pharo-hini;* 300 = *Pharo-thom;......*900 = *Pharo-sirkep.*

Further, in Karbi dialect thousand is termed as *'Suri'*, the multiple of thousand in the form of Thousand + Unit. It can be represented as:

1000 = *Suri-isi;* 2000 = *Suri-hini;* .... 9000 = *Suri-sirkep;* 10,000 = *Suri-kep;* 50,000 = *Suri-Phokep* etc.

It is to be mentioned here that, expressing any number above 20 is represented by inserting the term 'ra' in between thousand, hundred, tenth and the unit. If the number is 6539 then it will be = *Suri-Throk rapharo-pho rathom-keprasirkep*. This rule is practiced by a large number of Tibeto-Burman tribal group.

Further, when the number system is associated with an object either living or nonliving (i.e animal or human etc.) or the shape of the object can be taken into consideration, then such number becomes associated with a clarifier. Here the language structure of the said number system will be:

Object + Number + Clarifier (when the object is singular) and Object + Clarifier + Number (when the object is plural). In this aspect, One egg = Egg + One + Clarifier = *Voti-I-Pum (Voti* =Egg, *I* = One, *Pum* = Clarifier*)*. Four eggs = Egg + Four + Clarifier = *Voti- Pum- Phli (Voti* = Egg, *Phli* = Four, *Pum* = Clarifier*)*.

It is to be mentioned here that; the clarifiers vary according to the shape of the object. If the object is round in shape or spherical then *'Pum'* is termed as the clarifier. If the object is a human being then *'Bang'* is used as a clarifier for singular and *'Nut'* is used as a clarifier if the object is plural. So, a man is termed as '*Monit-I- Nut*' and two men are termed as '*Monit-bang-Hini*'. It is to be mentioned here that, if the object is a nonliving being then in case of two or three irrespective of '*Hini*' and '*Kethom*' only '*Ni*' and '*Thom*' are applied. However, in the case of living being, this rule is not followed. Further, the clarifier associated with flora is 'Romg' means the plant. Thus, one mango tree is termed as *Tharve-I- Rong*, four guava trees as *Menduram-Rong-Phli.* Meanwhile, when the objects are in a pair the '*chor*' is termed as the clarifier. So, six pairs of shoes will be *Keng-op-chor-throk*. It can be noted here that the common clarifiers are *Pak* = flat object, *Jon* = fauna, *Hum* = household, *Run* = room, *Hong* = elongated object, *Bong* = bottle or cylindrical object, etc. (Source: Field study and Teron, 2012: 28-33).

Amount / Grains etc

Some amount of grain is measured by:

1. *Chekipisi* ..... a Handful...
2. *Chepu isi* ..... Two hands joined ('palms wide open').
3. *Edang* .... 20 kgs
4. *Mon* .... Maund, 40 kgs.

Karbi people usually used different size of '*Ton*' or basket to measure the amount of grain.

Any Karbi family used to remain associated with a particular or more than one occupational pursuit both primarily and secondarily. However, in the remote villages, the presence of regular market could not be noticed. In such cases, the regular common minimum livelihood requisites were managed by the village dwellers from the traditional weekly markets or *haat*. Often it was maintained through the barter system. The quantity of the productions and the required amount was based upon the traditional number system among the Karbi people; whereas along with the other ethnic group's western mathematical weight system or monetary exchange used to take place.

The barter method in the studied areas is represented through the following diagram:

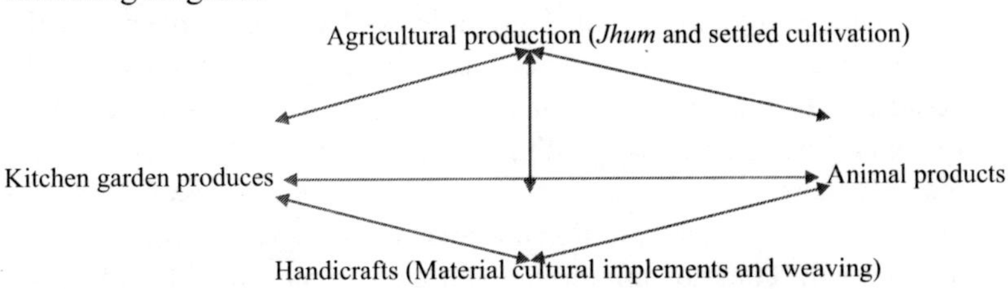

The Scope of Greater Cultural Interaction

It can be noted that due to several factors socio-political differences were quite noticeable in the district of Karbi Anglong, particularly with the neighbourhood states of Nagaland and Meghalaya. Along with that, even within the district, there were many unsettled political issues with the other tribal groups like Dimasa, Bodo, etc. But poverty and hunger could hardly recognize such differences of opinion. In the common minimum livelihood of the unlettered rural ethnic people, the question of survival under several inconveniences was the prime question. In the studied traditional markets, there was a much wider scope, where through economic exchange, people of different ethnic groups and distinctive cultural practices could come closer. It had widened up their scope to share each other's day to day problems and culturally interact with each other. Although the concerned people were of different ethnic groups and cultural practices, the problems related to their daily livelihood sustenance were quite similar. They had a very clear idea that only their inter-community level interaction and sharing of each other resources could meet up with their common minimum livelihood requirements, at least to some extent. Several settlements of the district were much isolated and remote from the highway communication. In such cases neither they had the scope of the regular market nor did they have the regular accessibility to the district headquarter of Diphu town. In such cases, the traditional weekly markets or the rural *haat* were the only options left for them. Their different products were well available and their sell and purchase provided the livelihood requirements of the concerned people of different ethnic groups. In this regard, the following case studies can be mentioned:

Case Study - 1: B.T, the eldest Karbi male among the studied people, stated that he had a six-membered family in Socheng and he was primarily associated with *jhum* cultivation. His son was also associated with the same. In spite of his age, B.T. regularly used to go to his nearest weekly markets of Socheng and Umcherra. According to him most of the rural Karbi people were dealing their livelihood under immense poverty. Geographically the district used to come under the rain shadow region and the cultivable land was not covered with irrigation facilities. Thus, the level of production was insufficient, which could satisfy their requirement of food as well as to procure other livelihood requirements by selling the productions in the market. Even most of their settlements were quite far from the access of regular markets. He stated that traditional weekly markets were the only option to acquire the common minimum livelihood for his family members as well as for the other families of the settlement. He stated that for the sake of survival, they had to depend on and share each other's productions. According to him, the difference in socio-political opinion between different ethnic groups was beyond their common level of understanding. They were struggling for a fold of rice and were least interested in such issues. Poverty, economic needs, and livelihood security had integrated them into the traditional weekly markets. Even such markets could play a vital role to settle down many of such issues through frequent cultural interaction.

Case study - 2: P.K. the eldest Karbi female among the studied families stated that her husband passed away quite at an early age and during the study, she was living alone after the marriage of her daughters. Although her son was settled in Diphu town, she was reluctant to leave her ancestral settlement of in-laws. Her age was not favourable to get involved with *jhum* or settled cultivation. She was involved with a kitchen garden and animal husbandry. Every week with such household products she used to attend in two weekly markets of Kheroni and Donkamokam. Through barter exchange against her products, she used to collect rice and other requirements, from those markets. She stated that, due to her age, it was not possible for her to go to the regular market of Hamren or other places. The local weekly markets and indigenous economic organization had actually saved her life. In the traditional markets, sometimes she used to sell her products against cash money and against that she used to purchase other livelihood requirements from the people of other ethnic groups. She stated that in the life of unlettered village communities like them, hardly there existed any interest to know about the issues of ethnic differences and conflicts. She felt that poverty and livelihood requirements had reduced their cultural differences. The question of survival had brought them much closer to one another and in this regard, their traditional weekly market had played a vital role.

Case study - 3: P.H., (the eldest Dimasa male) was settled in Dhansiri. He remembered the days of Karbi-Dimasa conflict, which had severely affected their daily livelihood. He was living with her wife and both of them were associated with kitchen garden production. Due to their age, agricultural works were no more possible for them. He had engaged some labourers to look after the land, but most of the paddy productions were taken by them. The traditional markets were the prime source for him to collect his livelihood requirements against his kitchen garden produces. He opined that he could not differentiate the poverty-stricken people of other ethnic groups from him. He stated that such markets were not merely for the exchange of goods but it used to play a vital role in the inter-ethnic cultural interaction.

Case study - 4: T.S.R. (the eldest Naga male) was settled in Chokiola. He expressed his disagreement related to conflict due to territorial distribution. He stated that such issues could never redress the poverty or inconveniences of the common people. On the other hand, it could create differences rather than likeness in between them. He viewed that, geographically Karbi Anglong had several obstacles and scarcity of rain is one of them. Again, the agricultural land was not supported with irrigation facilities. Thus, it was a very arduous task for them to generate crop productions. He felt that it was never possible for a person to procure the different types of food as he required. Only sharing of productions could distribute the food resources equally among everyone. For such purpose, the traditional *haat* was the only common medium. He felt that such markets were the place of fellow feeling for them where their intention was always to share instead of capture.

Case study - 5: D.B. (the eldest Bodo male), settled in Langhin stated that ethnic conflicts could only disturb their social peace. He recalled several incidences of ethnic conflicts in the district and as a result due to strike the markets used to remain close. Even under such circumstances, there was hardly any impact on their local traditional weekly markets. It was mainly due to the fact that they used to carry the products generated within their courtyard or surrounding localities and did not require heavy transport support. On the other hand, the people from the town adjacent areas used to come to their *haat* for livelihood requirements, when the markets used to remain closed during the strikes. Thus, according to him, the livelihood of poor people like them was far away from other issues, which could not resist their poverty. He stated that the traditional markets were the rich places of cultural and social sharing for them.

Case study - 6: A.M. (the eldest Garo male) was settled in Baithalangso. He became afraid to remember the days of conflicts, because it could make the survival more miserable only, instead of solving their problems. Although the strike was declared due to such issues, it had no impact on their traditional weekly markets. He stated that, although there might be different unsettled issues, they had never felt any ethnic difference when they used to come in the *haat*. He agreed that culturally there were many differences in between them, but their requirements and hardship to accumulate them were much similar. It was the cementing force for them and in this regard, their traditional weekly markets were immensely important.

Case study - 7: K.K. aged 71 years was unmarried. Her brothers got married and after the death of her parents, she found it very difficult to stay with them. The brothers provided a small portion of land to her and made her separated from their familial hearth. She used to cultivate different vegetables and had some domestic animals. She used to collect such produces and sold them in adjacent *haat*. Against such produces she used to purchase rice and other livelihood requirements. She stated that due to her age, it was not possible to go to the regular markets which were far from her settlement. The weekly *haat* had helped her to survive, without getting depended on others and being unwanted to them.

Case study - 8: L.T. aged 24 years became widow just after 4 months of her marriage. She was the lonely child of her parents and even after her marriage her parents also passed away. She was treated as inauspicious by her in-laws and expressed their reluctance on her stay with them. She came back to her parental place and had a son. But she had no idea how to run their livelihood. On the small portion of land, she started kitchen gardening because she could not do any cultivation work alone. On the other, she had domesticated two cows and a hen. In the adjacent traditional weekly markets, she used to take them for sale and in return, she could get rice or allied livelihood essentials, instead of going to the regular markets at farthest distance. She said that such weekly markets had paved her way to live with dignity even being alone in life.

From the above case studies, it can be summarized that the people of different ethnic groups in the studied areas were intimately depended on each other through their traditional markets. Such markets had integrated them, instead of their cultural differences and several other issues. Moreover, it had generated the scope for the womenfolk of the society, to live with self-dignity and identity, by becoming self-learner.

Observation and Remarks

Our feelings over borderland issues are primarily confined to the international boundaries and relationship with neighbouring nations. However, even within our nation, there are many unsettled issues in the borderland of states. Their solutions are also lying in those borderland areas, where many age-old ethnic traditions are getting preserved and practiced.

A number of the studied *haat* or traditional tribal markets were getting conducted in the villages existed in the borderland of Assam - Nagaland, and Assam - Meghalaya regions. Till date, there were many unsettled issues in those regions and the concerned people had their own different cultural practices. Instead of that, the need for economy, as well as other livelihood requirements, had brought them much closer to each other. Their traditional economic organization was primarily based upon locally available natural resources; however, being located in a rain shadow region and due to lack of infrastructural support like irrigation, the production levels were much less in the studied areas. Only through the economy, they could accumulate other livelihood requirements, whereas they used to sustain their derived need of economy only by sharing each other's resources. Poverty, scarcity was the prime factor which had reduced the barrier of their cultural differences. Again, the platform of their traditional economic organization that is the weekly markets or *haat* had emerged as a place of social and cultural integration for them. Such integration had often reduced the impact of different unsettled issues of the said regions and played a very vital role to sustain the livelihood of unlettered village people even in many adverse circumstances. Simultaneously, such markets had sustained their age-old cultural practices of barter exchange and traditional number system, which could be rarely seen in many other tribal areas of our country. Thus, in the studied areas, the derived need like the economic organization had generated an integrative need of traditional weekly markets or *haat* for them, which could play a vital role to resolve many of unsettled matters in the said borderland regions.

References

Bose, NK 1971, *Tribal life in India*, India Book House, Bombay.

Clifton, JA 1968, *Introduction to cultural anthropology*, Houghton Mifflin Company, Boston.

Dash, KN 2004, *Invitation to social and cultural anthropology*, Atlantic Publishers, New Delhi.

Ember, C, Ember, M & Peregrine, PN 2002, *Anthropology*, Pearson Education Asia, New Delhi.

Hoebel, EA & Frost, EL 1976, *Cultural and social anthropology*, McGraw Hill Book Company, New York.

Hunter, DE & Whitten, P 1976, *The study of anthropology*, Harper, andRow Publishers, New York.

Kessing, FM 1958, *Cultural anthropology: the science of custom*, Holt Rinehart, and Winston, New York.

Lyall, C 1997 (1982), *The Karbis*, Spectrum Publication, Guwahati.

Official Records of Karbi Anglong Autonomous Council 2016, Karbi Anglong, Diphu.

Phangcho, PC 2003 (1956), *The Karbis of North-East India,* Angik Prakashan, Guwahati.

Teron, D 2012, *The Karbi studies*, Assam Book Hive, Guwahati.

Vidyarthi, LP & Rai, BK 1976, *The tribal culture of India*, Concept Publishing, New Delhi.

Chapter – 12

Selection Intensity among the Ahoms and the Khamyangs of Upper Assam

Dali Dutta and Sarthak Sengupta

Introduction

One of the major evolutionary forces is a natural selection that causes population modification by bringing about change in genetic makeup. The index of total selection intensity indicates the maximum potential rate of change through selection assuming that variations in fertility and mortality are genetically determined and fitness is completely heritable. Livingstone and Spuhler (1965) suggest that if the computed value of the index comes to zero for a population, that means there would be no change in the genetic make-up of that population through selection.

Crow (1958) suggested an index of opportunity for selection in a population. It comprises two components, differential mortality, and differential fertility. Though several authors have pointed out the difficulties in using and interpreting the index, Crow's index is considered to be one of the most feasible means of inferring selection as it is difficult to measure selection directly in the human population. As such this is the index mostly used worldwide. Subsequently, Johnston and Kensinger (1971) extended Crow's original approach and separated the mortality component 'into a component due to variance in the prenatal loss and another due to post-natal mortality'.

In this chapter, an attempt has been made to examine the intensity of natural selection among the Ahoms and the Khamyangs of upper Assam as well as to compare the present findings with other available data of Northeast Indian population groups.

The Ahom is one of the major Mongoloid populations of upper Assam. They first established their kingdom in upper Assam and then extended their territory down the Brahmaputra valley and ruled for about six hundred years. They belong to the Tai or Shan family. Linguistically, they belong to the Siamese Chinese branch of the Sino-Tibetan language family. At present, the Ahoms are mainly concentrated in the districts of Dibrugarh, Lakhimpur, Dhemaji, and Sibsagar of upper Assam.

The Khamyang or Khamjang are popularly known as Noras and are a section of the Thai or Tai stock. It may be relevantly noted that Khamyang is a Tai word. In Tai language *Kham* means 'Gold' and *Yang* or *Jang* means 'to have'. So, etymologically, the term Khamyang stands for people whose occupation was gold painting. Originally, they came to Northeast India from Thailand via Myanmar but the date of their arrival is still in obscurity. Racially, the Khamyangs belong to the Mongoloid stock and linguistically belong to Tai-speaking group. They are Buddhists. At present, the Khamyangs are mainly inhabited in the districts of Tinsukia (Powaimukh village), Sivasagar (Chalapathar, Chala Bangaon, Moniting, Disangpani, and Rahan Shyam Gaon), Jorhat (Balijan, Betbari, and Na Shyam Gaon) and Golaghat (Rajapukhuri village) of upper Assam.

Material and Method

For the present study, the villages selected for the Ahom population are Handique *Gaon* and Chengamari Tekela *Gaon* of Dibrugarh district and Hiloidari *Gaon* of Lakhimpur district, Assam. Chalapather Shyam *Gaon* of Sivsagar district and Betbari Shyam *Gaon*, Balijan Shyam *Gaon* and Na- Shyam *Gaon* of Jorhat district is selected for the Khamyang population. The sample consists of 212 Ahom mothers (Handique *Gaon* = 38, Chengamari Tekela *Gaon* = 64, Hiloidari *Gaon* = 110) and 110 Khamyang mothers (Chalapather Shyam *Gaon* = 59, Betbari Shyam *Gaon* = 13, Balijan Shyam *Gaon* = 18, and Na-Shyam *Gaon* = 20) and the data on embryonic wastages as well as mortality of live-born offspring have been considered. While collecting data, we have taken cognizance of only those mothers, who are aged 40 years and above in these two population groups. In this context, it is worth mentioning that most of the earlier workers (Crow, 1958; Salzana, 1963; Spuhler, 1963; Basu, 1967; Neel and Chagnon, 1968; Ghosh, 1970; Johnston and Kensinger, 1971; Talukdar, 1971; Basu, 1972; Mukherjee, 1972; Deka, 1980; Debnath and Sen, 1983; Das and Ghosh, 1988 and many others) has considered the mothers aged 40 years and above for calculation of the total selection intensity. It was observed by earlier researchers that when a mother reaches 40 years of age, the fertility of the women declines drastically. However, some of the workers have taken into accounts of the mothers aged 45 years and above in their study.

In cases where the subjects were not aware of their real age, it was estimated in correlation with certain local events and thus is approximate only. Information given by the mothers were cross-checked and verified from their respective husbands or/and elderly women of the household. Thus, there are chances of minor recall lapses in the information.

In order to estimate the total selection intensity, we have followed the method proposed by Crow (1958). We have also used the modified formula of Johnston and Kensinger (1971) which takes care of embryonic deaths. This has been done with a view to identifying how these two estimates of the total selection intensity in the Ahom as well as the Khamyang population, differ from each other.

Crow's index was computed using the following steps-

$$I = I_m + I_f / Ps,\ I_m = P_d / Ps,\ Ps = 1 / P_d,\ I_f = V_f / X^2$$

where I = Index of the total selection intensity,

I_m = Index of selection due to mortality,

P_d = Probability of deaths up to pre-reproductive age.

Ps = Probability of survival up to reproductive age,

I_f = Index of selection due to fertility,

V_f = Variance due to fertility,

X = Mean number of live births.

Johnston and Kensinger's (1971) index were computed using the following steps-

$$I = I_{me} + I_{mc}/P_b + I_f / P_b \times Ps;$$

$$I_{me} = P_{ed} / P_b;$$

$$P_b = 1 - P_{ed};$$

$$I_{mc} = P_d / P_s;$$

$$P_s = 1 - P_d;$$

$$I_f = V_f / X^2$$

where I is the index of total selection intensity,

I_{me} = the index of selection due to embryonic mortality,

I_{mc} = the index of selection due to child mortality,

P_{ed} = the probability to die before birth,

P_b = the probability to survive till birth,

I_f = the index of selection due to fertility,

P_d = the proportion of premature deaths up to pre-reproductive age (i.e., deaths before 15 years of life),

P_s = the proportion of survivors up to the reproductive age and above $(1 - P_d)$,

V_f = the variance in the number of live births due to fertility and

X = is the mean number of live births

Results and Discussion

There are wide variations among the samples under consideration with regard to various demographic variables. The data presented in Table 12.1a shows that the average number of live births per married women, who completed their fertility, is comparatively higher among the Ahom women from Chengamari Tekela *Gaon* (4.55) than the women from Handique *Gaon* (3.97) and Hiloidari *Gaon* (3.91). The variance of fertility is conspicuously lower, particularly among the women from Handique *Gaon* (1.65). The proportion of premature death is also much lower in them.

Table 12.1a: Demographic variables used in calculating selection potential among the Ahom

Parameters	*Ahom*			
	Handique Gaon	*Chengamari Tekela Gaon*	*Hiloidari Gaon*	*Pooled*
Number of mothers aged 40 years and above	38	64	110	212
Number of pregnancies	154	306	441	901
Number of live births	151*	291	430	872
Number of embryonic deaths	4	15	11	30
Proportion of embryonic deaths	0.0260	0.0490	0.0249	0.0333
Number of dead children up to 15 years of age.	4	12	16	32
Proportion of child deaths	0.0265	0.0412	0.0372	0.0367
Survivors up to 15 years of age and above	147	279	414	840
Proportion of survivors	0.9735	0.9588	0.9628	0.9633
Number of live births per women of completed fertility	3.97 ± 0.21	4.55 ± 0.23	3.91 ± 0.19	4.11± 1.86
The variance of mean live births	1.65	3.46	3.95	3.46

Table: 12.1b: Demographic variables used in calculating selection potential among the Khamyang

Parameters	*Khamyang*				
	Chalapather Shyam Gaon	*Betbari Shyam Gaon*	*Balijan Shyam Gaon*	*Na-Shyam Gaon*	*Pooled*
Number of mothers aged 40 years and above	59	13	18	20	110
Number of pregnancies	194	39	61	58	352
Number of live births	186	35	58*	56*	335*
Number of embryonic deaths	8	4	4	3	19
Proportion of embryonic deaths	0.0412	0.1026	0.0656	0.0517	0.0540
Number of dead children up to 15 years of age.	8	1	3	4	16
Proportion of child deaths	0.0430	0.0286	0.0517	0.0714	0.0478
Survivors up to 15 years of age and above	178	34	55	52	319
Proportion of survivors	0.9570	0.9714	0.9483	0.9285	0.9522
Number of live births per women of completed fertility	3.15 ± 0.16	2.69 ± 0.31	3.22 ± 0.34	3.18 ± 0.22	$3.11 + 0.22$
Variance of mean live births	1.61	1.23	2.07	0.98	1.53

* includes twin birth.

Table 12.2a: Selection intensity among the Ahom

Population / Village	*Crow, 1958*			*Johnston & Kensinger, 1971*			
	I_m	I_f	I	I_{me}	I_{mc}	I_f	I
Ahom Handique *Gaon*	0.0272	0.1047	0.1348	0.0265	0.0272	0.1047	0.1639
Ahom Chengamari Tekela *Gaon*	0.0430	0.1671	0.2173	0.0515	0.0430	0.1671	0.2800
Ahom Hiloidari *Gaon*	0.0386	0.2583	0.3069	0.0255	0.0386	0.2583	0.3402
Ahom (Pooled)	0.0357	0.2048	0.2126	0.0344	0.0357	0.2048	0.4667

Table: 12.2b Selection Intensity among the Khamyang

Population / Village	*Crow, 1958*			*Johnston & Kensinger, 1971*			
	I_m	I_f	I	I_{me}	I_{mc}	I_f	I
Khamyang Chalapathar Shyam *Gaon*	0.0449	0.1623	0.2145	0.0430	0.0449	0.1623	0.2667
Khamyang Betbari Shyam *Gaon*	0.0293	0.1699	0.2042	0.1142	0.0293	0.1699	0.3307
Khamyang Balijan Shyam *Gaon*	0.0545	0.1996	0.2650	0.0728	0.0545	0.1696	0.3431
Khamyang Na-Shyam *Gaon*	0.0769	0.0969	0.1812	0.0576	0.0769	0.0969	0.2435
Khamyang (Pooled)	0.0502	0.1582	0.2163	0.0571	0.0502	0.1582	0.2858

Table 12.3: Selection intensities in population groups of Northeast India

Population	Crow (1958)			Johnston & Kensinger (1971)				Source
	I_m	I_f	I	I_{me}	I_{mc}	I_f	I	
ASSAM								
Ahom	0.036	0.205	0.213	0.034	0.357	0.205	0.267	Present study
Khmayang	0.050	0.158	0.216	0.057	0.050	0.158	0.286	Present study
Ahom	0.083	0.118	0.218	0.074	0.083	0.118	0.308	Sengupta, 2004
Khamti	0.179	0.113	0.312	0.005	0.179	0.113	0.319	Sarkar et al, 1994
Sonowal Kachari	0.192	0.141	0.360					Deka, 1978
Sonowal Kachari	0.185	0.179	0.364	0.103	0.185	0.179	0.541	Deka, 1980
Sonowal	0.167	0.163	0.358	0.053	0.167	0.163	0.432	Sengupta, 2004
Tengaponia Deori	0.108	0.181	0.309	0.073	0.108	0.181	0.403	Gogoi, 2006
Borgonya Deori	0.045	0.166	0.219	0.200	0.045	0.166	0.461	Gogoi, 2006
Dibongiya Deori	0.046	0.123	0.174	0.098	0.046	0.123	0.290	Gogoi, 2006
Boro Kachari	0.110	0.130	0.250					Guha & Mukherjee, 1990
Semsa	0.320	0.250	0.650					Choudhury et al, 2001
Semsa	0.471	0.098	0.616	0.038	0.471	0.098	0.677	Limbu & Khongdier, 2000
Pnar Khasi	0.104	0.234	0.363	0.047	0.104	0.234	0.428	Khongsdier et al. 2001
Oraon	0.098	0.131	0.243	0.102	0.098	0.131	0.369	Sengupta & Gogoi, 1997
ARUNACHAL PRADESH								
Singpho	0.437	0.406	1.020					Padmanabhan & Jaswal, 1982
Apatani (Guchi)	0.435	0.195	0.710					Padmanabhan, 1982
Apatani (Guth)	0.440	0.312	0.889					Padmanabhan, 1982
Gallong	0.750	0.180	1.070					Chakravarty & Ahmed, 1989
Khampti	0.388	0.398	0.934					Choudhury (Unpub)
Digaru Mishmi	0.813	0.264	1.294	0.273	0.813	0.264	1.922	Kotal & Barua, 2004
Muklom	0.107	0.188	0.315	0.021	0.107	0.188	0.342	Sarkar, 1997
MEGHALAYA								
Hajong	0.443	0.131	0.631	0.032	0.443	0.131	0.684	Barua, 1983
Jaintia	0.450	0.130	0.640					Deka, 1978
Jaintia	0.456	0.125	0.638	0.107	0.456	0.125	0.814	Deka, 1989
Pnar	0.236	0.133	0.401	0.201	0.236	0.133	0.680	Khongsdier, 1990
Pnar	0.106	0.281	0.416	0.127	0.106	0.281	0.596	Banerjee et al. 1994
Pnar	0.104	0.234	0.363	0.047	0.104	0.234	0.428	Khongsdier et al. 2001
War Khasi (Christian)	0.147	0.184	0.359	0.093	0.147	0.184	0.486	Khongsdier, 1994
War Khasi (Non-Christian)	0.180	0.225	0.446	0.084	0.180	0.225	0.567	Khongsdier, 1994
Dalu	0.499	0.231	0.847	0.031	0.499	0.231	0.897	Kapoor, 1997
Sankar Koch	0.262	0.070	0.351	0.038	0.262	0.070	0.402	Kotal & Sengupta, 2003
MANIPUR								
Hmar	0.072	0.250	0.340	0.028	0.072	0.250	0.379	Varte, 1998
Chote/Purum (I)	0.198	0.095	0.312					Dasgupta et al. 1985
Chote/Purum (II)	0.227	0.122	0.377					Dasgupta et al. 1985
NAGALAND								
Kheza	0.244	0.164	0.449	0.177	0.244	0.164	0.707	Devi et al. 1998

It is relevant from the Table 12.1b that among the Khamyang women from Balijan Shyam *Gaon* (3.22) have a comparatively higher average number of live births per married women than the Khamyang women from other three villages. The variance of fertility is lower among the women from Na Shyam *Gaon* (0.98).

In all the samples, the index according to the improvised method (Johnston and Kensinger, 1971) shows considerable higher values than that of the value obtained through original one (Crow, 1958), perhaps because of the inclusion of embryonic death in the former. Opportunity for selection in all the samples of Khamyang operates mainly through differential fertility. A similar observation has also been made by Sikdar (2008) among the different other population groups of Northeast India. In them in the total opportunity for selection contribution of postnatal mortality is greater than the prenatal (embryonic) wastage in Chalapather and Na-Shyam *Gaon* while it is just reverse in Betbari and Balijan Shyam *Gaon*. The index in all the Khamyang samples indicates a very moderate intensity of natural selection and the value is more towards the lower level of the range displayed by the Indian populations following Crow's (1958) method, which varies from 0.24 to 2.25 (Reddy and Lakshmanudu, 1979; Rao and Choudhury, 1986; Reddy and Chopra, 1990). This finding goes in conformity with several other studies done recently in different parts of India. Among those we can mention the studies among three endogamous population groups of Andhra Pradesh (Lakhsmi et al., 2005) and the studies among the tribal population groups of Madhya Pradesh (Basu et al., 1988). In Northeast India, index of selection intensity in the Digaru Mishmi of Arunachal Pradesh (Kotal and Barua, 2004) is reported as the highest followed by Gallong (Chakravarty and Ahmed, 1989), Singpho (Padmanabhan and Jaswal, 1982), Khampti (Choudhury unpublished) and Apatani (Guth; Padmanabhan, 1982) of Arunachal Pradesh while the lowest is observed in the Ahom of Assam. The state-wise comparison reveals that the population groups of Arunachal Pradesh show a higher index of intensity than the other states of Northeast India.

The value of selection intensity is relatively low in all the samples of both the populations in relation to the Indian ranges which indicate a low pressure of natural selection among them. The observed village-wise intra-group variation may be attributed to the varying contribution of the fertility and mortality indices. Such trend may be due to improved literacy rates, economic condition, better living condition, nutritional status, health awareness level, and excess to health care may have a positive impact on the lower contribution of mortality for the evolutionary mechanism through natural selection.

References

Basu, A 1967, 'Selection intensity in Pahiras', *Eugenics Quarterly,* vol.14, pp. 241 – 242.

Basu, A 1972, 'A demographic study of the Kota of Nilgiri Hills', *Journal of Indian Anthropological Society,* vol. 7, pp. 29 – 45.

Basu, S, Kshatriya, G & Jindal, A 1988, 'Fertility and mortality differentials among the tribal population groups of Bastar district, Madhya Pradesh, India', *Human Biology*, vol. 60, pp. 407–416.

Crow, JF 1958, 'Some possibilities of measuring selection intensities in man', *Human Biology,* vol. 30, pp.1-13.

Das, NK, & Ghosh, AK 1988, 'Two Muslims sects of 24 Parganas, West Bengal – a study in selection intensity', *Human Science,* vol. 37, pp. 237-242.

Debnath, SK, & Sen, T 1983, 'Selection intensity in the Toto of Jalpaiguri hills, West Bengal', *Journal of Indian Anthropological Society,* vol. 18, pp.79 – 81.

Deka, R 1980, 'Selection potential among the Sonowal Kachari of upper Assam,' *Bulletin of the Department of Anthropology, Dibrugarh University,* vol. 9, pp. 136-140.

Ghosh, AK 1970, 'Selection intensity in the Kota of Nilgiri Hills, Madras', *Social Biology,* vol. 17, pp. 224- 225.

Johnston, FE & Kensinger, KM 1971, 'Fertility and mortality differentials and their implications for micro-evolutionary change among the Cashinahua', *Human Biology,* vol. 43, pp. 356-364.

Lakhsmi, N, Rao, VT & Veerraju, P 2005, 'Opportunity of natural selection among three endogamous population groups of Andhra Pradesh', *Indian Journal of Human Genetics*, vol. 11, pp. 39-43.

Livingston, FB & Spuhler, JN 1965, 'Cultural determinants of natural selection,' *International Social Science Journal,* vol. 17, pp. 118-120.

Mukherjee, DP 1972, 'Some recent trends in population genetics in India' In *Genetics and our health*, I.C.M.R. Technical Report Series, vol. 20, pp. 234- 242.

Neel, JV & Chagnon, NA 1968, 'The demography of two tribes of primitive relatively uncultured American Indians', *Proceedings of the National Academy of Sciences,* vol. 59, pp. 680 – 689.

Rao, KR, & Choudhury, D 1986, 'Indices of selection intensity among four sub-groups of Telis of Vidarbha region, Maharastra', *Human Science,* vol. 35, pp. 328-333.

Reddy, BM & Chopra, VP 1990, 'Opportunity for natural selection among the Indian population', *American Journal of Physical Anthropology,* vol. 83, pp. 281- 296.

Reddy, PC & Lakshmanudu, M 1979, 'Indices of the opportunity of selection in Mala, Madiga, and other populations', *Journal of Indian Anthropological Society,* vol. 14, pp. 245-252.

Salzano, FM 1963, 'Selection intensity in Brazilian Caingong Indians', *Nature,* vol.199, no. 514.

Sengupta, S 2004, 'Opportunity for natural selection in North East Indian populations', *Bulletin of the Department of Anthropology, Dibrugarh University*, vol. 32, pp. 43-56.

Sengupta, S & Chakravarty, K 1998, 'Selection intensity in the Ahom of Assam', *Journal of Human Ecology,* vol. 9, no.1, pp. 83-85.

Sengupta, S & Kalita, M 1996, Selection intensity among the Sonowal of Assam. In S.Sengupta (Ed): *Peoples of North East India,* Gyan Publishing House, New Delhi, pp. 73-80.

Sikdar, M 2008, 'Influence of socio-economic transition on genetic structure: a case study in Upper Assam, India', *Annals of Human Biology*, vol. 35, pp. 112-120.

Spuhler, JN 1963, 'The scope of natural selection in man' in *Genetic selection in man,* ed.WJ Schull, University of Michigan Press, Ann Arbor, Michigan, pp. 1-111.

Talukdar, S 1971, 'Selection intensity in two Bagdi groups of 24 Parganas, West Bengal', *Journal of Indian Anthropological Society,* vol. 6, pp. 131-133.

Chapter - 13

Ethnoarchaeological Study on the Origin of Rice Cake Making in Assam

Anamika Gogoi Duarah

Assam is a land of a number of indigenous ethnic groups with their own cultural entities. The cultural configuration of this region including other parts of Northeast India has a deep root of its prehistoric origin, the remnants of which are still visible in the lifeways of the people of this region. This is an area where, if the clock of time is wound in an anticlockwise direction, then one may discover that the number of archaeological elements still survives in analogous form (Ashraf and Roy, 23: 2012). The geographical situation of this region is such that one encounters the ethnocultural groups showing different levels of technology ranging from food gathering, an incipient form of food production to the developed agricultural economy through their respective indigenous technology and cultural pattern.

Some evidence regarding the viability of the Neolithic lifestyle in this region is found in the existence of present-day ethnic economies as reminiscent of Neolithic cultures (Roy, 1981). Although there is no direct evidence of Neolithic economy of Northeast India, it is reasonably appropriate to believe that the Neolithic food producing and economy of Northeast India was analogous to that of the present-day shifting cultivation. This phenomenon can well be perceived through unindustrialized agricultural paraphernalia related to both past and present- where one will find no difference in the typology of the tools except using of two different raw materials in the form of stone and metal (iron) respectively.

Regarding the materials used in the manufacturing of the implements in the areas where cultivation of yam, varieties of tubers, rice, bottle gourd, and broad bean were the main cultivated plants. The cultivation was done with the help of digging stick and the ground stone Celts served as the blades of weeding hoes (Sharma, 1974:17-19). Similar evidences come from the Spirit cave in Northwest Thailand (Gorman, 1971) where there was a population who consumed large variety of plants such as bottle gourd, betel nut, almond, broad bean, Chinese water chestnut, pepper, cucumber, some of which were domesticated as early as 10,000 B.C. (the dates of these plants ranges from 11,690±560 B.P. to 7622 ± 300 B.P., which are the oldest dates for vegetative plant materials recovered in an archaeological context anywhere in the world).

The growing of the similar variety of vegetables, their remarkable consumption and above all the easiest method of their cultivation which is supposed to have been practiced since the Neolithic period is still in vogue in Northeast India and Southeast Asia. It compels one to believe at no drastic climatic and ecological changes in this part of the world for the last thousands of years. The specific geographical location of Northeast India, its ethnic composition, and the environmental condition has enabled a unique tradition in the midst of heterogeneity (Ashraf et al., 2012:138).

Pottery making, one of the most important ethno archaeological evidence manifests a settled village life in the passage of the cultural evolution of human being. Pottery is defined as a container or vessel made of clay that is baked to a certain temperature; and the artisans who are engaged in making pottery are known as potters (Singh, 2008). The tradition of making earthen pot originated during the Neolithic past in Assam and other parts of Northeast India (Sharma, 1966, 1978; Ashraf, 1990; Roy, 2004: 146). In a pan-Indian context, pottery is often found in association with certain cultural phases having Microlithic traditions (Sankalia, 1962: 65). The foothills of Assam witness the continuity of this tradition from time immemorial. The tradition of preparing verities of rice cake, especially in earthen utensil is an age-old process among the aboriginals of Assam in general and foothills in particular. Stone artifacts, particularly, the celts of Neolithic traditions-an example of archaeological corroboration are commonly found in association with the pottery in this region. For instance, the Kitchen Midden at Bambooti near Damra of Goalpara district holds a strong indication for the same.

Aims and Objectives

The present study aims to establish the continuity of the tradition of making rice cake since prehistoric past on the basis of ethnoarchaeological evidence.

Methodology

The study has been carried out by applying archaeological and ethnographic methods.

The Findings

Bambooti, geomorphologically a sloping site and culturally a habitation site is located on the right bank of the Bambooti *Chiring* (stream) III towards the north of the village Tengasoth, near Damra of Goalpara district. The site is located some 500 meters away from Assam–Meghalaya political boundary that passes through Tengasoth village. Bambooti is quite significant in the sense that for the first time in Northeast India it yielded artefacts consisting of pottery and ground lithic tools from a Kitchen Midden. The Bambooti excavations exhibit 45cms thick cultural deposit divisible into three layers.

Pottery collected from the surface and different layers of the excavated site at Bambooti are similar in fabric and types. These are either dull red or drab brown in colour. Grey ware is quite rare. In respect of the surface treatment of the pottery, none has been found with any kind of treatment.

The selection of substandard clay, improper levitation and use of medium-grained sand particles as tempered material make the pottery of Bambooti coarse in fabric and texture. All the pottery is devoid of any kind of surface treatment. The firing of pottery as a whole was not well controlled, and as such, most of them were ill fired. All the pottery is invariably handmade. Only two numbers of potsherds were cord impressed and a good number of rims were decorated with incised designs. Because of the ill fired state of the pottery, these become more susceptible to weathering and as such the state of preservation is not up to the mark.

The following types can well be deduced from the rim and base portions of the available potsherds: (i) pitcher *(Kalãh),* (ii) salver/platter *(Chãru),* (iii) shallow bowl, (iv) deep bowl, (v) culinary bowl, (vi) lid, (vii) urn, (viii) storage jar, and (ix) pot. In the entire collection, salvers outnumber the rest followed by culinary bowls.

The above Table 13.1 shows that the platters (*Salver=Chãru)*, are highest in number (26.84%) while the lid is lowest in number (2.01 %). The most interesting and important information provided by the above table is the introduction of salver (*Chãru)* at a time when ground and polished stone implements mostly in the form of shouldered celts still played a significant role in the life of the people. In the later stage, this particular

Plate 13.1 Six trenches laid out at Bambooti

type of earthenware (*Chãru)* continued more or less in the same form as a traditional item amongst the aboriginal communities, not only of the localities under study but the whole of Assam.

Table 13.1 Distribution of pottery types in Bambooti

Sl. No	*Type*	*Number*	*Percentage*
1	Pitcher	12	8.05
2	Platter /Salver (Sãru),	40	26.84
3	Shallow bowl	23	15.44
4	Deep bowl	24	16.11
5	Culinary bowl	14	9.39
6	Lid	3	2.01
7	Storage jar	17	11.41
8	Pot	5	3.35
9	Pitcher base	4	2.68
10	Body sherd	7	4.69
Total		149	99.97

Since the pottery from Bambooti are archaeologically *in situ* and occur together with the stone artifacts in the Kitchen Midden, therefore the age in absolute term of these pottery has been considered as a vital source of information to ascertain the chronology of the allied prehistoric material cultures of the foothills of Southwestern Assam. Three numbers of the pottery samples from Bambooti have been brought under the process of OSL dating. The estimated age of this pottery is shown in the following table.

Table 13.2 Quartz Optically Stimulated Luminescence (OSL) ages of the pottery samples along with elemental concentration (by ICP) used for dose rate calculation and equivalent dose (De)

Lab. No.	*Sample No.*	*U (ppm)*	*Th (ppm)*	*Potassium K (%)*	*Equivalent Dose (De) Gy*	*Dose rate (Gy/ka)*	*Age*
LD 1060	BBT/137 /2010	4.2±0.04	33.7±0.34	1.69±0.20	13.48±0.18	5.0±0.70	2.70±0.05 2700±0.05
LD 1061	BBT/138 /2010	3.1±0.03	26.9±0.27	1.70±0.20	14.14±0.22	4.30±0.06	3.29±0.07 3290±0.07
LD 1062	BBT/139 /2010	3.8±0.04	25.1±0.25	1.54±0.20	15.45±0.38	4.19±0.06	3.69±0.10 3690±0.05

ka=kilo years=1000 years; Gy=gray

Pottery in ethnographic perspective refers to that earthenware, which is used by the contemporary ethnic groups living in the foothill region of southern Assam. It includes both the varieties that are used in their day-to-day life as well as for occasional purposes. Some of these are handmade and some are wheel made. The ethnic groups acquire all these pottery from the markets or the vendors. The handmade pottery is made by the Hira potters and the wheel made potteries are made by the Kumar potters. The pottery types and their uses among these ethnic groups are more or less similar. No distinct variation is found in respect of the pottery types.

Table 13.3 Pottery types available among the contemporary ethnic groups

Sl. No	*Types of pottery*	*Name of the tribes*					
		Garo	*Rabha*	*Karbi*	*Bodo*	*Tiwa*	*Khasi*
1	Pitcher	Present	Present	Present	Present	Present	Present
2	Platter	Present	Present	Present	Present	Present	Absent
3	Shallow bowl	Present	Present	Present	Present	Present	Present
4	Deep bowl	Present	Present	Present	Present	Present	Absent
5	Culinary bowl	Present	Present	Present	Present	Present	Present
6	Lid	Absent	Absent	Absent	Absent	Absent	Absent
7	Storage jar	Present	Present	Present	Present	Present	Absent
8	Pot	Absent	Present	Present	Absent	Present	Absent

The above table indicates the use of Platter/Salver (*Charu*) by almost all the ethnic groups of Assam.

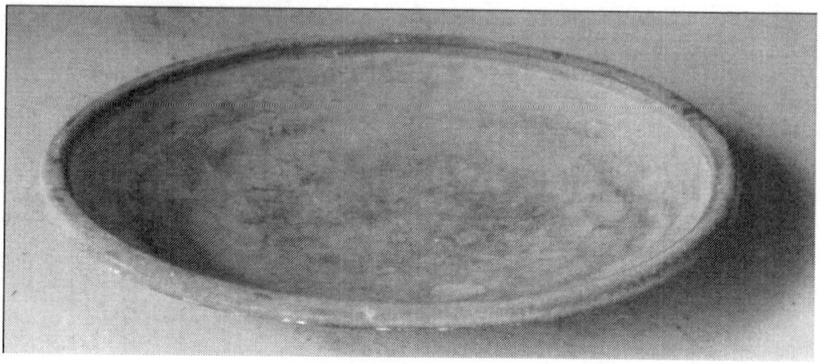

Plate 13.2 Pottery type: **Platter Local name:** ***Khola (Tiwa and Rabha)***

Utility: To prepare rice cakes, to fry rice, sesame, etc. Occasionally used as a platter to eat food.

Plate 13.3 Pottery type: Platter; Local name: Lungleafule (Karbi)

Utility: To prepare rice cakes, to fry rice, sesame, etc. Occasionally used as a platter to eat food

Discussion and conclusion

Presence of the highest numbers of platters especially from the excavated site of Bambooti suggests that the area was inhabited for a long period of time. The earthenware that was clustered with the stone artifacts, stand as strong supporting evidence to understand the actual utilization of the stone artifacts. The context of its occurrence clearly indicates that the stone artifacts were definitely used as household implements. At the same time, the presence of platter among the ethnic groups living in the neighbouring areas of Bambooti and their utilization especially for the making of rice cake indicates the continuity of this tradition since Neolithic age in this region. This definitely postulates an early phase of pottery culture as suggested by the OSL date of 3000 years BP.

Plate 13.4: 1st row: Contemporary Salver (Charu) from Bambooti, Damra

2nd row: Neolithic (OSL dating of 3000 years old) *Charu* from Bambooti excavations.

This is the earliest evidence of the use of Salver for rice cake (*Pitha* making *Charu*) in Assam.

References

Ashraf, AA 1990, *Prehistoric Arunachal: a study on the prehistory and ethnoarchaeology of Kamala Valley*, Directorate of Research, Itanagar.

Ashraf, AA & Roy, SK 2012, 'Ethno-archaeology of Northeast India' in *North-East India: a handbook of anthropology*, ed TB Subba, Orient BlackSwan, New Delhi, pp. 22-33.

Gorman, CF 1971, 'The Hoabinhian and after subsistence patterns in South Asia during the late Pleistocene and Early Recent periods', *World Archaeology*, vol. 2-3, pp. 300-320.

Roy, SK 1981, 'Aspects of neolithic agriculture and shifting cultivation, Garo Hills, Meghalaya', *Asian Perspective*, vol. XXIV, no. 2, pp. 193-220.

Roy, SK 2004, *Ceramics of Northeast India-ethnoarchaeological perspectives*, Himalayan Publishers, Itanagar, New Delhi.

Sankalia, HD 1962, *India courses towards urban life*, eds. RJ Braidwood & GRS Willey, Edinburg at the University Press, pp. 60-83.

Sharma, TC 1966, *Prehistoric archaeology of Assam - a study of Neolithic culture*. Ph.D. thesis, The University of London.

Sharma, TC 1974, 'Recent archaeological discoveries in Northeast India', *Puratattva*, no.7, pp. 17-19.

Sharma, TC 1978, 'On the significance of shouldered celts in the prehistory of Northeast India'. Paper presented at *Xth International Congress of Anthropological and Ethnological Sciences,* New Delhi.

Chapter - 14

Menstrual Cycle among the Meiteis of Manipur: Myths and Taboos

Zenia Thangjam and Sudipta Ghosh

Introduction

The onset of menstruation is one of the most important changes that occur among the girls during the adolescent years. Menstruation is a natural process experienced by women every month after attaining menarche and continues till menopause. Though menstruation is a natural process, it has been surrounded by taboos and secrecy in many societies. It is generally not discussed openly and instead alternatives such as 'crimson wave', 'mother nature', 'aunt flow' and 'on the rag' are used to refer to a woman's menstrual cycle (Lamborn, 2017). Menstruation is stigmatized in Indian society. This stigma is built up due to the traditional beliefs of impurity attached to the menstruating woman. Menstrual taboo is one such widespread social taboo. In other words, a menstrual taboo is a social restriction or negative connotation attached to menstruation and is not specific to one region or religious practice. According to Young and Bacdayan (1965), menstrual taboos are those customs often found in tribal societies that publicly restrict the behaviour of menstruation and applicable throughout most of the women's life. Manipur society is no exception to this in practicing such taboos. These social taboos are considered as not a curse but the benefit to Meitei society. They have been told by their forefathers what it ought to be done and generally, these became taboos. It is believed that the supernatural being always looks after them and those who break the rules are punished. This system operates in society in the form of 'Taboo' (Naorem, 2008). Meitei society has a culture of silence around menstruation which has been escalated by passing down generations after generations. The Meiteis consider menstrual cycle as inauspicious, unclean and impure. During this cycle, women are considered as untouchable. Interestingly, women themselves believe that too. Myths and mysteries have long been enveloped the aspect of menstruation and sometimes the taboos practiced during the menstrual cycle are perpetuated due to religious reasons. It is perhaps worth mentioning here that among the orthodox Nepali Chetris, families make every effort to get their daughter married before menarche. It is because they believe that pre-pubescent girls are pure (Bennet, 1983).

The topic of menstruation is caught in the strong web of socio-cultural practices. In the present study, the participants follow specific taboos like 'not entering kitchen', 'not entering religious places', 'not touching elders' and so on during the menstrual cycle. Similarly, a study conducted among the unmarried girls of Gazipur, East Delhi also suggested that majority (92.0%) of the participants follows the taboos such as 'not entering temples' and 'not performing prayers' during the menstrual cycle (Nair et al., 2007). Other studies conducted among the urban slum of Delhi (Talwar, 1997) and rural North India, (Singh, 2006) have also reported many menstrual taboos imposed on the daily life of women. Such taboos that are practiced during menstruation have impacted women's emotional state, perception, lifestyle, and most importantly health. Keeping these issues in mind, the present chapter tried to examine myths and taboos practiced and observed by the Meitei women of Imphal, Manipur during their menstrual cycle.

Materials and Methods

The present study was carried out among the adult Meiteis of Matai village of Imphal East district, Manipur. A total number of 63 respondents were interviewed. Of these 59 were women, who have already attained their menarche, and 4 were men. Information was gathered using a simple random sampling method. The respondents were informed about the purpose of the study and written consent was obtained. Care was taken about their willingness for participation and complete confidentiality was maintained throughout the study. To collect data, the interview was carried out using a structured questionnaire containing both closed and open-ended questions related to the menstrual cycle, menstrual taboos, and menstrual hygiene. The data was entered and analyzed using Microsoft Excel.

Results and Discussion

The results of the present study show that most of the participants (35.59%) attained menarche at the age of 13 years. The mean age of attaining menarche is 12.79±1.5 years, which ranges from 11 to 15 years (Table 14.1). Similar age at menarche (12.57±1.01 years) has been observed among

Table 14.1 Descriptive statistics of menstrual characters among the Meitei

Menstrual characters	*Mean (years)*	*Standard deviation (years)*	*Range (years)*	
			Min	*Max*
Age at menarche	12.79	1.15	11	15
Age at menopause	49.90	2.48	45	52

the Bengali girls of Tripura (Saha and Sil, 2015). On the other hand, studies conducted among the Mao Naga (Maheo, 2004) and Kabui Naga (Chakravarti, 1986) tribes of Manipur show a higher mean age of attaining menarche, as 14.59 years and 15.15 years respectively. The age at menopause of the Meitei women in the present study ranges from 45 to 52 years. Many (36.66%) of them attained their menopause at the age of 49 years. The mean age at menopause of the present study is found to be 49.90±2.48 years, which is considerably lower than the Ao Nagas of Nagaland (51.33 years; Purnungla and Sengupta, 2002). The reasons behind such variations could be multi-factorial. Menarche and menopause of woman are influenced by factors like nutritional status, size of family, medical facilities, educational levels, living standards, socio-economic conditions (Chandrika and Adilakshmi, 2014). So, the lower ages at menarche and menopause of the present study might be due to a comparatively better nutritional intake along with other environmental factors among the Meiteis.

It is observed that taboos related to religious practices are strictly followed by the majority of the Meitei women (Table 14.2). For example,

Table 14.2 Practice of taboos during the menstrual cycle among the Meitei

Statement/Activities	*Yes*	*%*	*No*	*%*
Discussing the topic in public	10	16.95	49	83.05
Attending social functions	59	100.00	0	0.00
Entering kitchen	0	0.00	59	100.00
Touching cooked food	1	1.70	58	98.30
Touch clean utensils	30	50.85	29	49.15
Touch anyone especially elders (preferably men)	26	44.07	33	55.93
Touching plants/ flowers	57	96.62	2	3.38
Plucking plants/ flowers	41	69.50	18	30.50
Cutting hair/nails	21	35.60	38	64.40
Doing prayers	0	0.00	59	100.00
Entering temple, shrines and sacred places	0	0.00	59	100.00
Touching infants	28	47.46	31	52.54
Using empty floor or mat to sleep	0	0.00	59	100.00
Using separate utensils	0	0.00	59	100.00
Taking bath daily	33	55.94	26	44.06
Washing hair daily	16	27.12	43	72.88

(Contd...)

Washing hair and taking a bath on the fifth day of menstruation	59	100.00	0	0.00
Wearing black pants only	0	0.00	59	100.00
Touching cupboards which have clean clothes	45	76.28	14	23.72
Having leftover foods by others	59	100.00	0	0.00
Having sex during cycle	0	0.00	59	100.00
Restrict food (esp. Sour)	44	74.57	15	25.43
Restrict meat	0	0.00	59	100.00
Washing all the clothes used during menstruation on the fifth day	59	100.00	0	0.00
Using clean clothes after having a bath on the fifth day	59	100.00	0	0.00
Seeing birds before bathing	59	100.00	0	0.00
Seeing men before bathing	59	100.00	0	0.00
Avoiding the chance of a dog eating the leftover food	0	0.00	59	100.00
Taking *Neem* twig while going out	0	0.00	59	0.00

they are tabooed to enter the temple (100.00%) and perform prayers (100.00%) during the menstrual cycle, which is similar like other part of the country (Nair et al., 2007). Perhaps, it is because menstruation is regarded as unclean and impure. Tamilselvi and Ramachandran (2012) also reported that in the Cuddalore district of Tamil Nadu, menstruation is considered as religiously impure and ceremonially unclean. More than half of the respondents of the present study follows taboos like 'not touching elders and men' (55.93%), 'not touching infants' (52.54%), 'not cutting hair and nails' (64.40%) during their menstruation cycle. In addition, the majority of them also follow social taboos like 'not touching cooked food' (98.03%), 'not washing hair' (72.88%), 'restrict sour fruits like lemon, wild apple, gooseberry, and banana flower' (74.57%) during the cycle.

Meitei women also believe that menstruation cycle completes only when they take bath and wash their hair on the fifth or sixth day of the cycle. A similar phenomenon of completing the menstruation cycle by taking a bath and washing hair is also observed among the inhabitants Simlitolas of Assam (Das, 2008). Moreover, taboos like 'not plucking basil plant and king chili', 'not touching water container', 'not fetching water from the pond', 'not touching bed of the father and husband', 'not crossing rope tied to the cow' still exists in Meitei society. It is found that the participants follow these taboos without knowing the reasons behind and consider their customs. They believe that misfortunes might occur to the husband and elders if they don't follow the taboos. A participant also mentioned that 'having sex during menstruation leads to birth defect'. Regarding menstrual taboo, the male participants opined that as Meitei society is a patriarchal society, most of the household chores are performed by the women folks. So, if they also work during menstruation, they will be exhausted and might get physical fatigue. Perhaps, considering the health status of these women folks and also to maintain family hygiene the taboos practiced. However, according

Table 14.3 Practice of taboos classified by educational attainment among the Meitei

Taboos	*Educational level*							
	Secondary		*Middle school*		*Higher secondary*		*Degree*	
	Yes	*No*	*Yes*	*No*	*Yes*	*No*	*Yes*	*No*
Discussing the topic in public	1 (5.89)	16 (94.11)	1 (20.00)	4(80.00)	0	6(100.00)	8(25.81)	23(74.19)
Attending social function	17(100.00)	0	5(100.00)	0	6(100.00)	0	31(100.00)	0
Entering kitchen	0	17(100.00)	0	5(100.00)	0	6(100.00)	0	31(100.00)
Touching cooked food	1(5.89)	16(94.11)	0	5(100.00)	0	6(100.00)	0	31(100.00)
Touching clean utensils	8(47.06)	9 (52.94)	0	5(100.00)	3 (50.00)	3 (50.00)	19 (61.30)	12(38.70)
Touching anyone especially elders (preferably men)	5 (29.42)	12(70.58)	1(20.00)	4 (80.00)	2(33.34)	6(66.66)	18 (58.07)	13(41.93)
Touching plants/flowers	16(94.11)	1(5.89)	4 (80.00)	1(20.00)	6(100.00)	0	31(100.00)	0
Plucking plants/flowers	14(82.36)	3(17.64)	2 (40.00)	3(60.00)	5 (88.34)	1(16.66)	20 (64.52)	11(35.48)
Cutting hair/nails	3 (17.65)	14 (82.35)	1 (20.00)	4 (80.00)	2 (33.34)	6 (66.66)	15 (48.39)	16 (51.61)
Doing prayers	0	17(100.00)	0	5(100.00)	0	6(100.00)	0	31(100.00)
Entering temples, shrines and sacred places	0	17(100.00)	0	5(100.00)	0	6(100.00)	0	31(100.00)
Touching infants	6 (35.30)	11 (64.70)	1(20.00)	4(80.00)	1(16.66)	5(83.34)	20 (64.52)	11(35.48)
Using empty floor/ mat to sleep	0	17 (100.00)	0	5 (100.00)	0	6 (100.00)	0	31 100.00)
Using separate utensils	0	17 (100.00)	0	5 (100.00)	0	6 (100.00)	0	31(100.00)
Taking bath daily	6 (35.30)	11 (64.70)	2 (40.00)	3 (40.00)	3 (50.00)	3 (50.00)	22 (70.97)	9 (29.03)
Washing hair daily	2 (11.77)	15 (88.23)	1 (20.00)	4 (80.00)	1 (16.66)	5(83.34)	12 (38.71)	19 (61.29)
Washing hair and taking bath on the fifth day of menstruation	17 (100.00)	0	5 (100.00)	0	6 (100.00)	0	31 (100.00)	0
Wearing black pants only	0	17 (100.00)	0	5 (100.00)	0	6 (100.00)	0	31 100.00)
Touching cupboards which have clean clothes	12(70.59)	5 (29.41)	1 (20.00)	4 (80.00)	5 (83.34)	1 (16.66)	27 (87.10)	4 (12.90)
Having leftover food from others	17(100.00)	0	5(100.00)	0	6(100.00)	0	31(100.00)	0
Having sex during cycle	0	17(100.00)	0	5(100.00)	0	6(100.00)	0	31(100.00)
Restrict food (esp. Sour)	15 (88.23)	2 (11.77)	4 (80.00)	1 (20.00)	4 (66.66)	2 (33.34)	21 (67.74)	10 (32.26)
Restrict meat	0	17 (100.00)	0	5 (100.00)	0	6 (100.00)	0	31 100.00)
Washing all the clothes used on the fifth day of menstruation	17 (100.00)	0	5 (100.00)	0	6 (100.00)	0	31 (100.00)	0
Using clean clothes after having a bath on the fifth day	17 (100.00)	0	5 (100.00)	0	6 (100.00)	0	31 (100.00)	0

(Contd...)

Using clean clothes after having a bath on the fifth day	17 (100.00)	0	5 (100.00)	0	6 (100.00)	0	31 (100.00)	0
Seeing birds before bathing	17(100.00)	0	5(100.00)	0	6(100.00)	0	31(100.00)	0
Seeing men before bathing	17(100.00)	0	5(100.00)	0	6(100.00)	0	31(100.00)	0
Avoiding the chance of a dog eating the leftover food	0	17(100.00)	0	5(100.00)	0	6(100.00)	0	31(100.00)
Taking neem twig while going out	0	17(100.00)	0	5 (100.00)	0	6 (100.00)	0	31 100.00)

Table 14.4 Practice of taboos classified by family type among the Meitei

Taboos	*Family types*			
	Nuclear family		*Joint family*	
	Yes	*No*	*Yes*	*No*
Discussing the topic in public	7(17.08)	34(82.92)	3(16.67)	15(83.33)
Attending social function	41(100.00)	0	18(100.00)	0
Entering kitchen	0	41(100.00)	0	18(100.00)
Touching cooked food	0	41(100.00)	0	18(100.00)
Touching clean utensils	12(29.27)	29(70.73)	8(44.45)	10(55.55)
Touching anyone especially elders (preferably men)	20(48.79)	21(51.21)	6(33.34)	12(66.66)
Touching plants/flowers	40(97.57)	1(2.43)	18 100.00)	0
Plucking plants/flowers	31(75.61)	10(24.39)	10 (55.56)	8 (44.44)
Cutting hair/nails	16(39.03)	25 (60.97)	5 (27.78)	13 (72.22)
Doing prayers	0	41(100.00)	0	18 (100.00)
Entering temples, shrines and sacred places	0	41(100.00)	0	18 (100.00)
Touching infants	21(51.22)	20 (48.78)	7 (38.89)	11 (61.11)
Using empty floor/ mat to sleep	0	41(100.00)	0	18 (100.00)
Using separate utensils	0	41(100.00)	0	18 (100.00)
Taking bath daily	23(56.10)	18 (43.90)	10 (55.56)	8 (44.44)
Washing hair daily	11(26.83)	30 (73.17)	5 (27.78)	13 (72.22)
Washing hair and taking a bath on the fifth day of menstruation	41(100.00)	0	18 100.00)	0
Wearing black pants only	0	41 100.00)	0	18 (100.00)
Touching cupboards which have clean clothes	34(82.93)	7 (17.01)	11 (61.12)	7 (38.88)
Having left over food by others	41(100.00)	0	18(100.00)	0
Having sex during cycle	0	41(100.00)	0	18 (100.00)
Restrict food (esp. sour)	33(80.48)	8 (19.51)	11 (61.11)	7 (38.89)
Restrict meat	0	41(100.00)	0	18 (100.00)
Washing all the clothes used on the fifth day of menstruation	41(100.00)	0	18 100.00)	0
Using clean clothes after having a bath on the fifth day	41(100.00)	0	18 100.00)	0
Seeing birds before bathing	41(100.00)	0	18 100.00)	0
Seeing men before bathing	41(100.00)	0	18 100.00)	0
Avoiding the chance of a dog eating the leftover food	0	41 100.00)	0	18
Taking neem twig while going out	0	41(100.00)	0	18 (100.00)

*Percentages are given in the parenthesis.

Table 14.5: Frequency and percentage of the maintenance of menstrual hygiene among the Meitei

Menstrual hygiene index	*Yes*	*%*	*No*	*%*
Toilet and bath-room facilities	59	100.00	0	0.00
Take bath daily	33	55.93	26	44.07
Usage of sanitary napkins	44	74.57	15	25.43
Usage of intimate wash	33	55.93	26	44.07
Physical illness (abdomen pain, back pain, and cramps)	24	40.67	35	59.33

Table 14.6: Maintenance of menstrual hygiene cross-classified by educational attainment and family type among the Meitei

Menstrual hygiene index	*Educational level*				*Family type*	
	Secondary	*Middle school*	*Higher secondary*	*Degree*	*Nuclear*	*Joint*
Usage of clothes	6 (35.29)	1 (20.00)	1 (16.66)	7 (22.58)	12 (29.26)	3 (16.66)
Usage of sanitary napkins	11 (64.71)	4 (80.00)	5 (83.34)	24 (77.42)	29 (70.74)	15 (83.34)
Usage of intimate wash	7 (41.17)	1 (20.00)	5 (83.34)	20 (64.51)	21 (51.21)	12 (66.66)
Usage of soap	10 (58.83)	4 (80.00)	1 (16.66)	11 (35.49)	20 (48.79)	6 (33.34)
Take bath daily	6 (35.30)	2 (40.00)	3 (50.00)	22 (70.97)	23 (56.10)	10 (55.56)

*Percentages are given in the parenthesis.

to previous researchers, it is a misconception to consider menstruation as impure, and hence these taboos shouldn't be followed (Das, 2008).

In Meitei society, adolescent girls have to go through a ritual called 'Laiming louba' (which means taking the name of God) before reaching their probable age at menarche. For this, the mothers would take her to the temple or will perform *Puja* (prayer) at home by Brahmin or priest, which might be for the wellbeing of their fertility and health (Devi, 2013).

According to Hindu mythology, women folks for the first-time experienced menstruation when Lord *Indra* (the king of Gods) beheaded *Vishwaroopacharya* (the second teacher of Gods). Since Lord *Indra* killed a Brahmin, he got cursed. To get rid of it he distributed the curse amongst the land, water, tree, and the women folks. The women from that day on started menstruating every 28-30 days and got the ability to give childbirth. As a result, it is believed that menstruation is a curse, also because blood is considered toxic and unclean in this society. Perhaps that is why touching a menstruating woman is considered as an inappropriate act (Swami, 1975). It is believed that if menstruating women cooked food and served to men and elders, it will bring bad luck to them. Similarly, few previous studies also reported unpleasant attitudes towards menstruating women by the family members (Drakshavani and Venkata, 1994; Dasgupta and Sarkar, 2008). In this connection, the significance of the day of attaining menarche is crucial in Meitei society. For example, Meitei women believe that if they attain their menarche on Wednesday, they become a prosperous woman who is believed to have all the luck.

An attempt is made in this chapter to analyze the role of educational attainment and family type of practices of the menstruation taboos. Taboos like 'not plucking plants or flowers' (44.44%); 'not touching infants' (61.11%) and 'not touching cupboards' (38.88%) are found to be practiced more among the Meitei women living in joint families (Table 14.3 and Table 14.4). However, with educational attainment and social awareness, many taboos that were practiced earlier such as 'not sleeping in the daytime'; 'using separate utensils'; 'sleeping on the mat or floor'; 'not going to the fields'; 'staying in menstrual hut' are not practiced anymore. Overall, educational attainment also has a role in menstrual hygiene practices in Meitei society (Table 14.6). For example, it is observed that women with graduation and post-graduation degrees mostly use sanitary napkins (77.42%) and intimate wash (64.50%) during their menstrual cycle.

It is observed that proper toilet and bathroom facilities are present in all the participants' houses. Little more than half of the participants (55.94%) took bath daily during the menstrual cycle. Some of them (44.06%) took bath only on the fifth day of the cycle as taboo of not bathing during menstruation is still practiced among them. Interestingly, a similar kind of menstrual taboo of 'not taking bath during menstruation' is also observed among the women of Mansoura, Egypt (El-Gilany et al., 2005).

The majority (74.57%) of the participants in this community preferred to use sanitary napkins instead of clothes as menstrual absorbents. Proper disposal of the used material is evident in this community. They wash the sanitary napkins with water, wrap with newspaper and dispose of it in the dustbin. On the other hand, those who use clothes (25.43%), they wash it, dry properly and keep them to use again for the next cycle. A study conducted by Kamaljit et al. (2012) suggested that the majority (73.7%) of the girls of Amritsar, Punjab also preferred to use sanitary napkins. While the study conducted by Khanna et al. (2005) reported that the majority (75.0%) of the adolescent girls of Rajasthan use clothes during menstruation. Little more than half of the respondents of the present study (55.93%) prefer to use an intimate wash to clean their reproductive organs during the cycle.

The results of the present study indicate that some of the participants (40.67%) have a physical illness such as abdomen pain, back pain, and cramps during the first three days of their menstrual cycle (Table 14.5). It is observed that although the Meitei women still practiced taboos related to menstruation, they have become more aware of menstrual hygiene.

Conclusion

From this study, it is observed that a strong belief of menstruation as unclean and impure still exist in Meitei society and the taboos related to menstruation continue to be practiced even today. Surprisingly, women folks of this community generally practice the taboos without knowing the reason behind or questioning much about it. In Indian culture, Hindu society is braided into a set of traditions, myths, and misconceptions about menstruation (Kaundal and Thakur, 2014). Menstruating women are forced into seclusion during this time through the taboos, perhaps because there are many misconceptions about the knowledge on menstruation. Several studies have reported this aspect (Ahuja and Tewari, 1995; Singh, 2006; Paul, 2007) and showed that there is a low level of understanding and awareness regarding menstruation among the girls when they attain their menarche. The taboos and negative attitudes of parents in discussing the issues related to menstruation have grossly discouraged young girls to understand it biologically. This might have led to many serious health problems. To put an end to the beliefs of these taboos associated with menstruation, a change in perception is required. The methods to bring about such change needs to be discussed.

The limitations of this study are less variable, time constraint, and less sample size. Hence, a similar study on a larger scale may help to arrive at a broader and more substantial conclusion.

References

Ahuja, A & Tewari, S 1995, 'Awareness of pubertal changes among adolescent girls', *Journal of Family Welfare*, vol. 41, no. 1, pp. 46-50.

Bennet, L 1983, *Dangerous wives and sacred sisters: social and symbolic roles of high caste woman in Nepal*, Columbia University, New York.

Chakravarty, R 1986, *The people of Manipur*, B.R. Publishing Company, New Delhi.

Chandrika, T & Adilakshmi, T 2014, 'Menarche and menopause among the Yanadi tribal women', *IOSR Journal of Humanities and Social Science*, vol. 19, no. 9, pp. 1-3.

Das, S 2008, 'Menstruation as pollution: taboos in Simlitola, Assam', *Indian Anthropologist,* vol. 38, no. 2, pp. 29-42.

Dasgupta, A & Sarkar, M 2008, 'Menstrual hygiene: how hygienic is the adolescent girl?', *Indian Journal of Community Medicine,* vol. 33, no. 2, pp. 77-80.

Devi, TM 2013, 'Meitei women and culture of Manipur', *Journal of Business Management and Social Sciences Research,* vol. 2, no. 1.

Drakshavani, DK & Venkata, RP 1994, 'A study on menstrual hygiene among rural adolescent Indian girls', *Indian Journal of Medical Science,* vol. 48, no. 6, pp. 139-143.

El-Gilany, AH, Badawi, K & El-Fedawy, S 2005, 'Menstrual hygiene among adolescent schoolgirls in Mansoura, Egypt', *Reproductive Health Matters*, vol. 13, pp. 147-152.

Kamaljit, K, Arora, B & Singh, KG 2012, 'Social beliefs and practices associated with menstrual hygiene among the adolescent girls of Amritsar, Punjab, India', *Journal International Science Academy*, vol. 25, no. 2, pp. 96-70.

Kaundal, M & Thakur, B 2014, 'A dialogue on menstrual taboo', *Indian Journal of Community Health,* vol. 26, no. 2, pp. 192-195.

Khanna, A, Goyal, RS & Bhaswar, R 2005, 'Menstrual practices and reproductive problems: a study of adolescent girls in Rajasthan', *Journal Health Management*, vol. 7, pp. 91-107.

Lamborn, AM 2017, *It's About 'that time' to break the cycle: a rhetorical analysis of challenging menstrual taboos*. Retrieved from http://digitalcommons.acu.edu/etd/67.

Maheo, LM 2004, *The Mao Naga tribe of Manipur-a demographic anthropological study*, Mittal Publications, New Delhi.

Nair, P, Grover, V & Kannan, A 2007, 'Awareness and practices of menstruation and pubertal changes amongst unmarried female adolescents in a rural area of East Delhi', *Indian Journal of Community Medicine*, vol. 32, no. 2, pp. 156.

Naorem, M 2008, *Taboos in Manipur*. Retrieved from http://ezinearticles.com/?Taboos--in--Manipur&id=1815677.

Paul, D 2007, *Knowledge and practices of adolescent girls regarding reproductive health with special emphasis on hygiene during menstruation: a report of an ICMR. funded research project*, National Institute of Public Cooperation and Child Development (NIPCCD), New Delhi.

Purnungla & Sengupta, S 2002, 'Menarche and menopause among the Ao Naga women of Nagaland, India', *Journal of Human Ecology*, vol. 13, no. 4, pp. 323-324.

Saha, S & Sil, KS 2015, 'Age at menarche and its relationship to body mass index and waist circumference among adolescents Bengali girls of Tripura, Northeast India', *International Journal of Multidisciplinary Approach*, vol. 2, no. 1, pp. 233-237.

Singh, AJ 2006, 'Place of menstruation in the reproductive lives of women of rural north India', *Indian Journal of Community Medicine*, vol. 31, no. 1, pp. 10-14.

Swami, CB 1975, *Srimad bhagwatam canto, 6(2), Ch.13*, The Bhaktivedanta Book Trust.C., Mumbai.

Talwar, R 1997, *A study of the health profile of adolescent girls in an urban slum and their knowledge about reproductive health.* MD Thesis, Department of Preventive and Social Medicine, Maulana Azad Medical College, New Delhi, pp. 155.

Tamilselvi, K & Ramachandran, S 2012, 'Socio-cultural taboos concerning menstruation: a micro level study in the Cuddalore district of Tamil Nadu, India', *International Journal of Scientific and Research Publications*, vol. 2, no. 8.

Young, F & Bacdayan, A 1965, 'Menstrual taboos and social rigidity', *Ethnology*, vol. 4, no. 2, pp. 225–240. doi:10.2307/3772731.

Chapter - 15

The Sedimentary Record of the Pre-Historic Sites of the Ganol-Rongram Valley, Garo Hills

Sukanya Sharma

Introduction

Ganol-Rongram Valley in Garo hills, Meghalaya have been an area of interest for Archaeologist from the middle of the last century. Almost thirty sites were discovered during explorations from the 1950s to the late 1980s by Sharma and Goswami. In 1959 Goswami and Bhagabati from the Department of Anthropology, Gauhati University had published a paper '*A Typological Study of Shouldered Celts from Renchengiri (Garo Hills)*'. In the Annual Indian Archaeological Review of 1963-64 published by the Archaeological Survey of India, finds from Rongram were first reported. They were two broken pieces of ring-stones and a bone, besides seventy-five celts of various shapes. In the next consecutive year finds from Chitra Abri, Dipu Abri and Rongram Chimbima were reported. In the next consecutive year finds from Rangigir, Selbalgiri and Thusekgiri were reported. In the Annual Indian Archaeological Review of 1966-67 Sharma and Goswami reported the first evidence of pebble tools similar to the Sumatraliths reported from Southeast Asia. Sharma studied the collection of tools from Garo Hills as part of his doctoral research and produced the first detailed study of the tools from Garo Hills. An inventory of the Neolithic tool types of Garo Hills was developed (Sharma, 1966). This established a strong foundation for future prehistoric research in the area. In the book '*Prehistory and Protohistory of India and Pakistan*' by Sankalia (1974), besides the Neolithic tool types, hand axe type tools and choppers and scrappers recovered from the pebbly gravel base of the terrace in Rongram, exposed as a result of fresh road cutting in the January of 1970 was described (Sankalia, 1974). Besides Rongram from Molchigiri and Rongchigiri, two other sites in the valley pebble choppers and scrappers were collected by Sankalia and Sharma. But only at Rongram and Rongdu, they were found in a stratified context while in the other sites they were found mixed with the Neolithic tools on the exposed cultural layer for which it was difficult to construct a Stone Age sequence for Garo Hills.

The focus of this chapter is on the specific characteristic of the deposits on which the tools occur. This is part of an already completed work on the development of a regional archaeological structure (Sharma, 2007). Initiated by ecological considerations this model was adopted to understand the adaptability conditions developed by the prehistoric inhabitants of the area. Situated between two different environmental systems the monsoonal tropics and the tropical rainforest zone the regional ecology of Northeast India have had a major role in the growth and development of human culture in the area.

The probable geomorphological processes that resulted in the formation of these thick deposits are tectonics caused by the upliftment of the Himalayas during the Middle Pleistocene (Himalayan Orogeny 4), excessive soil stripping caused by drier climatic conditions during the 18,000 BP glacial maxima and reworking of these sediments in the subsequent periods resulting in the deposition of the much finer material or alluvium. These fertile colluvial-alluvial deposits capable of supporting a very rich plant life, including edible foods and organic raw material, ample hunting ground and gathering area and cultivating fields, presence of perennial sources of water, dolerite dykes and river pebbles for making tools and dry ground surface to be used as dwellings even during rainy season are some of the resources which has governed human behaviour in the area. Distribution of the archaeological record conforms to the distribution of these resources. Artifact density and distribution reflect the pattern of resource utilization (Sharma, 2007).

Various post-depositional factors have operated in the area disturbing the accumulated artefactual material. The upper layers of the Rongram Inspection Bangalow site have been sliced down for the construction of a building, a locality of the site Gawak Abri, called Miching Grenchep is presently under use as homestead land, etc. All these various activities have caused considerable lateral and vertical movements of artifacts in certain areas resulting in their modified distribution and frequency. As a result of the study area, stray finds are often recorded but in the absence of proper context, their use is limited. This can be identified as one of the limitations of the data.

Methodology

By conducting site surveys areas with high artifact density are identified and plotted on a map through site surveys geographical and geological data was collected. A combination of site survey and landscape approach is adopted for recovering and interpreting the archaeological record of the Ganol-Rongram valleys. The basic data recovery technique in the present study consisted of systematic surface documentation of artifacts directed towards producing distributions of artifacts within a carefully controlled space. All artifacts were documented and recorded at the site itself and no artifact collection was made. An area with high artifact density is called a site and all other finds within a radius of one kilometer are identified as localities of that site in the study area. Sediments collected from specific depths were chemically analyzed. The type of analysis undertaken consisted of Calcium Carbonate determination by Rapid Titration method (Piper, 1978), Organic Carbon determination was done by the Colorimetric method, PH determination by BDH indicator papers and the soil colour was classified according to the Munsell Soil colour chart. Mechanical analysis of the samples was undertaken by Pipette method for identifying the type of sediments that constitute the alluvium and colluvium and their individual percent. The results of these various tests are used in the interpretations below. The sediments were also investigated using scientific techniques like X-Ray Diffractometer (XRD). XRD is a powerful tool to identify minerals in the soil, based on d-spacing and relative peak intensities.

Typology of Sites

In the Ganol- Rongram valleys there are surface sites, sub-surface sites, and buried sites. These characteristic features of these categories will be dealt with under the site description below. But it is noteworthy to mention that even though human habitation continues the appreciable destruction of the sites has not taken place. Certain situations under which the sites in the area are preserved will be discussed after each site has been discussed in detail. The few surface sites are on the bedrock. The bedrock is exposed at an altitude of 600 m msl at Missimagiri, which is a flat top tableland. Deposition is very thin on this surface on which lithic tools have been found. At Chitra Abri and Mokbol Bichik on the slope of the alluvial mound dolerite dyke exposures are very close to the bedrock. As dyke material was profusely used by the prehistoric settlers for making tools these are found littered on the bedrock surface with cores, flakes, and chips. Rongram is a sub-surface site. The top layers of the alluvial mound on which tools are found had been sliced down for the construction of an Inspection Bungalow exposing the implementiferous layer. Tools have been found in a half-buried condition at this site. Didami, Gawak Abri, Ida Bichik are fully buried sites. Various post-depositional processes act on the artifacts in these sites. On the basis of the state of preservation sites in this study are classified into three categories as follows:

Type1: In situ sites, which were buried immediately or shortly after their abandonment and remain buried. The degree of patination on lithics is nil or limited in such sites and this is the main criteria for identifying sites of type1.

Type2: In situ sites exposed by the removal of the overlain sediments without considerably disturbing the original arrangement of the tools.

Type3: Locations with scattered artifacts on the surface. The original sedimentary context is unknown.

Sites will be described below depending on which type they belong to. Under type1 there are two sites Gawak Abri and Didami. Rongram

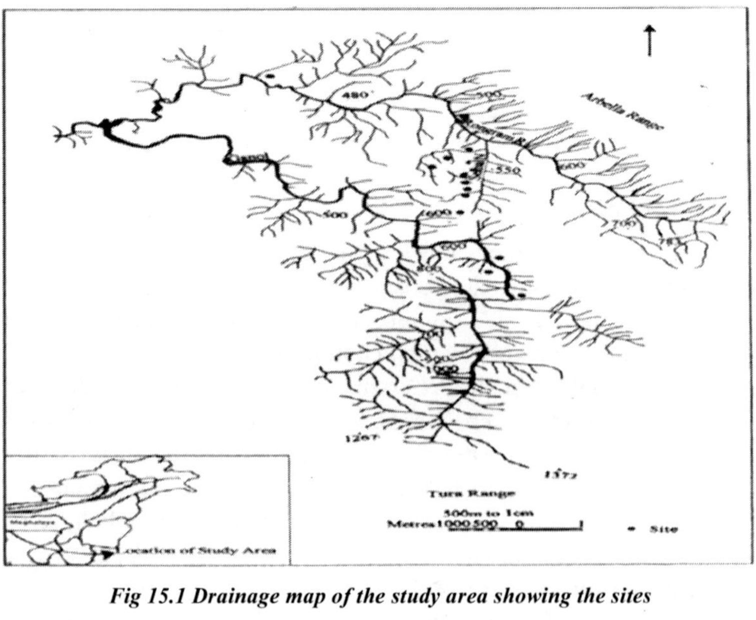

Fig 15.1 Drainage map of the study area showing the sites

Inspection Bangalow, Ida Bichik, Bibragiri, Missimagiri, Selbal Bichik, Mokbol Bichik II, are sites under type2. The two other sites, namely Chitra Abri, Mokbol Bichik I fall under type3. From Rongram Inspection Bangalow, Gawak Abri, Ida Bichik and Didami samples of the alluvium and colluvium were collected.

Gawak Abri- It is located approximately 8 km downstream from the source of the river Rongram. The river Rongram flows one and a half kilometer away to the west of the site. On its southeastern side less than half km away is the Selbal stream, a first-order channel of the river Rongram and on its southern side is the Ida stream, a second-order stream of the same river system. The altitude is approximately 550 m msl and the area is 3 sq km. Artifacts were recovered from the northern side of the mound. The deposit within which the tools are found is almost six meters in thickness on the southern side of the mound while on the northern side it is about four meters in thickness. The implementiferous layer is overlain by a deposit of 1 and 1/2 m on the northern side of the mound. The alluvium is strong brown in colour. There is a slight difference in shade between the alluvium above 47 cm and the alluvium below it. The former is 7.4 Yr, 5/8 while the latter is 7.5 Yr 4/6. Sedimentological analysis of the deposit has revealed that above 47 cm the percent of clay is much more than the lower levels while the percent of total silt also is comparatively higher. But the percent of sand both coarse and fine is very high in the bottom layers. In 20 gms of sediment, the percent of sand was 68.85 percent. The rest of the sediments consisted of silt of which coarse silt was 26.7 percent. In the upper levels also the percent of coarse silt was similar. This indicates that the material is coarse and not well sorted. Percent of clay is negligible in the whole deposit and the percent of medium and fine silt is also very low. The coarse sand particles and the quartz gravels separated by dry sieving are very angular. This indicates that the material has not been transported from a very long distance. The alluvium is acidic and the organic carbon content is high. Dolerite dyke exposures are present in the southern and southwestern corner of the site.

The total thickness of the implementiferous layer is almost one meter. Cultural material collected from the site consisted of lithic tools and pottery. A total number of 123 lithic artifacts and 50 potsherds were collected from a 2/2 m trial trench. It can be called a single culture site on the basis of the typological character of the tools. The lithic assemblage consisted of ground and polished celts, short axes, chipped celts, and a very high percent of micro size flakes, some of which were probably used. A thin patina is seen on the surface of the tools. The flake scars are sharp and fresh. The pottery consisted of two varieties classified on the basis of colour and fabric. One was very coarse black colour pottery and the other was also of coarse variety but comparatively finer with a thin grey slip. Very few rim sherds were recovered for reconstructing the shapes. The pottery from this site has been dated to 2.3 +/-0.2 ka (LD1727) which confirms that the site belonged to the late Neolithic phase.

Didami- This site is located at a distance of seven km towards the north, from the source of river Ganol. It is at an altitude of 916 m msl. It is on the bank of a first order stream called Didami Biphek which joins the Didami Chiring, a tributary of Ganol. The Ganol flows at a distance of about two and a half km on the southwestern side of the site. An exposed section on the eastern side of the mound was studied. This section is very close to the stream Didami Biphek, which flows on the eastern boundary on the bedrock. All other secondary and tertiary lithostratigraphic units are unexposed. The pebbly horizon identified in the region as Tertiary-Quaternary boundary is partially exposed. On it, the Quaternary alluvial deposit is seven meters thick. The implementiferous layer is approximately two meters thick. It sits on a meter-thick deposit and is buried by three-and-a-half-meter deposit. The eastern section is exposed for almost half a kilometer but the implementifeorus layer is not visible all along the section. The horizontal extent of the tool-bearing layer is approximately 3m. 65-70 percent of the colluvium consists of sand. Rest is silt while the percent of clay is negligible. Dolerite dykes in a half-buried state are noticed on the eastern side of the mound. The lithic assemblage solely consists of bifacially flaked artifacts, blade flakes, and probably utilized flakes. Seventy-five lithic artifacts were exposed in the two-meter section. Patination is almost absent and the flake scars are sharp and fresh. The total extent of the site could not be ascertained as the area is thickly vegetated. On the surface of the mound, no tools were found. The deposit on the western side of the mound is even thicker. An approximately two-meter vertical section exposed on the western side of the mound revealed no cultural material. In the study area, the altitude of this site is the highest. An XRD analysis of the deposit consisting of the tool bearing layer produced some intriguing results. The most important of this is the presence of calcite in the deposit. In both the strong brown and yellowish-brown colluvium calcite is present. Quartz is present in all samples as a primary mineral. According to Papachristodoulou and co-workers (2006), quartz is an indigenous mineral present in soil which might indicate the origin of the soil from primary rocks. The abundance of quartz indicates that soil samples might be from the Piedmont area (Ravisankar et al., 2010). This is a common feature of soil found all across

Northeast India. Kaolinite is identified in all the soil samples in varying quantity. The tabulated data indicates that kaolinite is the second most abundant mineral after quartz in all the samples (Fig 15.2 and 15.3) and (Table 15.1 and 15.2). Kaolinite is also a common mineral found in soils all across Northeast India. Biotite is identified in the mineralogical composition of the soil. The presence of a group of non-clay minerals, such as feldspars, biotite, hornblende, etc., which represent igneous material, may indicate the occurrence of volcanic-ash (Grim, 1953: 362).

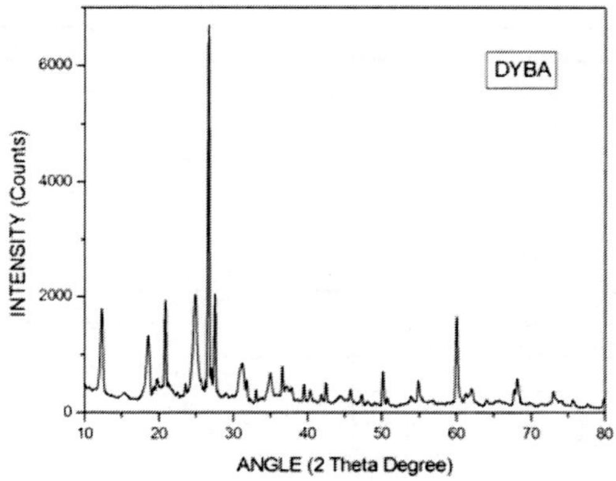

Fig 15.2 XRD Graph of Didami Yellowish Brown Alluvium/Colluvium

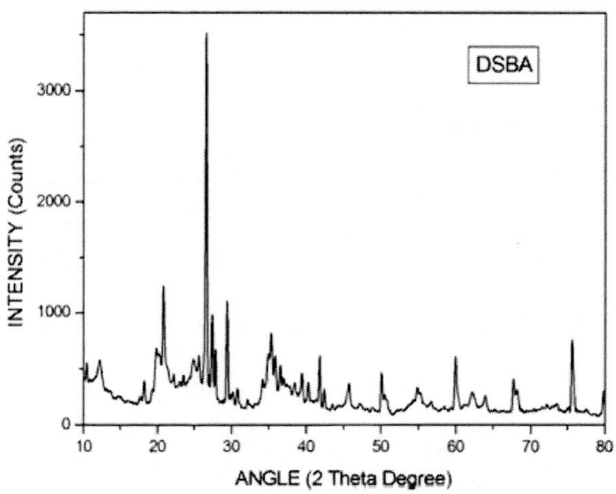

Fig 15.3 XRD Graph of Didami Strong Brown Alluvium

Table 15.1 XRD table of Didami Yellowish Brown Alluvium/Colluvium

Sl.No.	*Mineral group*	*d=λ/2sinθ (in Å)*	*Mineral identification*
		DYBA	
1	Amphiboles	8.325552494	Hornblende
2	Kaolins	7.161561673	Kaolinite
6	Kaolins	4.486145848	Kaolinite
7	Oxides, Hydroxides	4.255315045	Quartz
8	Kaolins	3.943216947	Kaolinite
9	Oxides, Hydroxides	3.769287033	Hematite
11	Oxides, Hydroxides	3.335870309	Quartz
12	Oxides, Hydroxides	3.235618594	Rutile
14	Feldspars	2.993835595	Anorthite
15	Feldspars	2.861297994	Anorthite
19	Kaolins	2.644437813	Kaolinite
20	Kaolins	2.563777385	Kaolinite
\21	Oxides, Hydroxides	2.453477657	Goethite
22	Oxides, Hydroxides	2.417950127	Goethite
23	Oxides, Hydroxides	2.374356988	Quartz
24	Oxides, Hydroxides	2.280223511	Quartz
25	Oxides, Hydroxides	2.233666098	Quartz
26	Oxides, Hydroxides	2.19677421	Quartz
27	Oxides, Hydroxides	2.159674289	Quartz
28	Oxides, Hydroxides	2.126766395	Quartz
29	Micas	2.036826607	Biotite
30	Oxides, Hydroxides	1.978417731	Quartz
31	Oxides, Hydroxides	1.918348098	Quartz
33	Oxides, Hydroxides	1.854629882	Quartz
34	Oxides, Hydroxides	1.817053623	Quartz
37	Kaolins	1.670755113	Kaolinite
38	Kaolins	1.618187306	Kaolinite
39	Oxides, Hydroxides	1.539898982	Quartz
40	Kaolins	1.511449853	Kaolinite
42	Oxides, Hydroxides	1.451664121	Hematite
43	Oxides, Hydroxides	1.381615691	Quartz
44	Oxides, Hydroxides	1.373829262	Quartz
45	Oxides, Hydroxides	1.29390471	Hematite
46	Oxides, Hydroxides	1.276979008	Hematite
47	Oxides, Hydroxides	1.255487467	Hematite
48	Oxides, Hydroxides	1.228450131	Hematite

Table 15.2 XRD table of Didami Strong Brown Alluvium/Colluvium

Sl.No.	*Mineral Group*	*d=λ/2sinθ (in Å)*	*Mineral identification*
		DSBA	
1	Amphiboles	8.469308652	Hornblende
2	Amphiboles	8.141331898	Hornblende
3	Kaolins	7.222985468	Kaolinite

(Contd...)

10	Kaolins	4.462592924	Kaolinite
11	Oxides, Hydroxides	4.26140071	Quartz
16	Oxides, Hydroxides	3.472552299	Quartz
17	Oxides, Hydroxides	3.345133211	Quartz & Illite
18	Oxides, Hydroxides	3.251310314	Quartz
19	Oxides, Hydroxides	3.199604282	Quartz
21	Feldspars	2.95735792	Anorthite
22	Feldspars	2.898105592	Anorthite
26	Kaolins	2.563777385	Kaolinite
27	Kaolins	2.539421139	Kaolinite
29	Oxides, Hydroxides	2.456406638	Goethite
30	Oxides, Hydroxides	2.428398441	Goethite
32	Oxides, Hydroxides	2.284406422	Quartz
33	Oxides, Hydroxides	2.237668877	Quartz
34	Oxides, Hydroxides	2.159674289	Quartz
35	Oxides, Hydroxides	2.128926715	Quartz
36	Micas	2.077665022	Biotite
37	Micas	2.043402093	Biotite
38	Oxides, Hydroxides	1.981498532	Quartz
39	Oxides, Hydroxides	1.925275822	Quartz
40	Oxides, Hydroxides	1.888393221	Quartz
41	Oxides, Hydroxides	1.859985364	Quartz
42	Oxides, Hydroxides	1.818074652	Quartz
43	Oxides, Hydroxides	1.805402618	Quartz
44	Kaolins	1.751431353	Kaolinite
45	Kaolins	1.736072758	Kaolinite
46	Kaolins	1.68612831	Kaolinite
47	Kaolins	1.672024073	Kaolinite
48	Kaolins	1.660264884	Kaolinite
49	Kaolins	1.622127242	Kaolinite
50	Oxides, Hydroxides	1.576994839	Quartz
51	Oxides, Hydroxides	1.556572023	Quartz
52	Oxides, Hydroxides	1.541652924	Quartz
53	Oxides, Hydroxides	1.490664584	Hematite
54	Oxides, Hydroxides	1.453801124	Hematite
56	Oxides, Hydroxides	1.382156681	Quartz
57	Oxides, Hydroxides	1.373296234	Quartz
60	Oxides, Hydroxides	1.306921796	Quartz
61	Oxides, Hydroxides	1.286387038	Hematite
62	Oxides, Hydroxides	1.256550464	Hematite
63	Oxides, Hydroxides	1.229454054	Hematite
64	Oxides, Hydroxides	1.200066565	Hematite

Rongram I B: The river Rongram flows through a relatively flat and narrow basin for a distance of about eight kilometers upstream from its confluence with the Ganol River. The Rongram Inspection Bangalow site is located four kilometers upstream from the confluence on the eastern bank of the river. Occurring at an altitude of 458 m msl it is the remnant of an ancient terrace. The approximate height of the mound from the present river bed is 10m. The mound measures 39 m x 27 m in size. The geological history of the Ganol-Rongram valleys is well preserved and visible in the exposed section of the mound. The floor of the mound is formed by an Archaean Gneissic rock. Over the Archaeans rest some Gondwana conglomerates. Sediments of the Tertiary age form the next layer. This is the Tura sandstone. A pebbly horizon composed of sand, clay, pebbles, and gravel sits on the Tura sandstone. In the northwestern, northern and northeastern section of the mound, this layer is highly ferricretised and compact. But in the southern corner, it is non-ferricretised and loose. This is the Tertiary-Quaternary boundary. This layer is capped by alluvium, approximately 1m thick. It is of two distinct varieties identified on the basis of colour. From the surface to 36 cms the colour of the alluvium is dark yellowish brown (10YR: 4/6, according to Munsell colour chart) and below it is strong brown coloured (7.5YR: 5/6, according to Munsell colour chart). The dark yellowish-brown alluvium consists of 50.0 percent sand and almost an equal percent of silt. Of this, coarse silt amounts to 27.82 percent. Fine silt and clay are very less. In the strong brown coloured alluvium percent of sand is even higher. It is above 65.00 percent of which fine sand is 36.86 percent. Total silt amounts to 30.65 percent of which 22.27 percent is coarse silt. On the basis of the angularity of the sand particles and gravel separated by dry sieving, it can be stated that the sediments have not been transported from a very long distance. In the study area, the altitude of this site is the lowest and the site lies at the farthest distance from the source of both the Ganol and Rongram rivers. The source of the Rongram is at a distance of 15km southeast of the site. Chemical analysis of the alluvium revealed that both the yellowish brown and strong brown alluvium is acidic. Calcium carbonate is absent while the content of organic carbon is medium. This evidence indicates high rainfall, humidity and thick vegetation in the area when the alluvium was deposited. But this data is insufficient for drawing conclusions on the past ecological condition of the area. The surface layer is implementiferous. Ground Neolithic celts were found in a half-buried condition. Till 36 cm below surface ground and polished celts, pestles and a few flakes were found. Below this level, the prolific occurrence of edge-ground tools, chipped tools, short axes, and pebble scrapers and choppers are noteworthy. At 55 cm level, flattish stones with average length and breadth of 16 cm and 15 cm respectively were uncovered. These could have been used as grinding stones. Considering the fact that they occur in one particular horizon in a cluster it can be inferred that they were part of a rammed floor. The implementiferous layer continues till 67 cm. The reddish-brown alluvial layer continues for another 50 cm below surface. This can be called the virgin layer. On the basis of tool typology and stratigraphy, this site can be called a multicultural site. Sixty-seven lithic artifacts were recovered from a 2/3m trench dug by the present owners of the site at the southwestern corner of the site. It was a controlled dig undertaken on request. A considerable portion of the colluvial deposit has been sliced down for the construction of an Inspection Bungalow of the Public Works Department exposing the implementiferous layer. On the basis of the height of an adjacent intact alluvial mound on the western bank of the river, it can be said that the original height of the alluvial deposit of the Rongram Inspection Bangalow site must have been approximately 10 m. Of this, approximately 2 m deposit is still intact. At present, the Meghalaya Police has an outpost on the site and a new building has been constructed on the site.

Ida Bichik: This site, as is true of most of the other sites, gets its name from a second order stream called the Ida Chiring. This stream joins the Selbal, a first-order stream of the Rongram river. The Ida Chiring has a course of one and a half and it forms the northern boundary of the site. The northern, western and southern boundaries of the site are formed by the Ida Chiring and on its eastern boundary is the Ida Biphek, a third-order stream. The site is at an altitude of 550 m msl. On the eastern boundary, there is a dolerite dyke across the Ida Biphek stream. All the streams here flow on the bedrock. The pebbly horizon is visible on the southern side of the mound and no other lithostratigraphic units are visible. This horizon is approximately 2m thick above the bedrock and the alluvial deposit is approximately 6m thick. The size of the mound is 1 sq km. The colour of the alluvium is Strong Brown (7.5 YR 4/6- Munsell colour chart) and it is acidic. Approximately 65.00 percent of sand is recorded from a 20gm sample of which 37.18 percent is fine sand. Silt content is 34.00 percent of which coarse silt constitutes 14.73 percent. This sample was collected from a depth of 2 m from the surface. Lithic tools were found in a half-buried condition on the southern side of the mound that had been cleared for cultivation and a part of it was sliced down to make a pathway across the mound. One hundred artifacts were collected. Surface exploration of the mound did not yield any tools. The implementiferous layer is sealed by deposits measuring 2 to 2 ½ m in thickness. The thickness of the implementiferous layer could not be ascertained. Ground and polished celts chipped celts, varieties of flake tools like points, scrapers, flake blanks, pebble cores were collected from the site. Almost 60.00 percent of the assemblage constitute of ground and chipped celts. A pebble core measuring 25cm x15cm x 15cm in size was found. Thus, river pebbles were also used to make tools besides dyke material. Just half a kilometer on the southeastern corner of this site across the Ida Biphek there is another tool scatter which is exposed on the surface. This mound has been extensively used for cultivation and a part of the mound has been dug and flattened. On this surface, tools are exposed. On the basis of distance, this is considered as a locality of Ida Bichik and is named Ida Bichik II. The tool assemblage is similar to Ida Bichik I and the density of tools are also almost similar. The size of this mound .75 sq km.

Bibragiri: It is located on the eastern bank of the Ganol river, eleven kilometers downstream at an altitude of approximately 800m msl. On its western boundary is a deep gorge at the bottom of which the Ganol flows on the bedrock. The site consists of a cluster of three colluvial mounds interspersed with dolerite dykes. The height of the colluvium in all the three mounds is different. The ferricretised pebbly horizon is exposed in the northeastern mound, on which there is a five-meter thick alluvial deposit. Just behind it less than half a kilometer on the southwestern corner there is another mound with approximately fifteen meters of colluvium. No other lithostratigraphic units are exposed. The colluvium is strong brown in colour with a very high percentage of quartz angular gravel. Through surface exploration, the presence of lithic tools on these two mounds has been confirmed. No tools were found on the third mound in the southeastern corner. The northeastern mound in this study will be referred to as Bibragiri I and the southwestern mound will be referred to as Bibragiri II. Almost three-meter deposit in Bibragiri I was sliced down and the surface leveled for constructing a soil conservation department office. At Bibragiri II an orange orchard was started on an experimental basis and pits were dug for the saplings. In the process, the surface layer was considerably disturbed and the implementiferous layer was exposed. Pathways were constructed crisscrossing the mound at different levels exposing the implementiferous layer at various depths. On this basis, it is ascertained that the implementiferous layer at Bibragiri II is more than two meters thick. At Bibragiri I pebble short axes, large and medium-sized flake tools constitute the assemblage. At Bibragiri II short axes only occur sporadically. Blade flakes dominate the assemblage. Fifty and 150 lithic artifacts were studied from Bibragiri I and II respectively from a 2x3m grid at Bibragiri I and 5x3m grid at Bibragiri II.

Missimagiri: This site located at an altitude of 750 m msl gets its name from a stream called Missima, a tributary of Ganol River. It is thirteen kilometers downstream of Ganol on its eastern bank. The Archaean gneissic bedrock is exposed at this altitude and patches of Gondwana conglomerate and Tertiary sandstone are also seen. Due to these exposures, a considerably flat surface occurs at this altitude forming a tableland. Deposition is very thin on this surface. Huge dykes of dolerite are seen in and around the site. At the northern boundary of the present habitation area, a 2 m thick deposit consisting of a gritty, strong brown colluvium is present. In extent, this layer is half a square kilometer, which dips downslope in the northern direction. Part of it was sliced down for constructing a house of the village headman in 1976. The implementiferous layer was exposed in the process. The north-south extension of the site is 145 m and the east-west extension is 100 m. Tools were found in fully buried and half buried condition. Blade flakes their size ranging from 2 cm to 10 cm dominate the assemblage. Roughly cylindrical cores are found in considerable number. In a grid of 2x2 m, seven such cores were recorded. This site is one of the richest sites in the area. In comparison to the site area, the tool density is very high. The easily available raw material in the form of the dolerite dykes and the flat hard bedrock surface provided a very convenient place for stone tool making. An inventory of artifacts collected from the site by a previous worker is reproduced below for a better understanding of the character of the site.

	Types of artifact collected	*Number*	*Percentage*
1.	Cores	73	2.90
2.	Cleaver type flakes	48	1.91
3.	Scrapers	242	9.64
4.	Blades	316	12.58
5.	Simple flake	596	23.83
6.	Levallois flake	56	2.23
7.	Knife	50	1.99
8.	Points	74	2.94
9.	Borer	32	1.27
10.	Arrowhead	30	1.19
11.	Spearhead (leaf points)	16	0.63
12.	Notched flake	26	1.03
13.	Waste flakes and chips	300	11.95
14.	Diverse group	501	19.96
	Total	2501	
(Reproduced from Sonowal 1987: 52)			

The presence of an appreciable number of cores (72), unmodified simple flakes (596) and debitage clearly indicated that this was a factory site. The size of the tools varies between 1cm to 15 cm. Core dimensions was equally varied.

Selbal Bichik: At an altitude of 550 m msl this site is located on the eastern bank of the Selbalgiri stream, a first-order stream of the Rongram River. It is at a distance of two kilometers towards the south of the Tura-

Williamnagar road. The footpath follows the channel of the river and this forms the western boundary of the mound. At present, the river flows on the bedrock and deposits sediments on the eastern bank. On the western bank, no recent deposit is seen. The alluvial deposit on the mound is approximately 4 m in thickness. The surface layer is formed by a 75 cm thick humus layer. This layer sits on a yellowish-brown silty layer below which is a strong brown layer. The sedimentological studies revealed that the composition of this colluvium is very much identical to the Rongram Inspection Bangalow site. Length-wise the mound is 200 m and breadthwise it is 100 m. Surface exploration undertaken under the present study yielded few tools. Only 25 artifacts were found on the surface. These two 2 grounds and polished celts, 1 chipped celt, 2 hammerstones, and 9 flakes. But still on the basis of previous reports (IAR 1965-66, 1969-70: 1) and collections made and reported by previous workers (Sharma, 1966; Mahanta, 1993) this site has been taken up for study. It is one of the most frequently visited site in the area and one of the oldest reported sites.

Mokbol Bichik II: This site is located north of the Missimagiri site at an altitude of 630 m msl. On its southern boundary is the Missima stream and on its northern boundary is the Mokbol Chiring, a second-order stream which joins the Selbal stream. On both of its boundaries, there are prominent dolerite dyke exposures. It is within 1 km radius of the Missimagiri site and also another site, the Mokbol Bichik. On the basis of the similarity of tools with the site of Mokbol Bichik, it has been categorized as Mokbol Bichik II. The size of the mound is half a square kilometer roughly. Tools are found in half buried condition on the surface of the site. Below the humus layer, the colluvium is strong brown. The total thickness of the implementiferous layer could not be measured as during the time of exploration the site was under cultivation. The total thickness of the alluvial layer is approximately 6 m. Lithic tools found on the site are slightly larger than medium size tools and they are mostly made of slabs extracted from the dykes. Large size flakes, that were probably utilized were also collected. No systematic collection could be attempted as the mound was under cultivation. Sixty-seven artifacts found within an area of 5x5 m approximately were studied. But horizontal and vertical displacement of the artifacts was noticed due to agricultural activity.

Citra Abri: The site is located on a steep ridge at the left bank of the river Rongram, at a distance of about two kilometers on the southwest of Rengsangiri village, which is at a distance of five-kilometer northeast of Rongram Inspection Bangalow site. It is located at an altitude of 500 m msl on the slope of the Arbella Mountain. On the contour map, this area is marked with closely clustered contour lines and not contorted. This indicates steep slopes, which at present are incessantly used by the inhabitants for shifting cultivation. The site is exposed on the bedrock. Ground and polished Neolithic celts and flake artifacts constitute the assemblage. Double shouldered celts were found only in this site in the study area. An inventory of artifacts made on the site showed a high percent of flakes (56.0%) in comparison to the ground and polished tools. Fifty artifacts were studied from a 5x5 m grid. But in the absence of a clear stratigraphy, it is hard to identify if the tools belong to the same context or they belong to two different contexts.

Mokbol Bichik I: This site gets its name from a second-order stream, the Mokbol Chiring. This stream is about one and a half kilometer in length and flows from the east to the west ultimately joining the Selbal stream. At present, it flows on the bedrock. At a distance of 300 km on the north, there is a huge dolerite dyke exposure at the foot of an alluvial mound. The site can be called a surface site as the artifacts are exposed on the bedrock. The tool assemblage mainly consists of tools made of slabs extracted from the dyke. Large size flakes, which were probably utilized are also found in considerable number. A few short axes and a huge chunk of waste flakes were the remaining types of artifacts. But as the original sedimentary context of the assemblage is unknown it is difficult to assess the time period of the assemblage. Eighty-two artifacts were collected from 5x5 m grid.

Table 15.3 Sedimentary analysis table

Site name and layers	Altitude above sea level (in meters)	% of clay	% of total silt	% of coarse silt	% of medium silt	% of fine silt	% of coarse sand	% of fine sand
Rongram IB Layer I	458	6.27	42.525	27.825	1.125	13.575	27.83	23.36
Rongram IB Layer II		5.75	30.65	22.275	4.4	3.975	26.73	36.87
Gawak Abri Layer I	550	10.07	40.7	24.825	9.3	6.58	30.60	18.66
Gawak Abri Layer II		0.625	30.525	26.7	3.35	0.475	33.508	35.35
Didami 2m	916	0.975	29.03	16.2	5.33	7.5	34.57	35.43
Didami 4m		7.95	26.48	10.93	15.08	.445	38.40	27.18
Selbal Chiring Modern Terrace	550	2.43	18.43	5.55	6.65	6.23	61.94	17.21

The Sedimentary Record of the Sites

The above site descriptions make it clear that the sediments within which the lithic tools are found contain a very high percentage of coarse angular sand and silt. Sedimentological analysis of samples collected from three sites located at different altitudes reveal certain patterns (Table 15.3).

The sediments are of coarser variety. Gravels separated by dry sieving are angular which suggest that the sediments have not been transported from a long distance. Percent of clay is negligible. The highest amount does not exceed seven percent. At Rongram Inspection Bangalow site and at Gawak Abri an upward-fining sequence is noticed. Percent of silt is comparatively more in the top layers (Rongram Inspection Bangalow - 42.53% and Gawak Abri - 40.7%) while the percent of sand is very high at the lower levels (Rongram Inspection Bangalow - 63.59 % and Gawak Abri - 68.84 %). Silt (25.0% to 30.0%) is also present at Didami which is at an altitude of 916 m msl. It is clear that when these sediments were deposited the rivers had the capacity to drain out only the clay while all the other material like silt and sand was deposited. Analysis of sediments from recent river deposits in the area shows the presence of a high percent (61.94%) of coarse sand. Thus, under the present climatic conditions deposition of the finer sediments is minimum. From this, we can postulate that climatic conditions different from the present prevailed during the period when these deposits were created. Deposition occurs when the river does not have the capacity to carry the material. Probably rainfall was lower than at present, so the rivers had less water or the drainage was obstructed. These sediments till date have been always defined as alluvium. But the sedimentary analysis clearly proves that the character of the sediments does not conform to the textbook definition of alluvium. The angularity of the gravel within the sediment indicates that the material has not been transported from a long distance. The coarse character suggests that there has been no sorting of the material. In the samples below 550-600 m, msl some amount of upward fining sequence is noticed but above it, no such situation exists. Also, it is difficult to perceive a situation when the rivers can climb up till the height above 600 m to 900 m msl when it did not have the capacity to carry down the silt. It is much more convincing to accept these deposits as mass wasting, gravity or debris flow materials and products of soil creep from the Arbella and Tura mountain ranges. This can thus be called colluvial silt. Colluvia includes coarse, unsorted talus and landslide or slump debris on steep slopes below cliffs, and texturally variable, bedded sediments mantling foot slopes. The definition of colluvium embraces deposits transported by mass movement rather than sediments deposited by running water (Botha and Partridge, 2000: 90). Such colluviation during the late Pleistocene has been reported recently from different parts of the world. Botha et al. (2000) have reported it from South Africa, Corvinus has reported it from Nepal and similar formations were observed in Thailand. In the Northeastern region of India also such formations have been reported from Manipur. In the Imphal Valley these deposits, dating between 25-11 ka, disconformably cap fluvio-lacustrine formations (Thokchom, 1987). From Garo Hills also Medhi (1977-78) reported terminal Pleistocene colluvial silts but the term alluvium prevailed within the scientific community for defining these deposits. Thus, though the term alluvium is used in this study initially to define these deposits it is proposed that for future studies these deposits should be referred to as colluvial silts. The deposits below 550m msl can be called sandy silt or silty sand. Pure alluvium is present beyond the boundary of the study area which is the confluence of the Ganol and the Rongram. In the Rongram IB site, some amount of alluviation has occurred for which the yellowish-brown younger alluvium and the strong brown older alluvium is distinctly visible. The percent of Fine Sand, Silt, and Clay, when added, is more than 70.00 percent at Rongram Inspection Bangalow in both the layers. In geological science, if the addition of the percent of Fine Sand, Silt, and Clay in any deposit is more than 70.00 percent that deposit is classified as loess. This loessic character of the Rongram IB sediments is intriguing. The count from Ida Bichik is 85.27 percent while at Gawak Abri 69.40 percent and 66.49 percent and at Didami 65.43 percent and 61.59 percent from Layer I and 2 respectively. These deposits are the result of some amount of fluvial activity, gravity or debris flow material deposits but it is difficult to envisage aeolian activity in the region. This high percent of silt and fine sand is the result of the loss of capacity by the rivers when these deposits were created. At present, the rivers are depositing more than 60.00 percent coarse sand. All the finer material are drained out from the area and deposited further downstream. The Himalayan orogeny four was responsible for large-scale denudation of the soil cover of the Tura Mountains which filled the valley. A phase of continental fluviatile sedimentation during the middle Pleistocene has been recorded in the Meghalaya plateau (Sinha et al., 1981-82: 39). These deposits probably were created during this event. Both these factors were aided by the fracture-controlled drainage of the region. Just at Rongram, only 4 km upstream of the confluence of the Ganol and the Rongram rivers (Fig 15.4) there is a fault. This is a fracture or a zone of fractures along which there has been displacement of the sides relative to one another. This fault extends for almost 5 km north-south interrupting the flow of both Ganol river and its tributary the Rongram river which flows westward from the south and southeastern corner of the study area respectively. The Pleistocene sediments were obstructed from flowing downstream and it might have also triggered a ponding environment. But these faults were no more active during the Holocene. Thus, the rivers were actively eroding, cutting through the sediments and depositing further downstream. As noted earlier on the basis

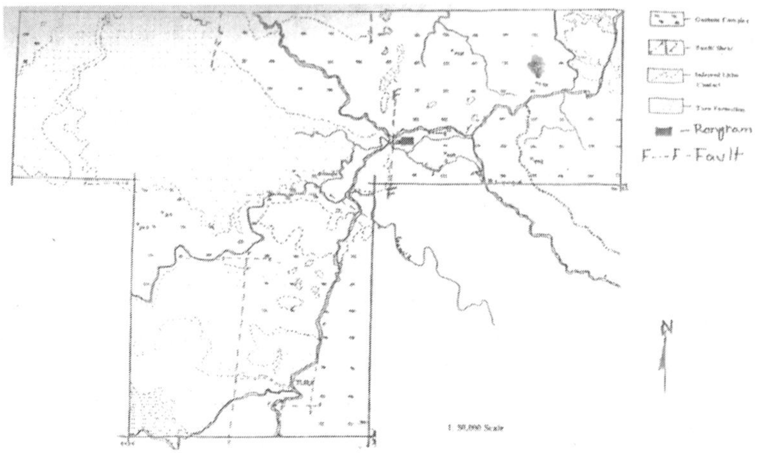

Fig 15.4 Fault Map

of physical characteristics this sediment in the study area can be divided into two stratigraphic units.

There is no soil formation in the area which indicates that the landscape was dynamic. The deposition was episodic which continued till the present climatic situation set in around 10,000 BP. Artifacts in the sites like Didami, Bibragiri, Missimagiri are found buried within these deposits. The authors of the flake-blade assemblage, the bifaces, and pebble tools settled on the Middle Pleistocene deposits maybe during the late Pleistocene or early Holocene when the climate was much drier than at present. Denudation from the hills continued till the beginning of the Holocene. At the end of the Pleistocene when the rainfall increased the rivers started eroding these deposits resulting in the deposition of much finer sediments downstream at sites like Rongram Inspection Bangalow. On these sediments, the authors of the celt assemblage lived. That is why most of the earlier workers reported the sites with the celts as surface sites as deposition was very less after the rainfall increased and these sites were either surface or subsurface sites. The strong brown color of the colluvial silt has formed as a result of pedogenesis. This proves that it is older than the yellowish-brown sandy silt within which the cells occur. Radiometric dates from different parts of Northeast India of these two layers (Ramesh and Rajagopalan, 1999: 13-35) confirms the middle-upper Pleistocene origin of the strong brown layer and Holocene origin of the yellowish-brown layer. In the study area, the two main rivers are flowing on the bedrock. Deposition by a few first-order streams in the study area is still continuing. These streams are eroding their catchment areas during the rainy season. These deposits are about a

Plate 15.1 Recent deposits

meter thick from which no cultural material of archaeological importance has been recovered (Plate 15.1).

Thus, it can be stated that this geomorphic unit which supported the Stone Age people and also the present-day inhabitants has been formed as a result of

(1) Crustal movements related with the morphotectonic upliftment of the Himalayan orogen, which simultaneously buckled up the pre-Cambrian massif of Meghalaya, triggering a phase of continental fluviatile sedimentation, and;
(2) Excessive soil stripping and heavy seasonal rainfall in response to semi-arid conditions prevailing during the last glacial maximum (LGM).
(3) Once precipitation increased with the onset of the Holocene, the rivers were eroding the catchment and cutting through the sediments and depositing them in the lower courses, which were also triggered by major eustatic changes. Massive valley filling is recorded.

Location of the sites clearly indicates that the settlers of the prehistoric period had chosen the area in between the Ganol and the Rongram River where the slope is comparatively gentle, for habitation. On the left bank of the Ganol river, no site is recorded while on the right bank of the Rongram River only three sites are recorded. This selection made by the prehistoric inhabitants is noteworthy. The alluvial mounds in between the right bank of Ganol River and left bank of Rongram River was chosen specifically by the Stone Age people for habitation. The depressed trough or basin in between the Tura and Arbella ranges is enclosed in the three sides by steep slopes and dense vegetation. There is a narrow opening on the western side through which the rivers flow out of the basin. This enclosure provides a natural boundary that protects the basin from strong winds and heavy clouds that blow from the south, southwest and southeast and north and northeast. The luxuriant growth in the hill slopes is the home of a large number of edible plants and faunal species. Organic raw material like bamboo, cane, and wood used as construction material and for making tools are found in abundance besides dolerite dyke material for making lithic tools. Also, the slopes can be used for shifting cultivation. The alluvial terraces on which the lithic tools have been found is formed when a floodplain is abandoned through valley incision, thereby isolating the terrace surface from flooding. This provided a dry dwelling surface. Thus, the chief factors behind the selection of the area by the Stone Age inhabitants are:

- (i) Extreme fertility of the alluvium capable of supporting very rich plant life, including edible foods and raw material for construction of shelter, etc.
- (ii) Ample hunting ground and gathering area and cultivating fields.
- (iii) Presence of perennial sources of water.
- (iv) Availability of dolerite dyke exposures in the area and river pebbles making procurement of raw material for lithic tools an easy task.
- (v) Protection from bad weather and environmental hazards and defensibility.
- (vi) Dry ground surface to be used as dwellings.

References

Botha, GA & Partridge, TC 2000, 'Colluvial deposits' in *The cenozoic of Southern Africa*, eds. TC Partridge & RR Maud, Oxford University Press, Oxford, pp. 88-99.

Geological Survey of India-Miscellaneous Publication 30, *Geology and Mineral Resources of India, part IV-Arunachal Pradesh, Assam, Manipur, Meghalaya, Mizoram, Nagaland, and Tripura*, Government of India, Calcutta.

Goswami, MC & Bhagwati, AC 1959, 'A typological study of shouldered celt from Renchengiri (Garo Hills)', *Journal of the University of Gauhati*, vol. 10, no. 2, pp. 105-122.

Grim, RE 1953, *Clay mineralogy*, McGraw-Hill Book Company, INC, New York.

IAR-Indian Archaeological Review, 1963-64 to 1979-80.

Medhi, DK 1977-1978, 'Some aspects of quaternary studies in the Garo Hills, Meghalaya', *Bulletin, Deccan College PG, and Research Institute*, vol. 37, no. 1, pp. 71-78.

Papachristodoulou, C, Oikonomou, A, Ioannides, K & Gravani, K 2006, 'A study of ancient pottery by means of X-ray fluorescence spectroscopy, multivariate statistics, and mineralogical analysis', *Analytica Chimica Acta*, vol. 573 - 574, pp. 347–353.

Ramesh, NR & Rajagopalan, G 1999, 'Late quaternary sediments of North-Eastern India: a review', *Gondwana Geological Magazine*, vol. 14, no. 1, pp. 13-35.

Ravisankar, R, Kiruba, S, Chandrasekaran, A, Naseerutheen, A, Seran, M & Balaji, PD 2010, 'Determination of firing temperature of some ancient potteries of Tamil Nadu, India by FT-IR spectroscopic technique', *Indian Journal of Science and Technology*, vol. 3, no. 9, pp. 1016-1019.

Sankalia, HD 1974, *The prehistory and protohistory of India and Pakistan*, Deccan College, Pune, pp. 283-298.

Sharma, S 2007, *Celts, flakes, and bifaces - the Garo hills story*, BAR international series, South Asian archaeology series no. 7, John and Erica Hedges Ltd., Oxford.

Sharma, TC 1966a, *Prehistoric archaeology of Assam - a study of Neolithic cultures*. Ph.D. dissertation, University of London.

Sharma, TC 1966b, 'Researches on the prehistoric archaeology of Assam', *Journal of the Assam Science Society*, vol. 9, no. 1-10.

Sonowal, M 1987, *Studies on the flake and blade industries of the Garo Hills, Meghalaya*. Ph.D. thesis, Gauhati University, Guwahati.

Thokchom, ASA 1987, *Quaternary studies in the Manipur valley*. Ph.D. thesis, Deccan college, Pune.

Chapter - 16

Lepchas of Sikkim: A Review of Ethnographic Texts from Colonial to Current Times

Charisma K. Lepcha

'Sikkim equates snow; so, we have to see snow'.

My friend sounded eager and excited as she told me she was coming to Sikkim. Hailing from Meghalaya which does not get any snow, she had been looking forward to the trip and packed appropriately –new gloves, hats, and woolens to keep her warm for her first snow experience. But once she arrived in Gangtok, she was in for a big disappointment. The reason was not that it did not snow but the fact that it snowed too much. The roads were blocked and they were not allowing vehicles to traverse the roads that led to the snow. To understand the location of the place, she needed to travel about 40 km from Gangtok in order to reach her snow destination. Unfortunately, she returned to Meghalaya without seeing snow. I am not sure if she still equates Sikkim with snow but if we listen to the creation tale of the Lepchas, she might not be too disappointed perhaps.

Who are the Lepchas?

Lepchas are the oldest inhabitants of Sikkim. They call themselves *Rong* from the Lepcha words *Rongkup* or *Rumkup* meaning the children of snowy peak/ children of God. Tradition has it that their creator God, Itbumu, created their progenitors Fudongthing and Nazongnyu from the pure snow of Mt. Kanchenjunga. The couple was instructed to live like siblings but they violated the rules and gave birth to several children. Itbumu is believed to have summoned the two and said, you have committed a sin. I cannot allow you two to live in this sacred mountain any longer. As a punishment, both of you now must live in the foothills of Mt Kanchenjunga as humans and fend for yourselves. In the meantime, the abandoned babies grew up to be evil spirits and started troubling the people. After getting rid of seven children, the couple decided to keep their child who is now considered to be the first Lepcha. With their legends pointing to Kanchenjunga as the place of origin, it is only understandable to find Lepchas living in the foothills of this mountain for a long time. While they profess no migration history, it is opined that they migrated from the east during the first wave of migration as J.C. White, the first Political Officer of Sikkim, writes, 'their origin is doubtful, as they did not enter Sikkim across the Himalayas or from Tibet, but are supposed to have come from the east along the foothills from the direction of Assam and upper Burma' (White, 1909: 7). Archaeological findings of stone tools in Sikkim show Neolithic assemblages that can be categorized firstly with the south-east Asian Hoabinian culture dating around 10,000-8,000 BC and secondly, the polished tools that resemble the Sichuan and South China cultural assemblage of 8,000-4,000BC (Mullard, 2011). Bringing his expertise from the linguistic history of Tibeto-Burman languages, van Driem (1998, 2006) proposed a theoretical model of the migration pattern of ancient Tibeto-Burman language family in which he estimated that the ancestors of Lepchas might have migrated in the third and fourth millennium B.C.

Sikkim: A Brief Profile

Sikkim is one of the eight Northeast states although a recent addition to the already existing seven sisters. It is the second smallest state in India with a total population of 6.19 lakhs. It is surrounded by Tibet / China in the north and the east, Nepal on the west, Bhutan in the east and Darjeeling, West Bengal in the south. It does not share borders with any of the Northeast states and is seen as 'geographically not contiguous with the remaining seven states' (Subba and Wouters, 2013: 195). In that, Sikkim often finds itself at an-in-between place, not fully accepted nor rejected when it comes to Northeast India. But there are certain corresponding features of frontier regions including proximity and the politics of border areas that Sikkim shares along with 'ecological and cultural similarities' (*ibid)* and colonial interest on the tribes of the region -specifically the Lepchas that could be seen as the much-needed continuity of Sikkim with the rest of Northeast India.

Commencement of Colonial Ethnography

While Sikkim was off limits to most colonial explorers, even leading to the arrest of Dr. Archibald Campbell and Dr. Joseph Dalton Hooker in

1849, the first Europeans to write about the Lepchas. Both mentioned Lepchas in their writings early on. 'Note on the Lepchas of Sikkim, with a Vocabulary of their Language', by Campbell (1840) was published in the *Journal of the Asiatic Society of Bengal*. While Hooker's *Himalayan Journals* (1855) also finds a considerable mention of the Lepchas of Sikkim.

'They are wonderfully honest, theft being scarcely known among them; they rarely quarrel among themselves, and I have never even seen them strike one another. 'Do you ever fight?' was asked of an intelligent Lepcha; 'No, never, (was the reply) why should we, all Lepchas are brothers, to fight would be unnatural' (Campbell, 1840: 386).

Likewise, Hooker, the world-famous botanist also found them to be 'timid, peaceful, and no brawler' (Hooker, 1855: 118). There is a 'paternalistic admiration for their childlike nature' (Didur, 2011) as he goes on to write, 'a group of Lepchas is exceedingly picturesque' (*ibid*) and describes them as 'amiable and obliging, frank, humorous, and polite, without the servility of the Hindoos' (*ibid*: 120). This description of the Lepchas is widely shared by earlier travelers and explorers as Waddell also mentions the distinctive physical and moral traits of a Lepcha. He writes, 'the Lepcha is naturally indolent and easy-going. His close companionship with nature has made him a naturalist, a tender lover of flowers, and something of a philosopher' (Waddell, 1899: 93). J. Claude White, the first political officer of Sikkim (1887-1908), also describes Lepchas as 'people of a mild, quiet and indolent disposition, loving solitude, and their homes being found in the most inaccessible places' (White, 2000: 7). One after another, the descriptions of a docile Lepcha laid the foundation for the gradual construction of the image of a shy, simple Lepcha that was to be reiterated by scholars and anthropologists in the coming years.

Archibald Campbell also mentioned the printing of four gospels into Lepcha language by a German missionary. The work of the missionaries might have even started among the Lepchas earlier than most parts of Northeast India. The earliest gospel translation was St. Matthew's in 1845, followed by Genesis and part of Exodus in Lepcha' (Sprigg, 2005: 53) published in 1849. That same year in 1849 - the St. John's Gospel was also printed along with a revised version of St. Matthew's Gospel. These publications were printed at the Baptist Mission Press, Calcutta. These were the first books to be printed and published in Lepcha language with the help of modern technology, i.e., the movable printing press. Another notable mention in Campbell's article was General Mainwaring's work in compiling a Lepcha dictionary. Colonel George Byres Mainwaring took a keen interest in the language, literature and the people as he collected information on Lepcha narratives. He was the first person to write a grammar of Lepcha, which was published in 1876. In his introduction to *A Grammar of the Lepcha Language,* he wrote that the Lepcha language was 'unquestionably far anterior to the Hebrew or Sanskrit' (Mainwaring, [1876] 1971: xix). He went on to add,

> 'I may, without fear of misrepresentation, state it to be, the oldest language extant. It is a most comprehensive and beautiful one; and regarded alone, as a prolific source of the derivations and etyma of words, it is invaluable to the philological world.
>
> But, like everything really good in this world, it has been despised and rejected. To allow the Lepcha race and language to die out would indeed be most barbarous and inexpressibly sad' (*ibid*: xx).

Anthropological Writings

The beginnings of anthropological writings about Lepchas started with the coming of anthropologists' Geoffrey Gorer and John Morris who spent three months each accounting the village life and culture of the Lepchas in the Lepcha reserve of Dzongu, North Sikkim. Dzongu is a homogenous Lepcha terrain where non-Lepchas are not allowed to reside permanently. During the King's rule, it was separated and 'preserved' as a Lepcha only area and many anthropologists have found it to be a haven for ethnographic study even today. *Himalayan Village: An Account of the Lepchas of Sikkim* (1938) by Geoffrey Gorer was an extensive study of the Lepcha life, environment, housing pattern, family, kinship, marriage, various rites of passage, religion, political organization, economy, and the Lepcha lifestyle. Gorer also found them to 'lack aggression' (Gorer, 1987: 449) and called them a dying race (Gorer, 1987: 37). Agreeing with him was another anthropologist John Morris who was actually on his way to Nepal but was denied entry so he tagged along with Gorer and wrote *Living with Lepchas* (1938). Both monographs are extensively read although Gorer's book is more popular and has gone for reprint several times. He not only accounted the life of the Lepchas but also saw that the Lepchas had come in contact with various other cultures as he wrote, 'the Lepchas have been very greatly influenced and their ways of life much modified by the contact and pressure of their more highly developed neighbours, the Sikkimese, the Nepali, and above all the Tibetans' (Gorer, 1987: 45). In these writings, we notice the anthropologists' concern regarding the loss of Lepcha culture as they came in contact with other cultures. Prior to their coming to, the work of C. de.

Beauvoir Stocks (1925) is noteworthy who collected the folklore, myths, legends and Lepcha customs. Gorer refers to Stocks in his monograph as Stocks provides a detailed collection of Lepcha folktales in *Sikkim: Customs and Folklore* (1925). Another extensive writing on the Lepchas was done by René von Nebesky-Wojkowitz, a Czech ethnologist who visited Sikkim and Kalimpong in the 1950s and wrote a combined paper with Gorer about 'The use of thread-crosses in Lepcha Lamaist ceremonies' (1951) and was of the opinion that the Lepchas' religion was also being diluted as 'they practice simultaneously, and without any feeling of theoretical discomfort, two (or possibly three) mutually contradictory religions' (Gorer, 1987: 181). But Nebesky-Wojkowitz also wrote about the '*Ancient funeral ceremonies of the Lepchas*' (1952) and '*Hunting and Fishing among the Lepchas*' (1953). Since he was a Tibetologist, he noticed the hesitancy of Lepchas acceptance to Buddhism and mentioned 'the priests of the old tribal religion offered particular stubborn resistance' (1955: 121). While the geopolitical scenario of Sikkim was undergoing massive change, the population and the communities were comparatively studied by Chie Nakane, a Japanese anthropologist wrote about '*A Plural Society in Sikkim: A Study of Interrelations of Lepchas, Bhotias, and Nepalis*' (1966), and talked about the inter-community relationship between the three communities of Sikkim and likened the language of Lepchas to be closer to the Khasis.

Around the same time, another important ethnography on Lepchas was carried out by Halfdan Siiger from the Third Danish Expedition to Central Asia in the 1940s who studied the Lepchas, Boros and the Kalashas. Siiger spent several months in Sikkim and Kalimpong and documented the socio-cultural, linguistic and religious aspects of Lepchas. He also worked on word-to-word translations and analysis of 39 ritual texts that had only existed as oral traditions before. Siiger was one of the first to collect and methodically compile a comprehensive and coherent approach to understanding society. His work among the Lepchas produced one of the most solid ethnographies on the subject so far (Lepcha and Torri, 2016: 149). His magnum opus - *The Lepchas: Culture and Religion of a Himalayan People.* Part I and Part II appeared in two volumes in 1967. Siiger also published articles on '*Fate in the Religion of the Lepchas*' (1967), 'A Himalayan Goddess of Procreation: From the Lepchas of Sikkim' (1972), '*The Gods of the Lepchas of Sikkim*' (1975) and '*The Abominable Snowman: Himalayan Religion and Folklore from the Lepchas of Sikkim*' (1978). His contribution to Lepcha studies is commendable and is still referred by young scholars working on Lepchas.

Indian Scholars

The twentieth century saw the dawn of Lepcha research undertaken by a number of Indian scholars, who looked at Lepchas as the minority community under threat in their own land. Amal Kumar Das (1978) introduces Lepchas as 'true sons of soil who have been exploited through generations and centuries' (1978: v) as he outlined the Lepcha village and settlement pattern, economic and domestic life, social organization, religious beliefs and practices, myths, tales, songs, proverbs, dances, and language. In conclusion, he says the Lepchas, 'think themselves to be inefficient in comparison with others, and their lack of competitive zeal indirectly influences their mentality as a loving community in the struggle for existence' (1978: 258). Indira Awasty also calls Lepchas to be a 'sinking and shrinking race' (1978: 36) as the introduction of Buddhism and Christianity were seen to divorce them from their traditional culture. In *The Himalayan Gateway* (1983) by George Kotturan discusses the history, culture, and people of Sikkim and touches on Lepchas as how certain monasteries would not necessarily be open to Lepchas even though they had accepted Buddhism as their newfound religion. The acceptance of newfound religions was seen as a problem in *Himalayan Lepchas* (1988), as Thakur is also wary of the religious influence and calls the culture change to be 'an irreparable loss' that would affect the community in the long run. He, however, doesn't miss to mention that Lepchas were 'small, shy, silent' (1988: 109) and their voice was being subdued by the more dominant cultures at that time. During these times, the writings on Lepchas were mostly lamenting their culture change and the loss of culture. There were also a few comparative studies on the communities of Sikkim that further highlighted the culture contact and its consequences among Lepchas. Tanka B. Subba's article '*Dynamics of a Hill Society: Case Study of the Lepchas*' (1989) mentioned the strained relationship between Lepchas and Bhutias while suggesting that 'Lepchas could perhaps never accept fully the religion of those who plundered their property – cultural as well as material' (Subba, 1989: 126). *Ecology, Culture, and Change: Tribals of Sikkim Himalayas* (1989) by Veena Bhasin, an anthropologist compared the Lepchas and the Bhutias of Sikkim and noted the changes too. Tapan Chattopadhyay's *Lepchas and Their Heritage* (1990) details the traditions, myths, religion, and music of the Lepchas.

Lepcha Scholars

During this time, we also see research undertaken by members of the Lepcha community itself. The general theme of these writings was on the disappearing culture and religion of the Lepchas. So much so Kharpu Tamsang, a Lepcha scholar who spent some time in School of Oriental and African Studies (SOAS) went on to write *The Unknown and Untold Reality about the Lepchas* (1982) hoping to uncover various aspects of Lepcha culture, history, and religion in detail. But it was Arthur Foning's *Lepcha, My Vanishing Tribe* (1987) that garnered considerable acclaim. While he was not an anthropologist, he managed to look at the Lepcha world from lived experiences and critically looked at the coming of Buddhism, Christianity, and modernization. It was an honest account of a native Lepcha in the wake of external influences from the Tibetans, the British and the Nepalis through culture, religion, and language simultaneously. Foning talked about the split between Christian Lepchas and Buddhist Lepchas that divided the community but credits the Buddhist missionaries for translating Buddhist texts into Lepcha with a 'completely Lepcha aura' (1987: 154). He is also thankful to Christian missionaries for their contribution in producing and printing the gospels by the modern means of the printing press. However, it was the book title that was to remain in the imagination of many as Lepchas started believing that they were a vanishing tribe. Rip Roshina Gowloog, the first Lepcha anthropologist conducted a diachronic study of Gorer's ethnography in *Lingthem Revsited* (1995) and compared the changes in the village life since Gorer's time. She noted the definite spread of Lamaism and a decline of the traditional tribal religion. But that the Lepchas of Lingthem village was not particularly bothered about this phenomenon.

Culture Change, Revivalism, and Development

In 2006, Helen Plaisier, a linguist published *A Grammar of Lepcha,* which was seen as a very readable and modern linguistic grammar (Jacques, 2007) of the Lepcha. It was also very timely as there was a lot of documentation of culture changes and loss of traditional culture, and the input of a linguist in terms of making grammar accessible to not just Lepcha language speakers but also to linguists of the same language family allows a thorough study of the Lepcha language too. But the writings of Lepchas were mostly focused on preserving culture, cultural revivalism and development issues. Jenny Bentley, a Swiss anthropologist wrote about '*Change and cultural revival in a mountain community of Sikkim*' (2007) and talked about the different Lepcha associations 'involved in activities to try and enhance the social and economic conditions of the Lepchas of Sikkim' (Bentley 2007: 73). They talked about preserving, promoting and even modifying Lepcha culture to ensure the survival of the same.

Interestingly, Lepchas garnered quite a bit of attention around this time with the coming of hydel projects in Dzongu –the ethnographer's paradise in North Sikkim. '*Lepchas and their hydel protest*' (Wangchuk, 2007) discussed the protest movement against hydel projects that were slated in the Lepcha reserve of Dzongu, North Sikkim. Kerry Little wrote 'Lepcha narratives and their threatened scared landscapes' (2008) about the protests against dams in Dzongu. She examined the protest movement in great detail and provided different angles to the story. '*Deep Ecology, Dams and Dzongu land*' (2009) and 'From the village to the cities—the battlegrounds for Lepcha protests' (2010) have all contributed to the voice from Dzongu. The protests were however seen to be of non-violent nature as Vibha Arora has extensively documented the Gandhian methods to protest hydro projects in Dzongu in '*Gandhigiri in Sikkim*' (2008). Following the fight for safeguarding their sacred environment, Davide Torri, an Italian anthropologist thinks the survival of Lepchas has a lot to do with the unification of religious differences 'Lepchas from all backgrounds (Buddhist, Christian and 'shamanic') try to look at each other mostly without animosity today' (2010: 161) as the battle against dams actually brought the community together despite their religious differences. Lepcha (2008) also discussed the predicament of the dams as development in '*Dzongu in Dilemma*'. Interestingly, there was a blog that was dedicated to the anti-dam movement that garnered worldwide attention as Arora (2014) talks about how 'blogging enabled Lepchas living in the peripheries of the Indian state to situate themselves in global networks of oppositional politics' (Arora, 2014: 363). Subba also wrote about '*Power Projects, Problematics of Belonging in Dzongu, Sikkim*' (2014) and discusses the politics of belonging when development projects are introduced in protected areas.

Conclusion

The above review on familiarizes us with the idea that Lepchas of Sikkim and the anthropological interest on this tribe has been there for a long time. It shows the gradual progression of the study of Lepchas from administrative to ethnographic to more specified accounts today. The works of colonial administrators introduced Lepchas of Sikkim to the world and the next batch of ethnographers contributed to descriptive anthropology on their language, rituals and mythological stories focusing on a single village study giving a detailed account of the lives of the people. Recent publications show a great deal of what is happening in the Lepcha cultural revival movement and the Lepcha assertion in light of development projects in Sikkim. There are also works being done on the anthropology of Christianity and conversion by both anthropologists and theologians which has not been discussed in detail here. This only brings us to the conclusion that the Lepcha case is no different than the study of various tribes in different parts of Northeast India. There is a similar pattern of the effects of culture contact and its influence and the threat to loss of traditional culture. The inroads of cultural revivalism and development dilemmas also make us realize that the issues are the same and it unites the tribal communities with their common quest for survival.

With the establishment of the Department of Anthropology, Sikkim University in 2013, native scholars are taking initiative on research and collaboration about the anthropological study of Sikkim. The anthropology department has been able to collaborate with the Social Justice, Empowerment and Welfare Department, Govt. of Sikkim in conducting research on the tribal communities of Sikkim and the establishment of Tribal Research Institute in Sikkim. While Sikkim is still making its toddler steps in an already established anthropological scenario in Northeast India, the case of Lepchas hopes to make the much-needed connection with the kind of studies being done in Sikkim and the rest of Northeast India. This brings us back to the creation story of the Lepchas which is actually very similar to the creation story about a god who created the first man and first woman in various folktales of Northeast India. 'Oh, we also have an Adam and Eve story, we also have the story of Noah, we also have the story of Babel' (Longkumer, 2010: 88); and we realize that Lepcha folktales also includes the great flood and the tower of earthen pots. The folk tales could perhaps be told in another occasion and studied extensively in a comparative manner across the region, but for now, there is that solace that Sikkim has found its footing in the larger picture of the anthropology of Northeast India.

References

Arora, V 2008, 'Gandhigiri in Sikkim', *Economic and Political Weekly*, vol. 43, pp. 27-28.

Arora, V 2014, 'weepingsikkim.blogspot.com Reconfiguring Lepcha belonging with cyber-belonging' in *Facing globalization in the Himalayas: belonging and the politics of self*, eds G Toffin & J Pfaff-Czarnecka, Sage Publications, New Delhi.

Awasty, I 1978, *Between Sikkim and Bhutan: the Lepchas and Bhutias of Pedong*, B.R. Publishing Corporation, Delhi.

Bentley, J 2007, 'Change and cultural revival in a mountain community of Sikkim', *Bulletin of Tibetology*, vol. 43, no. 1-2, pp. 59-79.

Bhasin, V 1989, *Ecology, culture, and change: tribals of Sikkim Himalayas*, Inter-India Publications, New Delhi.

Campbell, A 1840, 'Note on the Lepchas of Sikkim, with a vocabulary of their language', *Journal of the Asiatic Society of Bengal,* vol. IX, pp. 379-393.

Chattopadhyay, T 1990, *Lepchas and their heritage*, B.R. Publishing Corporation, New Delhi.

Chie, Nakane 1966, 'A plural society in Sikkim: a study of the interrelation of Lepchas, Bhotiyas and Nepalis' in *Caste and kin in Nepal, India, and Ceylon*, ed. CV Furer Haimendorf, Asia Publishing House, Bombay.

Das, AK 1978, *The Lepchas of West Bengal*, Indian Editions, Calcutta.

Didur, J 2011, 'Cultivating community: counter landscaping in Kiran Desai's *The inheritance of loss*' in *Postcolonial ecologies: literature of the environment*, eds EDe Loughrey & GB Handley, Oxford University Press, New York.

Foning, A 1987, *Lepcha, my vanishing tribe*, Sterling Publications Ltd., New Delhi.

Gorer, G 1987 (1938) *Himalayan village: an account of the Lepchas of Sikkim*, Pilgrims Publishing, Kathmandu.

Gowloog, RR 1995, *Lingthem revisited: social change in a Lepcha village of North Sikkim,* Har Anand Publications, New Delhi.

Hooker, JD 1855, *Himalayan journals*, Ward, Lock & Co., London.

Kotturan, G 1983, *The Himalayan gateway: history and culture of Sikkim*, Sterling Publishers, New Delhi.

Lepcha, C & Torri, D 2016, 'Fieldwork in Dzongu: in Siiger's footsteps and beyond' in *The footsteps of Halfdan Siiger–Danish research in Central Asia*, eds UH Johnsen, AW Geertz & PB Andersen, Moesgaard Museum, Aarhus.

Lepcha, C 2008, 'Dzongu in dilemma', *The North Eastern Hill University Journal*, vol. IV, pp. 121-126.

Little, K 2009, 'Deep ecology, Dams, and Dzonguland', *The Trumpeter: Journal of Ecosophy,* vol. 25, no. 1.

Longkumer, A 2010, *Reform, identity, and narratives of belonging: the Heraka movement in Northeast India*, Continuum International Publishing Group, London.

Mainwaring, GB 1876, *A grammar of the Rong (Lepcha) language as it exists in the Darjeeling and Sikkim Hills*, Daya Publishing House, Calcutta.

Morris, J 1938, *Living with the Lepchas: a book about Sikkim Himalayas*, Heinemann, London.

Mullard, S (2011) 1979, *Opening of the hidden land: state formation and the construction of Sikkimese history*, Brill, Leiden.

Nebesky –Wojkowitz, RD von 1952, 'Ancient funeral ceremonies of the Lepchas', *Eastern Anthropologist*, vol. 5, no.1, pp. 27-39.

Nebesky –Wojkowitz, RD von 1953, 'Hunting and fishing among the Lepchas', *Ethnos,* vol. 18, pp. 21-30.

Nebesky –Wojkowitz, RD von 1955, *Oracles, and demons of Tibet: the cult and iconography of the Tibetan protective deities*, trans. MS Wien, translated of German hab. Diss.

Plaisier, H 2006, *A grammar of Lepcha*, Brill, Leiden.

Siiger, H 1978, 'The abominable snowman: Himalayan religion and folklore from the Lepchas of Sikkim' in *Himalayan anthropology: the Indo-Tibetan interface*, ed JF Fisher, The Hague, Paris, pp. 421 – 430.

Siiger, H 1967, 'Fate in the religion of the Lepchas' in *Fatalistic beliefs in religion, folklore, and literature,* ed H Ringgren, Scripta Instituti Donneriani Aboensis*II*, Almqvist and Wiksell, Stockholm, pp. 150-57.

Siiger, H 1972, 'A Himalayan goddess of procreation, from the Lepchas of Sikkim', *Ex Orbe Religionum, Studia Geo Widengren, Pars Altera*, Leiden, pp. 236-245.

Siiger, H 1975, 'The Gods of the Lepchas of Sikkim', in *Studies in the history of religions: proceedings of the XIIth international congress of the international association for the history of religions, 1970*, Leiden, vol. XXXI, pp. 298-304.

Siiger, H 1967, *The Lepchas: culture and religion of a Himalayan people*, The National Museum of Denmark, Copenhagen.

Sprigg, RK 2005, *Shedding some light on the history, language, and literature of the Lepchas*, ILTA, Kalimpong.

Stocks, C de Beauvoir 1975 (1925), *Sikkim: customs and folklore*, Cosmo Publications, Delhi.

Subba, T & Wouters, J 2013, 'North-East India: ethnography and politics of identity' in *In the modern anthropology of India: ethnography, themes, and theory*, eds P Berger & F Heidemann, Routledge, New York.

Subba, TB 1989, 'Dynamics of a hill society: a case study of the Lepchas', *Journal of Social and Economic Studies,* New Series, pp. 117- 130.

Subba, TB 2014, 'Power projects, protests and problematics of belonging in Dzongu, Sikkim' in *Facing globalization in the Himalayas: belonging and the politics of self*, eds G Toffin & J Pfaff-Czarnecka, Sage Publications, New Delhi.

Tamsang, K 1982, *The unknown and untold reality about the Lepchas*, Lyangsong Tamsang, Kalimpong.

Thakur, RN 1988, *Himalayan Lepchas*, Archives publishers and Distributors, New Delhi.

Torri, D 2011, 'In the shadow of the devil: traditional patterns of Lepcha culture reinterpreted' in *Health and religious rituals in South Asia. disease, possession, and healing*, ed F Ferrari, Routledge (South Asian Religion Series), pp. 148-165.

van Driem, G 1998, 'Neolithic correlates of ancient Tibeto-Burman migrations' in *Archaeology and language II*, eds R Blench & M Spriggs, Routledge, London.

van Driem, G 2006, 'The prehistory of Tibeto-Burman and Austro-Asiatic in light of emergent population genetic studies', *Mother Tongue*, vol. XI, pp. 160-211.

Waddell, LA 1978 (1899), *Among the Himalayas*, Ratna Pustak Bhandar, Kathmandu.

Wangchuk, P 2007, 'Lepchas and their hydel protest', *Bulletin of Tibetology*, vol. 43, no. 12, pp. 33- 57.

White, JC 2000 (1909), *Sikhism and Bhutan twentyone years in the North-East frontier 1887-1908*, Asian Educational Services, New Delhi.

Chapter - 17

Health, Illness, and Therapeutics: A Study on Power Healing among the Lepchas

Sumitabha Chakraborty

'Health is a state of complete physical, mental and social well-being and is not merely the absence of disease or infirmity' as propounded by the World Health Organization (WHO, 1946/1948: 100). Life of an individual is always concerned with 'health'. The idea of ill-health disturbs the rhythm of life and the performances of the individual being. All human groups, no matter how small or technologically primitive, have always been devising ways and means for taking care of the health. Many definitions represent health and illness, which have conceptualized health as 'modes of relationship' – equilibrium and disequilibrium between man and his environment; involving human factors, ecological aspect and social structure (Lehriche and Danglas, 1973: 54). Health and illness have an integral association with the individual as well as society, where the health is a property and illness is a state. In one of his interpretation, Valabrega mentioned two notions of health and illness – first, the illness, behaviour of the sick and medical practices are considered by endogenous (illness is caused by the magical theft of the individual soul) and exogenous (illness is caused by the real or symbolic intrusion of some objects into the patient's body) concept; secondly, illness may be caused by the action of another man or sorcerer or religious origin, produced by a god or a spirit (1962).

Health and illness have close linkages with therapeutic and preventive practices, which have shown variations throughout the ages. These therapeutic and preventive practices led by the human being is termed as 'ethnomedicine', which is referred to beliefs and practices relating to disease which are the products of indigenous cultural development (Hughes, 1968: 88). In the sphere of ethnomedicine, man only depends on their surrounding 'biome' and developed an attachment to the biotic and abiotic creature for coping up various health disorders and illness. The traditional way of nature cure with herbal medicine got tremendous popularity during the historical period. The first recorded treatise on the collection of 800 plant and plant products was mentioned in *Charak Samhita* (1000 – 800 B.C.) followed by *Sushruta Samhita* (800 – 700 B.C.). These are still identified as the baseline guidance for the practice of traditional herbal medicine forever. In the path of development of ethnomedicine, there were two types of healing prevalent during the Vedic period – one relied on the magicoreligious system while the other combined with medicinal herbs and medicines.

In India, the concept of utilizing the natural and plant products to cure the ailments had appeared in the remote past, dating back to 4500-1600 B.C. during Rig Veda. In anthropological arena, the study of ethnomedicine came into being in the early part of the twentieth century, when the famous scholars like, Evans-Pritchard (on Azande); Kluckhon and Spencer (on Navaho); Redfield, Gillion, and Adams (on Maya) had done outstanding research on tribal health care system and much later the scholars like, Joshi; Singh; Bist; Rizvi and many others in Indian context had been studied ethnomedicine.

The Lepchas of Sikkim Himalayas has tremendous significance and value in ethnomedicine because Sikkim is the rich repository of many of such effective herbal plants and the Lepchas being the son of the soil acquire an age-old traditional system of therapeutics from their forefathers and practice when they feel to be effective. The present chapter is based on the concept of health, illness and its curative measures of the people; how far modern treatment can dilute the traditional system of the application.

The Area

Living on the western flank of the Eastern Himalaya Sikkim, one of the smallest states in India is flavoured with floral bounty and land-locked terrain. It is located between 27°05' - 28°09' N latitude and 87°57' - 88°56' E longitude, having an area of around 7096 sq.kms., and is known as the paradise of a nature lover. The state is bounded by Nepal in the west, Bhutan in the east, Tibet in the north and northeast and West Bengal in the south. The Chola range separated the state from Tibet and Bhutan, while the Singalila range separated it from Nepal (Gazetteer, 1931). Historical information revealed that before 1641 the area was ruled by the Lepcha Kings. In the 13thcentury, a blood treaty was signed and an oath was taken between the Lepchas and the Bhutias. In the year 1641, Phuntsong Namgyal was consecrated as the first Bhutia King of Namgyal dynasty. This kingdom ruled the area up to 1975 before the formation of an independent sovereign state (Sharma, 1983; p.18). A number of mountain passes, like, Nather La (4392 m.), Gelep La (4388 m.), Donkia La (5520 m.), Kongra La (4809 m.) along the ranges have sustained two-way traffic of traders, pilgrims, and adventurers from Tibet and central Asia. About 36.3 percent (2656 sq. km.) of the total area of the state is under forest coverage. The topography of Sikkim is quite varied. The elevation ranges from 1250 meter to 8558 meters, with almost no flat piece of land anywhere. Mt. Khangchendzonga (8598 meters), the world's third highest mountain is treated as 'sacred mountain' to the Sikkimese as their guardian deity and considered as the holiest of the holy. Teesta and Rangeet is two life-line river of the state.

The Study Area

The area under the study is mainly chosen from the buffer areas of the Khangchendzonga Biosphere Reserve mostly lies in the west and north district, viewing the rich concentration of almost all life-saving herbs. In the west district, the study had been carried out in (a) Yuksam (under Yuksam–Dubdi Gram Panchayat), (b) Tsozo (under Tsozo Gram Panchayat) and (c) Khecheopalri (under Khecheopalri Gram Panchayat). A total number of 636 households with a total population of 3385 (Census of India, 2001) souls are inhabited in west districts, of which about 75.00 percent are tribal residing in the remote hamlets (*bustees*).

In West district, the Lepchas are inhabited in many places but due to historical importance and also considering the population concentration the three areas were chosen. In Yuksam, there are many hamlets (*bustees*) of which the Lepcha are inhabited in three hamlets (bustee) namely Nubgang, Dosthang, and Ramgyathang. The Ramgyathang is totally inhabited by the Lepchas while the other two are not. Likewise, Tsozo has different hamlets of which Lethang, Lingay, and Tsozo have a full concentration of Lepcha. It had been noticed due to shyness and having a preference to live in isolation on the lap of nature, most of the Lepcha *bustees* were found in a remote corner amidst the forest.

In the northern district of Sikkim, the Lepchas are only inhabited in isolation in Dzongu. The Tibetan word 'Dzongu' means the land of nine hillocks (*dzon* is hillock, *gu* is nine). The area, Dzongu is separated into two areas – (a) the lower Dzongu and (b) upper Dzongu. In lower Dzongu, there are altogether two GPU (Gram Panchayat Unit) – (i) Gor-Sangtok and (ii) Hee – Gyathang. The upper Dzongu has five Gram-Panchayat Units (GPU) namely (i) Lingthem – Lingdem, (ii) Sakyong – Pentong, (iii) Shipgyard Salim Pakhel, (iv)Tingbong – Linzya and (v) Lingdong - Berfok.

The study was conducted in Linzya and Bay hamlet of upper Dzongu and Samdong hamlet of lower Dzongu.

It was found that most of the hamlets in upper Dzongu revenue villages are situated in very inaccessible terrain. The people have to cross the river Teesta with their traditional bamboo made suspension bridge and have to travel a long distance on foot through the forest land and inaccessible terrain.

People

Once the ruling race, the Lepchas are the earliest settlers of Sikkim profoundly proclaimed as '*Rongkup*' (the son of the snowy peak) '*motanchi*' (the term for intra-community identity). The history revealed that formerly the ruling dynasty of the Lepchas was extended from the Himalayas down to Titaliya, the plains of Bangladesh. To the east it was extended up to Gipmochi Mountain of present days Chinese Tibet and to the west it was up to Aroon river of Nepal (Tamsang, 1983). The Lepcha tradition depicted that in the beginning the first primo-genitors of the Lepchas, *Fodongthing* and *Nazaongnyo* were created by God from the pure, virgin snow of *Kingtsoomzaongboochoo's* (Khangchendzonga)) pinnacle and sent them down to live, prosper and spread up all over the fairyland. Therefore, most of the Lepcha clan thus claims to have mythical connections with this mountain peak, which they worship as their guardian deity.

The derogatory word 'Lepcha' is derived from the Nepalese term *Lepchey*, which means scurrilous speakers. Originally, the term *Lepchey* was anglicized by the British people and coined the present term 'Lepcha', who proclaimed themselves as *Rongkup* or in short *Rong* that is 'snowy peak'. According to the tradition, there were ten divisions of ancient Lepcha families claiming their descent from the ten sons of *Fodongthing* and *Nazaongnyoo*. Those ten divisions of the ancient Lepcha families were called as '*Rong kupkati*', which means ten Lepchas. The Lepcha is also recognized as '*Rong Migyit*'. They have hereditary fixed clan or caste which called *agyit*, means a group of Lepcha people or family under the common ancestor.

The Lepchas are thought to have been living mostly through hunting and gathering from the forests. Since later phase of last century, they took to settled cultivation and subsequently adopted the system of cash crop plantation, like cardamom, tea, and ginger, in their terrace agricultural field; the Lepchas raise maize, paddy, wheat, barley, and millet. The rice is the most important staple food millet is commonly used for making local bear '*Chi*'. Fish is taken occasionally but meat – both fresh and dried are taken regularly. They do not have any inhibition in consuming beef, pork, rabbit, porcupine, monkey, deer, etc. The Lepcha language as dubbed by many scholars as a 'mystery' language, because it is not related to any other language, prevalent in this region. Some have a belief that the language belongs to the Tibeto – Burman family, while others have found its root in the Austro-Asiatic family. Dr. Suniti Kumar Chatterjee had mentioned that the Lepcha language belongs to the Himalayan group of the Tibeto-Burman sub-family (Thakur, 1988).

Health, Illness, and Disease: The Lepcha Wisdom

The concept of health and illness among the Lepchas is fully guided by the belief in the supernatural. According to the belief of the people, the cause of illness can be classified into two categories – (i) disease caused by supernatural beings, their displeasure and actions, which are beyond their control; and (ii) diseases caused by the magical means. According to them, the system of the cause, effect, and cure is a circular and enclosed system of knowledge, which provides the manifestation of explanation and control in the face of disorders, chaos and inexplicable circumstances. It is their belief that if the cause of the illness is a spirit, the effect is then spirit possession or another way it can be the cause of controlled spirit possession. The idea of health, illness, and disease have own individual importance in Lepcha mind. The Lepcha feel that any kind of health disorder may not cause any disease all the time. Simple cough and cold, headache, body ache are not experienced as an illness or disease to them. According to them, the disease is of two categories – (a) curable and (b) non-curable. The people also have the opinion that due to carelessness some disease can be turned into a non-curable disease. According to their perception 'illnesses' has two aspects – i.e. (a) psycho-analytical (based on the existence of spirits, ghosts, evil doers), (b) medicinal (based on the existence of some noncurable fatal diseases like tuberculosis, cancer, cholera, diarrhea, etc.). The psycho-analytical aspect of the illness is cured only by means of propitiation of deities and appeasement of spirits, ghosts, etc., while the 'medicinal' aspect is cured by the application of traditional herbal medicine first and if not cured then they apply for modern allopathic medicine.

During the discussions, it is also pointed out that the faith in supernatural power, i.e. gods - *Rum* and demons – *Moong*; is an age-old tradition. Both *Rum* (God) and *Moong* (demon) can be doing harm in the form of fatal injury, epidemics, mishaps, disease, etc. and also can snatch out ones' life, if they are really dissatisfied. At that time, the *Mun* and *Boongthing*, the folk-healer is to be consulted. The *muns* and *boongthings* are considered by the Lepcha to be the media for communication to God (*rum*) and the devils or demons (*moongs*). It is believed by the people that the *boongthings* are supposed to be able to communicate with all the devils/demons (*Moongs*) except the '*Dom moong*', who causes *Leprosy*. It is the opinion of the *mun* and *boongthing* that different types of illness are responsible by the deeds of different *moongs* (devil/demon) which can be treated with worship and devotion of respective *moongs* accompanied by animal sacrifice. The folk-healer (*mun* and *boomgthing*) stated that if that *rum* and *moong* (God and devil/demon) are ignored or any disrespect is shown to them by defiling or polluting by nature's call etc. may invite the suffering of the particular individual – the people may suffer from serious sickness and sometimes even die. They mentioned one of such *moongs* is 'Lungzee normally reside in the big stone present at the entrance of a *bustee* (hamlet). *Mun* and *boongthing* also agreed that if *Rum* (god) is angered it appears in the malicious guise and then referred to as a demon, and may cause sickness and other misfortune. The sickness, the disease may also cause by magical means, which is treated by exorcism. In this sphere, the folk healer (*mun* and *boongthing*) took initiative steps. By counting the rosary beads and throwing off the dice, the folk-healer divines what is actually troubling the patient and then suggested that sacrifice is actually necessary or not. In a psycho-analytical aspect of illness, the disease may cause by the evil spirit and according to them, all evil spirit resides in the upper part and as well as in the lower part of the earth. To get rid of that evil spirit, in almost all Lepcha houses of both in Yuksam and Dzongu, a kind of structure was found, what they termed *Namgo* (for the evil spirit of an upper part of the earth) and *Sago* (for the evil spirit of a lower part of the earth). It is a common belief that this structure seemed to protect all kind of malevolent spirit.

It was informed that there is a number of spirits, demons, and deities in the Lepcha society, whose harmful action is responsible for disease and illness. Among all of them, few important, spirits, demons and deities are mentioned as follows:

(i) The demon *Mung-nong-chuk* and its evil action.
(ii) The deities *Rum-na-na-cho* become arrogant.
(iii) The spirit *Thing-na-na-cho* and its malevolent action.
(iv) Jungle spirit *Muzom-na-chuk-chumboo* and its harmful activities.
(v) Household deities *Sakya-tofion-lee-Rum* and its harmful action.
(vi) Principal household deities *Mukung-Rum* and its evil action.

(vii) The deity *Veek-Run* and its evil action believed to be present in the surrounding of a house, of a person.

(viii) Nature spirit *Yougebo* and its evil action.

(ix) Nature spirit – *Dzongo* and its evil action.

(x) The deity *Lungno* and their evil action.

(xi) The spirit *Makryum, Sor, Dut-chaim* and their malevolent effect.

(xii) The spirit *Muzom, sipundi, Anee* and their malevolent effect.

(xiii) The demon (*mong*) – *Dut, Tshen, Mamn, Cu, Gey-bo, Cyang-shergnyu, eetgnyn, Thyakdum, Pankar, Tong-Thing.*

It is narrated that due to the harmful effect of demon, deities, and spirits the people become sick by heart disease (*alut-dak*), stomach disorder (*tubok-dak*), rheumatism (*aku-dak athung-dak*), vision problem, nose bleeding (*jukmar-vee*), etc. which can be cured by the magico-religious performances.

Cosmology in Relation to Health and Illness

During the study, they also informed that they have strong faith in cosmology in relation to health, illness, and disease. Both eclipses (Solar and Lunar), stages of waxing and waning of the moon, falling of stars, sudden visibility of any constellation in the sky, etc. are believed to have a direct effect on peoples' health, especially on the pregnant lady, newborn baby and the children of the lactating stage. Since pregnancy, both would be father and mother have to follow certain taboos, which are believed to be essential for a safe delivery and as well as for the protection of any deformities of would be a child. They also informed that any kind of disrespect of that taboos may cause epilepsy and blindness to the newborn child. It is also in their faith that sacredness of the natural objects, like streams, lakes, rivers, trees, stones has a direct or indirect relation to the illness and disease. They informed that whenever the sacred river, lakes, and streams got polluted by any means of sinful activities, it becomes either dried up or displaced from its place of origin and this may cause an epidemic in that area. They also have the opinion that the high-density water in the sacred rivers and lakes would maintain the seasonal change, and indirectly would not affect the health of the people, on the other hand, the low density of water would disturb the seasons and the people may fall ill or their health may be disturbed.

Beliefs and Illness

The Lepchas, in one hand belief on ghost, demons and on the other hand they have the belief in gods and goddesses. They also have a religious attitude towards various natural objects. All supernatural being, good and bad, though eternally living outside the world, have innumerable manifestations. These manifestations, or replicas, of the supernatural, chose various natural phenomena for semi-permanent habitation, agreeable phenomena - lakes, or fruit trees or fruitful land – if the supernatural is generally benevolent, disagreeable places – useless trees, waterfalls, rocks or barren ground – if the supernatural is generally malevolent. Each type of supernatural has a preference particular kind of habitation, thus all the *Dent moong* – fever devils – live in big isolated trees, *Sabdok moong* – skim disease devils – in outcrops of rock. According to them, everything in the world possesses a soul, for the soul is the animating principle of all life, without whose intermediary nothing could move or grow. During the fieldwork, there is few such devil's habitations were come across as per their information. One such spot was in between the area of Tingboong and Linzya just beside the roadside gorge, where the two outcrops are believed as the homes of two malevolent spirits, i.e. *Sabdok moong* and his wife *Loo moong*. This female devil causes specific skin disease, and if a person/ or a passerby urinate on that spot should suffer from a non-curable genital disease. Her stone will be anointed with holy water by a lama and with milk by a *Mun*.

It is believed to be informed that there is a lake 'Luksom partam', high up in Dzongu, from whence birth is meant to have originated. Sterile couples who wish for children should visit this lake, spend the night on its bank copulating, and then in the morning throw into the water a silver rupee and a *chimi* (altar light) to please the gods. If necessary, this may be repeated annually for three years. The connection between water and birth runs all through *Mun* mythology. It was informed that in a divine world where the two gods *Tak-bo-thing* and *Narzong-nyou* live there is a stream called *Lungfung* which represents the birth of male children and a well called *Rungzeloong-lap* which represents the birth of female children. This well is guarded by a supernatural boy called *Sathim ong*, and on occasion, a family which has many girls and no boys will get a *Mun* to make sacrifices to the boy and the two gods to make the two pieces of water change place.

Rituals Curing of Illness: Practice of Power Healing

The rituals are performed for the benefit of individuals, households and the habitation area at large. The people have the belief that performances of these rituals are essential for curing the illness. In these rituals, *Mun, Boongthing,* and *Lama* play an overwhelming role as a witch, sorcerer or priest.

Cherim Ceremony - The *cherim* ceremony, held twice in a year; once at the beginning of rains, and again at the beginning of winter; to keep off epidemic diseases like malaria, typhoid, etc. from the community. Altogether there are three separate rituals performed, two by *Mun,* and the third by *Lamas.* In such communal sacrifice, at least one individual from each household has to be present, and each household contributes a little number of grains. The first ceremony, *rum* consists of an off sing to the devils by giving a number of chief articles as a sacrifice to the demon. When the offerings have been made, the *mun*, sitting opposite to the people, intones a long chant to invoke the gods (*rum*) and then takes the eggs and holds them to his forehead while he shuts his eyes and concentrates; the line which he envisages inside the eggs foretells the future health of the community.

The second ceremony – '*Tsandong*' is also performed by *Mun,* consists of offerings to the Gods of Khangchendzonga and to the plains. The offerings consist of rice, butter, *chimi*, a rupee and eggs. The sacrifice is in two parts; first grain and strained *chi* are thrown out by the *Mun* and her assistant and later a goat is dedicated and then killed. In this ceremony, prayers are also attributed to the God of mountains (*Sungmul*) from the protection of snow, hailstorm, and blizzard. The people present in this ceremony are busy cooking, eating, gossiping and watching the preparation.

The third ceremony - It is performed by the *Lamas* with the preparation of a very elaborate ceremonial object. The chief of these is the '*deu*', the 'nine-storied palace', consisting of elaborate regular polyhedral in different colour threads supported on bamboo splinters through a central bamboo. The foreground of the structure was occupied by elaborate representation of the female demon *Mamoo Moong*, portrayed as a snake-haired female riding on a tiger, and surrounded by hundreds of lesser objects. The *Mamoo Moong* herself was summoned and gratified with the offerings of copper pots and clothes. It is a perception that if any animals have not devoured within three days, it is a sign that there will be serious sickness in the coming season. Before taking out the image a *Mun* sang a song alone for thanking the god for coming and begging them now to go back. On these occasions, *Mun* always sang more or less sacred songs.

Shokbu – Rum ceremony - This ceremony is followed by the Lepcha people during the month of the summer season to propitiate the *Yomgebo* god (*rum*) and nature spirit. It is a belief to the people that during the onset of summer season people are affected by various seasonal diseases like diarrhea, dysentery, cough and cold, etc. which may cause by the ill effect of that *yomgebo* deity (*rum*) and the spirit residing in nature. According to them, the sun god, *Yomgebo* is most powerful among them all. People should have to appease that sun god. The Lepcha people offered millet, maize, buckwheat flour to the *Yomgebo* and the nature spirit. No animal is sacrificed in this ceremony. *Boongthing* plays an important role to propitiate the god and the spirit without taking any food. By seeing the yoke of the egg offered by every individual household, *Boongthing* can felt about the future health status of that particular household. Either the member of the household would really be affected by any diseases or not during the coming season can be foretold by the *Boongthing.* At the time of initiation of this ceremony, *Boongthing* sits facing the east because the sun rises in the east side, he also decorated the place by making a platform made of bamboo poles, a bamboo vessel for the offerings, wooden bowl for *Maung chi* (country millet beer), etc. The whole propitiation is preferably done on the bank of a river or a stream, because, they have faith in the sacred river Teesta.

Parnap- This ceremony is performed to appease a demon, known as *Zengo*, who is believed to reside in Tolung gompha. This ceremony is performed every year turn wise by every household. It is the perception of the people that the appeasement of the demon *Zengo* may protect their health from any dreadful diseases. It is also told that the Lepcha men, whenever completed the construction of his house, organized this ceremony in his newly built house as if to purify the house and no any demon can do any harm to the house. *Boongthing* or *Mun* is responsible to propitiate the rituals in their traditional way. On the day of the ceremony, one cock and one hen is sacrificed to the demon and on the next day, the house-owner organize a feast where the relatives, kith and kin members and the neighbours are invited. On the other hand, during the span of one year every household within a *bustee* contribute the food grains (millet, maize, and buckwheat), money and *Maung-chi* (millet-beer) as per their capacity and assimilated together. At the time of the yearly festival, furring the month of June, one of the members of that *bustee* carried away those assimilated articles to the Tholung monastery and performed worship by a Lama. This *parnap* ceremony, according to them is performed for overall prosperity, happiness, and well-being of the *bustee*. The people believed any kind of disregard and carelessness to that demon may cause harm to them and the people even died of the dreadful diseases.

Apang Moong/Sor moong - If get rid of genitor-urinary disease or violent death, a goat is tittered by a long rope which has three knots tied in its length, first of all, all the members of the afflicted household must touch the knots and then the *Mun* will call on all the devils to contend with the blood of the sacrifice and not take the patient, after which he throws the rope into the air. It the rope falls ends outwards (i.e. the end away from the goat falls towards the door), it means the devils will be satisfied and if it falls towards the house the prognosis is bad. After this the animal is killed and the *gazook* (the liver) and *sha-fot* (head) offered to the devil/demon and a pot filled with rice, a rupee and a ceremonial scarf (*Khada*), together with some of the invalid's ornaments and clothing and also a cup of *chi* with different grains in it. Then the *Mun* constructs a phallus out of wood, which is called in its guardian function *moong long tik*. This phallus is set up between two stones leaning slightly forward, somewhere in the forest, and anointed with the blood of the slain animal and *chi*. This will keep the devil/demon away from the area and household.

Num-een moong - The young children who become died from the infantile diarrhea is believed to be caused by a demon of a dead child named as *Num-een moong*. To drive away that demon (*moong*) the Lepcha people sacrificed a goat or a sheep. Even after the sacrifice of an animal if the person troubled by the *moong*, goes down to a narrow stream. The troubled person stands on the right of the stream and the *Mun* on the left of it. Then a 'gateway' is made over the stream of two bundles of elephant grass and brambles, while the *Mun* holds in each hand a bundle made out of wild raspberries, nettles and all other thorny and prickly plants. These bundles are dipped in water and peek over the sufferer several times. A bamboo filled with blood and *chi* are shut up at both ends, and a leaf filled with fried rice and meat and blood are peeked over the patient and thrown through the gateway for the demon. The branches of thorny plants are thrown through the gateway and finally, the gateway is filled up with thorny plants so that it looks like a tree. The *Mun* does this at two other places, one is some way apart on the streams, and the other is either above or below the first one. After completing the *Mun* must return straight to his own house without meeting anybody. It was told that *Num-een moong* is the demon released by the death of young children under the age of about ten. This devil pursues living people and especially other children. Older people who die do not let loose a devil/demon. The *Num-een moong* persists for about three years after the child's death.

Supernatural Power and the Illness

According to their opinion, the illness may occur due to the displeasure or dissatisfaction of the supernatural power beyond their control. These supernatural powers are sometimes benefited them and sometimes cursed them in the form of illness and diseases. This type of harmful supernatural power has its own jurisdiction which is given hereunder:

Malevolent power by God (*rum*)

Position	***Local name***	***Cause of diseases***
Village God	*Long run*	Responsible for a headache, fever, drowsiness
Household deity	*Tongthing*	Eye infection
Household deity	*Lee-run*	Cause the disease like diarrhea, dysentery, stomach, disorder, etc.
Common deity	*Tsandong run*	Cause epidemic like malaria, jaundice
Common deity	*Lung-no run, Ajo Gyantho*	Responsible for severe stomach pain, diarrhea, dysentery.
Seasonal deity	*Shukbu-run*	Responsible for various seasonal disease like cough and cold, pneumonia, diarrhea, dysentery, etc.

Malevolent power by the demon/devil/ghost (*moong*)

Position	***Local name***	***Cause of diseases***
Place of dense forest, rock, and cave	*Duet-Tshen moong*	Responsible for rheumatism (akn-dak / athmg dak), headache, body ache, joint and limb pain, high fever
Places of flowing streams, rivers	*Manoo moong* (female ghost)	Responsible for whole body pain.
Places of flowing streams, rivers	*Loo-moong* (female demon)	Responsible for specific skin disease, wounds, fatal injury
Places inside the bustee	*Gey-bo-moong*	Responsible for a severe headache, severe heart attack
Places of a village boundary	*Lyang shergynu* (female ghost)	Responsible for miscarriage, frequent vomiting; loss of appetite of the female folk.
Places of outcrops of a rock	*Sabdok moong*	Skin disease, sore, etc. are caused due to the ill effect of the moong
Places of roadside area	*Arof moong*	Accident, suicide

Malevolent power by the evil spirit

Position	***Local name***	***Cause of diseases***
Reside in nature as a whole	*Dzengo*	Cause of different dreadful diseases like TB, Pneumonia, Lung disease.
Reside in the tree trunk	*Apang moong sor moong*	Cause of genitor-urinary disease. Cause of violent death.
Reside in the dead child's soul	*Num-een moong*	Cause of infantile diarrhea
Reside in the open barren field	*Sipundi*	Cause of food poison and jaundice
Reside in the fruits, vegetables, and grains	*Amee*	Cause of limb pain, whole body pain
Reside in a huge tree, a crag, a taru, a cave, a cluster of trees, a hillock	*Lung-zee*	Cause of various infectious disease. The whole village got affected.
Reside in the huge stone situated at the entry point of the bustee	*Sandong Long-chuk*	Cause of various common diseases like a headache, body ache, limb pain, nose bleeding (*jukmar-vee*), heart disease (*alut-dak*), stomach disorder (*tubok-dak*)
Reside in the open air just outside the house	*Maknyam*	Cause of vomiting, stomach pain, diarrhea
Reside in the dense forest	*Sor*	Cause of loose motion, piles, abnormal delivery, etc.

From the list of a few supernatural powers, it can be assessed that the Lepcha world of vision is completely guided by beliefs. Even nowadays, this tradition got importance. The Lepcha take the measure, to propitiate those supernatural evil power first by the *Boongthing* and *Mun*, if it is not cured, they opt, for the better option of traditional herbal medicine by consulting the medicine-men - *maondaok*. If the health situation becomes aggravated then they go to the Primary Health Center and opt for modern medicine.

The Role of Boongthing and Mun

The Lepcha have their own ancient religion, named as *Boongthingism* and *Munism.* They believe in the existence of God called *Run* and to him, the *Boongthing* and *Mun* offer their prayers and thanksgiving. *Boongthing* and *Mun* perform all the rituals and religious ceremonies of the Lepchas. Many of the earlier writing mentioned that for the God-fearing Lepchas, prayers supplication and worship is performed through *Boongthing* and *Mun*. It is not a superstition, not any flight of eloquence and not even lips homage to God. The living quality of *Boongthingism* and *Munism* is demonstrated by the loyalty it has commanded from its followers, the Lepchas. *Boongthing* and *Mun* is the mediator between God (*Rums*), devil/ demons (*Moongs*) and the Lepchas. The *Boongthing* ward-off evil spirits by sacrificing animals and other things. Both of them are invited to officiate during clan/community rituals or even for worshipping the family deities. Their assistance is also invariably sought to cure the sickness of individuals. *Boongthing* is supposed to be able to communicate with the malevolent and benevolent demons/devils (*Moongs*). The institution *Mun* is hereditary in nature, but the institution *Boongthing* can be learned from the other *Boongthing*. The Lepcha believed that apart from the service of warding off the malevolent a spirit, *Boongthing* is also sought for during the wedding to invoke the gods and goddesses. The *Boongthings* are considered more popular among the Lepchas in general as their service is more frequently sought for particularly during illness. *Muns*' performance is restricted to different social functions. *Mun* plays a pivotal role in agricultural performance. *Muns* participation is compulsory in different ritual associated with agriculture. According to them, the *Muns* are hierarchically classified with their status. Every classification has definite performance. *Pilden Muns* is the superior one who has the capacity to communicating with the dead person's soul. Some of the *Muns*, known as *Mun Mook-Mun*, is thought to be the evildoers who cause hardship to the people. The *Mun-Jyum-Mun* category *Mun* perform the activities as like the *Pilden Mun*, except for that they cannot communicate with the dead person's soul, but they can cure the sick person by herbal medicine. The *Mun,* having the specialized knowledge of using herbs is considered as *Tangli Mun*.

Findings of Healthcare System among the Lepchas of West Sikkim

From the study, it was noticed that the Lepchas of Ramgyathang hamlet follows the dual system (both traditional and modern allopathic medicine) of medical practice, while the Lepchas of another setup, i.e. Lethang and Khecheopalri, the peoples' preference is different. They preferred the traditional way of health care more than the modern one. It was reported and informed that the Lethang Lepchas are the original migrant in the west district. Being an original migrant group, they have had a tendency to maintain the age-old tradition. On the other hand, in Khecheopalri monastery *bustee* the Lepchas are influenced by the monastery and the healing practices of the *Lama*. In this context, they informed that whenever the intensity of illness becomes severe, they prefer to go to the Health Centre. The age-old person always prefers the traditional medical practice by appeasing the supernatural power and by applying the ethnomedicine. To them, a kind of regular health disorder, like, loose motion; a cough and cold; snake bite; injuries, etc. are not at all cared seriously. The acute ailment like, eye infection; severe chest pain; continuous fever; tuberculosis; malarial infection, etc. carry some importance and for that purpose they initially consult the *Boongthing, Mun* and after that take the ethnomedicine. If it is not cured, then they have to consult the doctor. It is noticed that education plays a key role in the Lepcha society of West Sikkim district. The Lepcha, who have no education generally, prefers to follow the traditional medicine for their illness, while the person who has gained education prefers to consult the doctor. Of course, there are some exceptions found in the Lethang hamlet, where few high school students want to give much value to their traditional medical practices by following the ethnomedicine. Amongst them, those who are affluent in these three set up prefer to consult the modern medical system. The role of *Boongthing* and *Mun* are highest in Lethang *bustee* followed by Ramgyathang *bustee*. In Khecheopalri, the role of the lama is much more than the services of *Boongthing* and *Mun*.

Findings of Healthcare System among the Lepchas of North Sikkim

From the study, it was noticed that the health care system in lower Dzongu is more traditional and dual mode than the modern system. But in the upper Dzongu maximum number of Lepcha population prefer only to the age-old tradition of keeping the faith on the service of *Mun, Boongthing* and even *Lama*. Living in close proximity to nature and forest the people take the ethnomedicine and ethno-biotic components for healing up their illness. People informed that the lower Dzongu area is situated in the close proximity of the district headquarter Mangan and they have easy access to go there and treated their ailments in the district hospital, but for the Lepcha who reside in the farthest place like Linzya and Bay, they have to adapt their traditional system as an effective means of health care. In all, it is noticed that the infants are looked after very carefully, whenever the infants are in trouble the *maondaok*, traditional medicine man, is consulted along with *Boongthing*. Another important point is the impact of education and awareness which plays an important role in the healthcare system. People of upper Dzongu especially the areas, like, Linzya, Bay, Salim-Pakhel; the Lepchas have less access to take up the modern health facilities. The Lepchas of upper Dzongu depend on the traditional system first, then dual-mode (traditional as well as modern medicine) and finally, when health becomes severe the modern medicine is being applied. The reason behind is the belief in a supernatural power, strong religious faith compels them to stick on the age-old tradition.

Conclusion

In the prolonged discussion of the foregoing pages, it tries to delineate that irrespective of caste, class, and creed; 'health' is an important feature to all human groups. The ill-health disturbs the rhythm of life and the performances of the individual being. On having separate identity health and illness is always remained on both sides of the same coin. If health is a property, then illness is a state. The failure of health causes illness, whose cure is very necessary. Being an original inhabitant of nature the Lepcha of the Khangchendzonga Biosphere (KBR) in West and North district of Sikkim is not an exception to that. But according to their perception, every health disorder or health hazards are not contemplated as an 'illness'. Like another original son of the soil, the Lepcha also have a dependency on age-old ethnomedicine. The health, illness, the behaviour of the sick and medical practices among the Lepchas primarily follow the path of endogenous path of conception. Became according to their belief, everything in the world possesses a 'soul', and illness is the reflection towards the disorder of that 'soul'.

While describing the illness and therapeutics, it has been found that the illness of the Lepcha is either caused by the dissatisfaction of various natural being which is considered to be an animate object, the arrogance, and dissatisfaction of spirits, demons, and ghosts, believed to be residing in the nature; or by the displeasure of various deities related with nature. In accordance with the rules of prevention against the illness and diseases, the Lepcha primarily follows the path of appeasement of various deities by worshipping them; or propitiating the malevolent spirits, demons, a ghost by employing the service of the traditional spirit healer and priest, called as *Mun* and *Boongthing*. Unless they also prayed the service of the Buddhist monk; called *Lama* for the readings of holy Buddhist scripture. The second option for that is applying the herbal therapeutics with the consultation of traditional medicine men (*maondaok*). According to them, the disease and illness will be cured by these, if it is not, then they are advised to go to Primary Health Centre or District Hospital for modern treatment. Somebody goes and some are not as it is their mental make-up and also the respect towards the age-old tradition.

In relation to therapeutic practice, it was observed that the Lepcha of Dzongu area of north Sikkim possessed better mythology of illness and its traditional pharmacopoeia other than the Yuksam of West Sikkim. In all respect, the wisdom of pharmacopoeia and therapeutics is still maintaining its traditional essence. The interesting feature is that the people of the interior portion have the highest usage of the traditional system. But in spite of availing every facility, the Lepchas of Lethang hamlet of west Sikkim also shows the much dependency on the traditional way of treatment. The reason may perhaps is the mental make-up of the people. To them it is their age-old tradition, it should be kept alive.

References

Department of Forest, Report of Khangchendzonga National Park and Biosphere Reserve (unpublished).

Gazetteer 1931, *Gazetteer of Bengal and Sikkim – A.E. Porter*, vol. V, part-I and II, Usha Publication, Delhi.

Govt. of India 2001, *Population atlas*, Census Report, Sikkim.

Hughes, CC 1968, 'Ethnomedicine' in *Encyclopedia of social sciences*, ed DL Sills, vol. 9-10, pp. 88.

Khangchendzonga Conservation Committee 2007, *Brochure of Khangchendzonga and its people* (unpublished).

Lehriche, C & Danglas, G 1973, *Health and illness: a social psychological analysis*, Academic Press, London.

Sharma, R 1983, *Images of Sikkim: the land, people, and culture*, Ringsum Publication, Department of Tourism, Gangtok, Sikkim.

Tamsang, KP 1983, *The unknown and untold reality about the Lepchas*, Lyangsong Tamsang, Kalimpong.

Thakur, RN 1988, *Himalayan Lepchas*, Archives Publisher and Distributors, New Delhi.

Valabrega, JP 1962, 'La Relation Therapeutique, Malade et Medecin' cited in *Social factors in relations to chronic illness*, by Graham Smith (1963).

World Health Organization 1946-1948, 'Health and illness', *Bulletin*, New York.

Chapter – 18

Variation of Angular Photogrammetric Analysis of the Facial Profile: A Study on Tripuris and Bengalee Hindu Caste Population

Debalina Roy, Priyanka Das,
Kusum Ghosh, Diptendu Chatterjee,
and Arup Ratan Bandyopadhyay

Introduction

The face is crucial for human identity and damage such as scarring or developmental deformities have effects stretching beyond those of solely physical inconvenience. Nevertheless, the face is morphologically important for human classification in many ethnic classifications (Comas, 1960) and it holds the expression of every emotion. Facial appearance is vital for human recognition and communication. Facial shape is also an important determinant of ethnic classification and particularly facial symmetry seems to be the imperative paradigm of the developmental index. The muscles of the face play a prominent role and vary among different individuals, giving rise to additional diversity in expression and facial features. The face comprises of two types of tissues: Hard tissues and Soft tissues. Hard tissue (also termed calcified tissue) is tissue which is mineralized and has a firm intercellular matrix. It is influenced by the bone structure of the skull, and each face is unique through the anatomical variation present in the bones of the viscero-cranium and neurocranium. In anatomy, soft tissue includes the tissues that connect, support or surround other structures and organs of the body, not being hard tissue such as bone.

Facial soft-tissue thicknesses vary with craniofacial dimensions has implications for forensic identification, facial aesthetic surgery, an approximation of the facial features of missing individuals (Simpson and Henneberg, 2002).

Several methods have been attempted to evaluate facial characteristics for example craniofacial anthropometry (Kolar and Soltar, 1997) photogrammetry (Anibor and Okumagba, 2010; Reddy et al., 2011; Wamalwa et al., 2011), cephalometric radiography (McIntyre and Mossey, 2003) stereophotogrammetry (Sforza and Ferrario, 2006), computed tomography and laser scanning (Al-Khatib, 2010). Anthropometric measurements on photographs are called photogrammetry. Some Author (Stoner, 1955; Fernandez-Riveiro et al., 2003) standardized the photographic technique and record taking in natural head position (NHP) and gave average values for different ethnic groups (Arnett and Bergman, 1993) and demonstrated populations vary genetically and geographically in their craniofacial features.

Being at the crossroads of migration, Indian populations have undergone complex and ancient admixture events over a long period and have been the melting-pot of disparate ancestries originating from different parts of Eurasia and Southeast Asia (Sarkar, 1958). Contemporary ethnic India is a land of enormous genetic, cultural, and linguistic diversity (Karve, 1961; Majumder 1998).

Recent studies (Roychoudhury et al., 2000; Reich et al., 2009; Basu et al., 2016) exploring Indian genomic diversity demonstrated four major ancestral genetic components in mainland India that included four dominant ancestries in populations from mainland India: Ancestral North-Indian (ANI), Ancestral South-Indian (ASI), Ancestral Tibeto–Burman (ATB), and Ancestral Austro-Asiatic (AAA).

Measurement of the different craniofacial variables is being considered as important for studying human growth because facial proportions change with age, for studying sexual differences as sex differences are presented by variations in skeletal dimensions and muscle development and also for clinical treatments as normative value of craniofacial dimensions help in determining abnormality and thus treatment planning (Kolar and Salter, 1997).

Review of literature regarding photogrammetry from Asian countries is scanty (Ferdousi et al., 2013) and at the same time from the Indian context. In the present study an attempt has been made to understand the variation of craniofacial dimension in terms of angular measurements among the females from two different ethnic groups, Tripuris from Northeast India (Tripura) and Bengalee Caste Hindu population from Eastern India (West Bengal).

Materials and Methods

To achieve the purpose 100 females from Hindu Caste population of Kolkata (age range 22 to 25 years) and 100 age-matched (age range 22 to 25 years) Tripuri females from Tripura were taken as participants. Prior to the study verbal consent for taking photographs was obtained from each participant. Furthermore, all the participants were asked for at least four generation endogamies to include in the present study.

All right profile photographs were obtained with a Sony DSCW800/B 20.1 MP Digital Camera with 10 X optical zoom and at a 20.1-megapixel resolution. A dark colour curtain was used as a background, and the flash mode was also used as and when needed. To take the photograph, the camera was positioned approximately 1.0-meter distance from the participant and was raised to the ear level of the participant to get to enhance the quality of the image and to prevent distortion of the face (Ozkul et al., 2009). All the photographs were taken with the participants sitting in a relaxed position with their heads held in the close to the approximate of the eye-ear plane (Fernandez-Riveiro et al., 2003). Analysis of the facial photographs was done by a computer Adobe Photoshop CS 4. The landmarks for the photogrammetry and the five angular measurements are Naso-frontal angle, Naso-mental angle, Naso-labial angle, Naso-facial angle, and Nasal tip angle respectively (Figure 18.1 to 18.6). All the measurements were taken twice then recorded and analyzed in the SPSS (Version 20.1) data form. Descriptive and inferential statistics were done in appropriate places. Cut off was set at $p=0.05$.

Results and Discussion

Distribution of Cephalo-facial angles of the two ethnic groups has been presented in Table 18.1 along with mean population differences. Significant ($p<0.05$) differences in Naso-frontal, Naso-labial, and Naso-facial angles have been found between the Caste Hindu Bengalee females and Tripuri females. Nevertheless, the population difference was highest in Naso-facial angle (9.37°) followed by Naso-frontal angle (8.2°) and least being Naso-mental angle (0.85°).

Significantly ($p<0.05$) higher Naso-frontal angle (Fig 18.2), however, suggested less elevation (flat) of nasal bone among the Tripuris due to their ethnic affiliation to Mongoloids. A similar trend also has been noted with regard to Naso-mental angle (Fig 18.3) among the Tripuris in comparison to Bengalee females. So far, the significant ($p<0.05$) less Naso-labial angle (Fig 18.4) among the Tripuri females compared to that of the Bengalee

Table 18.1 Distribution of craniofacial angles of Bengalee Hindu caste and Tripuri females

Cephalo-facial angles (in degree)	*Population*	*Range*	*Mean ±SD*	*Population difference (in degree)*
Naso frontal angle (g-n-prn)	Tripuri	120-142	130.5 ± 6.35	8.2
	Bengalee	117-168	138.7±10.84 *	
Naso mental angle (n-prn-pg)	Tripuri	112-135	125.1±12.5	0.85
	Bengalee	107-138	125.8 ±7.16	
Naso labial angle (cm-sn-ls)	Tripuri	34-90	69.1±14.2	5.1
	Bengalee	36-89	74.1±13.2 *	
Nasal tip angle (n-prn-sn)	Tripuri	28-89	75.3 ±16.8	1.48
	Bengalee	47-88	73.8 ±11.02	
Naso facial angle (g-pg/n-prn)	Tripuri	12-39	26.8 ±9.07	9.37
	Bengalee	27-43	36.2 ±4.24*	

*p<0.05

females suggested the less elevation of the nose and higher alveolar prognathism. The higher Nasal tip angle among the Tripuris (Fig 18.6) in comparison to the Bengalee females was due to less nasal depth as one of the major nasal traits of Mongoloid feature. Finally, the significantly ($p<0.05$) higher Naso-facial angle (Fig 18.5) indicated less prognathous face and higher nasal elevation among the Bengalee females compared to the Tripuri counterparts.

The present study envisaged photogrammetric analysis had advantages in facial profile analysis especially on angular measurements, as they are not affected by photographic enlargement, non-invasive and commonly used

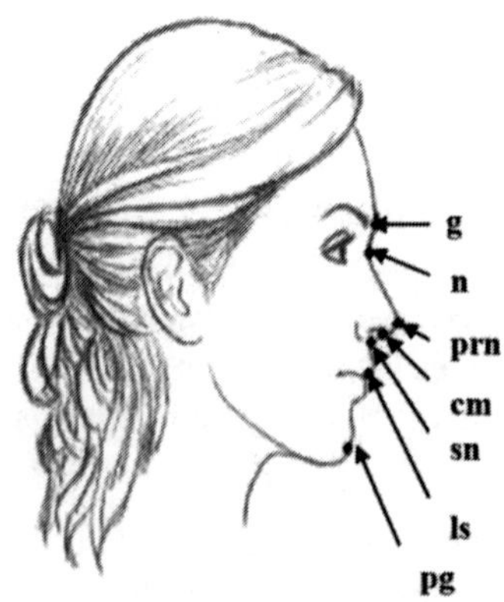

Fig 18.1: Landmarks used in this investigation: G. glabella; N. nasion; Prn. Pro- nasale; Cm. columella; Sn. Sub-nasale;Ls. labial superior; Pg. pogonion

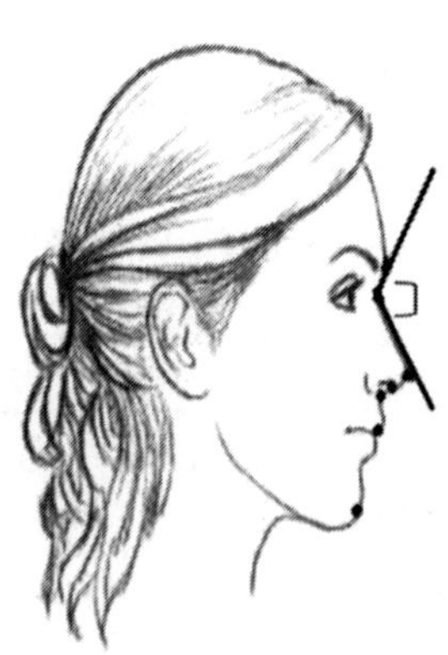

Fig 18.2: Naso-frontal angle (G-N-Prn)

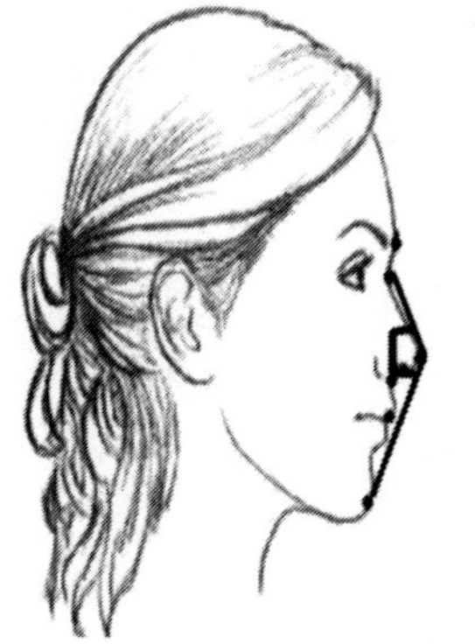

Fig 18.3 Naso-mental angle)
(N-Prn-Pg)

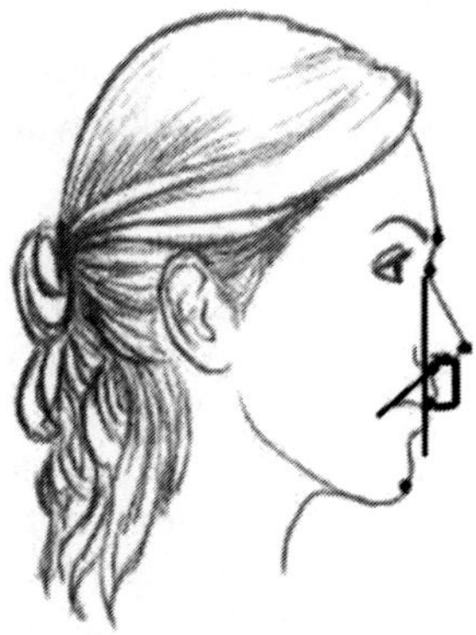

Fig 18.4. Naso-labial angle
(Cm-Sn-Ls)

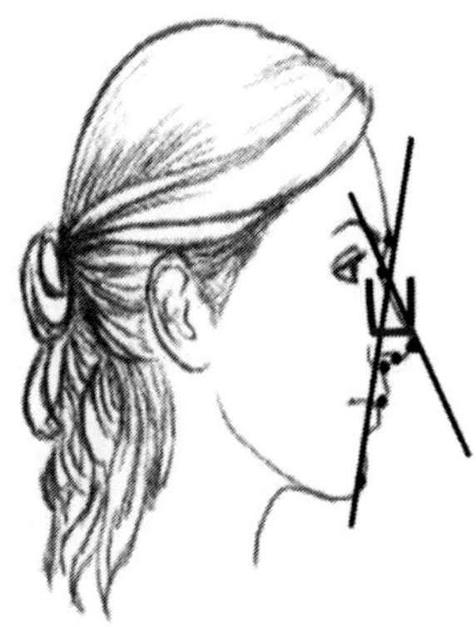

Fig 18.5: Naso-facial angle
(G-Pg/N-Prn)

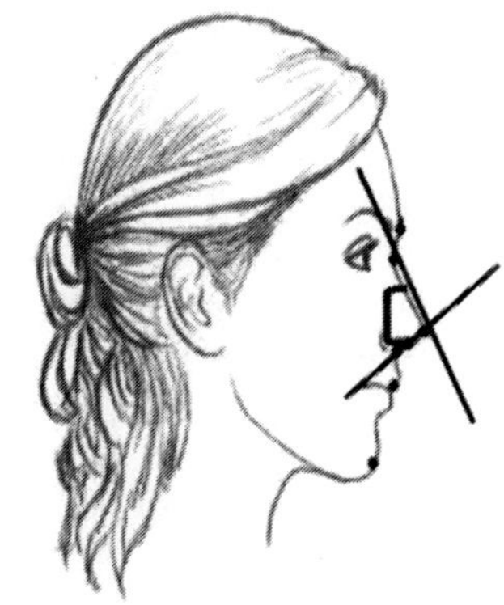

Fig 18.6: Nasal tip Angle
(n-prn-sn)

method to investigate pre- and post-operative changes and provides a permanent record of patients (Sforza and Ferrario, 2006). Nevertheless, in anthropological research, the facial features could additionally be analyzed quantitatively. Compared with other methods, the photogrammetric analysis does not require expensive or complex equipment and offers digital results that are easily evaluated using computer software. Furthermore, there is no radiation exposure, so it is ethically more acceptable to develop population norms through population-based studies. The present study, however, stimulates more population studies for better understanding the variation of facial features from known age sex individuals, which in turn can be extrapolated and or simulated for forensic anthropological studies.

Acknowledgements

Authors are grateful to the study participants for their cooperation. The financial support is acknowledged from the University of Calcutta [BI 65 (8&9)].

References

Al-Khatib, AR 2010, 'Facial three-dimensional surface imaging: an overview', *Archives of Orofacial Sciences*, vol. 1, pp. 1-8.

Anibor, E & Okumagba, MT 2010, 'Photometric facial analysis of the Urhobo ethnic group in Nigeria', *Archives of Applied Science Research*, vol. 3, pp. 28-32.

Arnett, GW & Bergman, RT 1993, 'Facial keys to orthodontic diagnosis and treatment planning-Part I', *American Journal of Orthodontics and Dentofacial Orthopaedics*, vol. 103, pp. 299-312.

Basu, A, Sarkar-Roy, N & Majumder, PP 2016, 'Genomic reconstruction of the history of extant populations of India reveals five distinct ancestral components and a complex structure', *PNAS*, vol. 113, pp. 1594-1599.

Comas, J 1960, *Manual of physical anthropology*, Charles C Thomas, Springfield, Illinois, vol. 63, pp. 1150-1152.

Ferdousi, MA, Al Mamun, A, Banu, LA & Paul, S 2013, 'Angular Photogrammetric analysis of the facial profile of the adult Bangladeshi Garo', *Scientific Research*, vol. 3, pp. 188-192.

Fernandez-Riveiro, P, Smyth-Chamosa, E, Suarez-Quintanilla, D & Suarez-Cunqueiro, M 2003, 'Angular photogrammetric analysis of the soft tissue facial profile', *European Journal of* Orthodontics, vol. 25, pp. 393-399.

Karve, I 1961, *Hindu society: an interpretation*, Deshmukh Prakashan, Poona.

Kolar, JC & Salter, EM 1997, *Craniofacial anthropometry: practical measurement of the head and face for clinical, surgical and research use*, Charles C Thomas Publisher Ltd., Springfield, Illinois.

Majumder, PP 1998, 'People of India: biological diversity and affinities', *Evolutionary Anthropology*, vol. 6, pp. 100-110.

McIntyre, GT & Mossey, PA, 2003, Size and shape measurement in contemporary cephalometrics', *European Journal of Orthodontics*, vol. 25, pp. 231-242.

Ozkul, T, Ozkul, MH, Akhtar, R, Al-Kaabi, F & Jumaia, T 2009, 'A software tool for measurement of facial parameters', *The Open Chemical and Biomedical Methods Journal*, vol. 2, pp. 69-74.

Reddy, M, Ahuja, NK, Raghav, P, Kundu, V & Mishra, VA, 2011, 'Computer-assisted angular photogrammetric analysis of the soft tissue facial profile of North Indian adults', *The Journal of Indian Orthodontic Society*, vol. 3, pp. 119-123.

Reich, D, Thangaraj, K, Patterson, N, Price, AL & Singh, L 2009, 'Reconstructing Indian population history', *Nature*, vol. 461, pp. 489-495.

Roychoudhuri, S, Roy, S, Dey, B, Chakraborty, M, Roy, M, Roy, B, Ramesh, A, Prabhakaran, N, Usha Rani, MV, Vishwanathan, H, Mitra, M, Sil, SK & Majumder, PP 2000, 'Fundamental genomic unity of ethnic India is revealed by analysis of mitochondrial DNA', *Current Science*, vol. 79, no. 9, pp. 1182-1192.

Sarkar, SS 1958, 'Race and race movements in India' in *Cultural heritage of India, The early phases,* Ramakrishna Mission Institute of Culture, vol. 1, pp. 17-32.

Sforza, C & Ferrario, VF 2006, 'Soft-tissue facial anthropometry in three dimensions: from anatomical landmarks to digital morphology in research, clinics and forensic anthropology', *Journal of Anthropological Sciences*, vol. 84, pp. 97-124.

Simpson, E & Henneberg, M 2002, 'Variation in soft-tissue thicknesses on the human face and their relation to craniometric dimensions', *American Journal of Physical Anthropology*, vol. 118, no. 2, pp. 121-133.

Stoner, MM 1955, 'A photometric analysis of the facial profile', *American Journal of Orthodontics*, vol. 41, pp. 453-469.

Wamalwa, P, Amisi, SK & Chen, S 2011, 'Angular photogrammetric comparison of the soft-tissue facial profile of Kenyans and Chinese', *The Journal of Craniofacial Surgery*, vol. 3, pp. 1064-1072.

Index

N

W

W